Humana Festival 2019
The Complete Plays

About the Humana Foundation

The Humana Foundation was established in 1981 as the philanthropic arm of Humana Inc., one of the nation's leading health and well-being companies. Located in Louisville, Kentucky, the Foundation seeks to co-create communities where leadership, culture, and systems work to improve and sustain positive health outcomes. For more information, visit www.HumanaFoundation.org.

Humana and the Humana Foundation are dedicated to Corporate Social Responsibility. Our goal is to ensure that every business decision we make reflects our commitment to improving the health and well-being of our members, our associates, the communities we serve, and our planet.

Humana Festival 2019
The Complete Plays

Edited by
Amy Wegener and Jenni Page-White

Lanham • Boulder • New York • London

Published by Limelight Editions
An imprint of The Rowman & Littlefield Publishing Group, Inc.
4501 Forbes Boulevard, Suite 200, Lanham, Maryland 20706
www.rowman.com

6 Tinworth Street, London SE11 5AL, United Kingdom

British Library Cataloguing in Publication Information Available

Library of Congress Cataloging-in-Publication Data

ISSN 1935-4452
ISBN 978-1-5381-3636-2 (pbk. : alk. paper)
ISBN 978-1-5381-3637-9 (electronic)

♾™ The paper used in this publication meets the minimum requirements of American National Standard for Information Sciences—Permanence of Paper for Printed Library Materials, ANSI/NISO Z39.48-1992.

Contents

Acknowledgments

The editors wish to thank the following persons for their invaluable assistance in compiling this volume:

John Cerullo
Janelle Renee Dunn
Robert Barry Fleming
Elizabeth Greenfield
Mary Kate Grimes
Carrie Hagovsky
Melissa Hines
Jane B. Jones
Steve Knight
Meredith McDonough
Zachary Meicher-Buzzi
Erin Meiman
Emily Moler
Kevin E. Moore
Hannah Rae Montgomery
Alonna Ray
Rebecca Redman
Jessica Reese
Jeffrey S. Rodgers
Charlotte Stephens
Michael Tan
Emily Tarquin
Lex Turner
Paul Werner
Sharifa Yasmin
Susan Yassky

Beth Blickers
Michael Finkle
Di Glazer
Ron Gwiazda
Rachel Viola
Amy Wagner
Ross Weiner
Derek Zasky

Actors Theatre of Louisville Staff 2019 Humana Festival

MANAGING DIRECTOR, Kevin E. Moore

ARTISTIC

Artistic Producer. . . . . Emily Tarquin
Artistic Manager . . . . Zachary Meicher-Buzzi
Company Manager . . . . .Dot King

Literary

Literary Director . . . . Amy Wegener
Literary Manager. . . . . .Jenni Page-White
Resident Dramaturg . . . . Hannah Rae Montgomery
Literary Associate . . . . .Jessica Reese

Education

Education Director . . . . Jane B. Jones
Education Associates. . . . . .Janelle Renee Dunn, Abigail Miskowiec
Teaching Artists . . . . Liz Fentress, Keith McGill,
Talleri McRae, Letitia Usher

ADMINISTRATION

General Manager . . . . Jeffrey S. Rodgers
Human Resources Manager. . . . . .Marie Tull
Systems Manager . . . . Dottie Krebs
Executive Assistant . . . . .Norman P. Dixon

AUDIENCE SERVICES & SALES

Ticket Sales Director. . . . . .Kim McKercher
Season Tickets Manager . . . . .Julie Gallegos
Patron Services Managers . . . . .Steve Clark, Kristy Kannapell
Patron Services Associates. . . . . LaShana Avery, Sophia Bierman,
Kristine Farley, Marty Huelsmann, Tyler Walls

Volunteer and Audience Relations

Director . . . . Allison Hammons
Lobby Manager. . . . . Tiffany Walton
House Managers. . . . . Tiffany Bush, Elizabeth Cooley,
Jordan Kelch, Stephen Minotti,
Abigail Rogers, Bryn Weiler
Audience Services Associates. . . . . Kelly Carr, Matt Dalton,
Hillary Jones, Rebecca Redman

DEVELOPMENT

Interim Director of Development. . . . . Carrie Hagovsky
Director of Individual Giving. . . . . .Katherine Lander
Grants Manager . . . . .Allie Summers
Donor Relations Coordinator. . . . . Matthew Brown

FINANCE

Director . . . . Peggy Shake
Accounting Coordinator . . . . .Jason Acree
Accounting Assistant. . . . . Christine England

MARKETING & COMMUNICATIONS

Director . . . . Steve Knight
Marketing Manager. . . . . Melissa Hines
Festival & Events Manager. . . . . Erin Meiman
Public Relations Manager . . . . Elizabeth Greenfield
Graphic Designer . . . . Mary Kate Grimes
Assistant Graphic Designer . . . . Sheyenne Santiago
Group Sales Manager . . . . Sarah Peters
Outbound Customer Service Representative. . . . . .David Meredith

OPERATIONS

Director of Operations . . . . .Carlo Stallings
Operations Manager. . . . . .Barry Witt
Building Services Supervisor . . . . Ricky Baldon
Building Services . . . . .Deonta Burns, Kevin Burns,
Michael Sweatmon, Cedrick Yelder

PRODUCTION

Production Manager . . . . Paul Werner
Associate Production Manager. .Michael DeWhatley
Production Stage Manager. . . . . Paul Mills Holmes
Resident Stage Managers. . . . . Stephen Horton, Jessica Kay Potter
Resident Production Assistants. . . . . Margaret Rial, Katherine Thesing

Scenic

Technical Director. . . . . Justin Hagovsky
Associate Technical Director . . . . Braden Blauser
Scenic Charge Artist . . . . Rachael Claxton
Scene Shop Manager. . . . . Javan Roy-Bachman
Master Carpenter . . . . Alexia Hall
Scenic Carpenters . . . . Hannah Allgeier, Josh Blum,
Daniel Cutler, Brooke McPherson,
Pierre Vendette, Kasey Williams

Assistant Scenic Charge . . . . .Colleen Doty
Deck Carpenter . . . . Gracie Lawson

Costumes

Costume Director . . . . Mike Floyd
Crafts Master . . . . Shari Cochran
Draper/Tailor . . . . .Jeffery Park
First Hands . . . . Rachel Gregory, Natalie Maynard
Stitchers . . . . Faith Brown, Christina Marcantonio
Costume Design Assistants . . . . Isabel Martin, Isabelle Tabet
Wig Supervisor . . . . .Katherine Ward
Wig and Makeup Assistant . . . . Rebecca Traylor
Wardrobe Manager . . . . .Anna Jenny
Wardrobe Assistant . . . . Chloe Hixson
Wardrobe Technician . . . . Katy Vest

Lighting

Supervisor . . . . Jason E. Weber
Associate Lighting Supervisor . . . . .Dani Clifford
Electrics Shop Manager . . . . .Steve Burdsall
Lead Lighting Technician . . . . Wylder Cooper
Lighting Technicians . . . . Will Blair, Lindsay Krupski,
Tyler Warner, Steven Youk

Sound

Supervisor . . . . Paul Doyle
Assistant Sound Supervisor . . . . Lindsay Burdsall
Sound Technicians . . . . Marion Ayers, Victoria Campbell

Properties

Director . . . . Mark Walston
Associate Properties Master . . . . .Heather Lindert
Assistant Properties Master . . . . .Katelin Ashcraft
Carpenter Artisan . . . . Ryan Bennett
Soft Goods Artisan . . . . Jessie Combest
Properties Artisan . . . . .Connor O'Leary

Video

Media Technologist . . . . .Philip Allgeier

PROFESSIONAL TRAINING COMPANY

Director . . . . Christine Albright-Tufts
Artistic Coordinator . . . . .Jonathan Ruiz

Acting . . . . Amber Avant, David Ball, Silvia Daly Bond,
Laura Lee Caudill, Avery Deutsch,
Rebby Yuer Foster, Josh Fulton,
Ashley N. Hildreth, Rasell Holt, Emma Maltby,
Kevin O'Connell, Jonathan Moises Olivares,
Ashley K. Patlan, Kayla Peters, Angelica Santiago,
Brett Daniel Schultz, Julian Socha, Seun Soyemi,
Russell Sperberg, Reagan Stovenour
Communications. . . . . Laura Mullaney
Company & Artistic Management. . . . . .Ben Otten
Costumes . . . . Jessica Land
Development . . . . Kelly Carr
Directing . . . . Sharifa Yasmin, Emily Moler
Dramaturgy/Literary Management . . . . Alonna Ray, Susan Yassky
Education/Teaching Artist . . . . Rachel Bischoff, Emma Leff
Festival & Events Management . . . . Henrietta Key
Lighting . . . . Seth Torres
Marketing. . . . . Charlotte Stephens
Producing & Casting Management .Rebecca Redman
Production Management . . . . .Bryn Weiler
Properties. . . . . .Kayla Carroll
Scenic Painting. . . . . Petra Stoppel
Sound . . . . Cheyenne S. Zuck
Stage Management . . . . Andie Burns, Annalise Fosnight
Elizabeth Gordon, Em Hornbeck

USHER CAPTAINS

Dolly Adams, Shirley Adkins, Marie Allen, Terryl Allen, Katherine Austin, Libba &
Chuck Bonifer, Tanya Briley, Judy Buckler, Brenda Cease, Maleva Chamberlain,
Donna Conlon, Terry Conway, Laurie Eiden, Doris Elder, Joyce French, Carol
Halbleib, LuAnn & Tom Hayes, Candace Jaworski, Holly Kissel, Yvonne Mead,
Barbara Nichols, Teresa Nusz, Dalen Payton, Beth Phipps, Nancy Rankin, Tim
Unruh, Peyton Weibe

Actors Theatre's Company Doctor

Dr. Andrew Mickler, F.A.C.S.

About the Humana Festival of New American Plays

For more than four decades, Actors Theatre of Louisville has been home to the internationally acclaimed Humana Festival of New American Plays, which has introduced over 450 plays and launched hundreds of subsequent productions around the world. Every year, producers, critics, artists, and theatre lovers of all kinds gather in Louisville to encounter groundbreaking world premieres, all fully designed and produced in rotating repertory. It's an invigorating annual celebration of the art form, and its success has marked the Humana Festival as one of the nation's preeminent powerhouses for new play development. Plays first brought to life in Louisville include three Pulitzer Prize winners, as well as multiple Pulitzer finalists and winners of the Obie Award, Kesselring Prize, Steinberg/ATCA New Play Award, Yale Drama Series Prize, Susan Smith Blackburn Prize, and many other prestigious honors. More than 400 Humana Festival plays have been published in anthologies and individual acting editions, making Actors Theatre a vital force in building the American dramatic repertoire.

Beyond its far-reaching impact, the Humana Festival is also good fun. The sense of excitement is palpable when these brand-new plays meet their audiences for the first time. Actors Theatre's buildings buzz with creative energy as boldly imagined worlds come to life onstage, and theatregoers mingle with a fiercely talented company of artists and staff in the lobbies. Louisville is a vibrant cultural destination, known not only for its horse racing and bourbon, but also for its bustling arts scene and spirit of curiosity. The city thrives on innovation and embraces difference, so it's no wonder that the Humana Festival has taken root in Louisville, where an adventurous ethos guides both the audience and the curation of each season. Year after year, the festival champions the extraordinary breadth of American playwriting by seeking out and amplifying new voices and diverse viewpoints. Each spring's lineup offers a dynamic mix of styles, stories, and theatrical vocabularies—tales that whisk you to other worlds or move you to consider the one you know with fresh eyes.

The enduring influence of Actors Theatre's decades-long commitment to the full production of new work—and the philosophical shift it helped catalyze—is immeasurable. When the festival began back in 1977, it gained widespread renown within a few short seasons, and found a generous, visionary sponsor in the Humana Foundation. In the years that followed, this venture would help change the ecology of American theatre, leading a movement among the nation's regional theatres to discover and support playwrights. The Humana Festival's significance has continued to be concretely demonstrated in the work itself: year after year, extraordinary plays spark lively conversations both in Louisville and in their lives beyond our stages, making these exciting world premieres the crucial first chapters of much longer stories.

EVERYBODY BLACK
by Dave Harris

ABOUT *EVERYBODY BLACK*

- *This article first ran in the* Limelight Guide to the 43rd Humana Festival of New American Plays, *published by Actors Theatre of Louisville, and is based on conversations with the playwright before rehearsals for the Humana Festival production began.*

"Hi. I'm Black." This cheerful introduction is the launching point of Dave Harris's blisteringly funny satire *Everybody Black*. As the historian addressing the audience goes on to explain, being black has landed him in a surprisingly lucrative position: a group of white historians have offered him a big ol' check to write the definitive version of The Black Experience™. These earnest white historians want an official record that captures the Truth of Blackness—and by that, they mean they want the boats, the chains, the Negro spirituals, the baby mama drama, the crack rocks, and the police brutality. It's a preposterous request. But then again, it's a whole lotta money. So the black historian has gleefully agreed.

In Harris's no-holds-barred comedy, the process of documenting Black History is a laughably compromised endeavor, distorted by the promise of profit and inherently biased toward a particular narrative. And the worldview of the black historian provides another challenge: despite his mandate, he feels no fidelity to "facts" or "truth." (In fact, he confesses with a wicked laugh, he's never even met another black person. Not one!) So from the outset, the project is fundamentally flawed. The play unfolds as a series of short scenes, orchestrated by a self-professed madman who shamelessly proclaims that he's just "making shit up about black people."

So perhaps it is unsurprising that the characters who populate this "Black History" play are not the ones that you might find in a dusty public school textbook. There's an argument between a slave and a black millennial about whose day was harder. There's a talk show segment about black people who are addicted to dating white people. There's even a visit with Every Black Father Ever—and later, Every Black Mother Ever. Each new character we meet is simultaneously a provocative flirtation with stereotype and also a subversive resistance to it, challenging our implicit expectations about who might appear in a play called *Everybody Black*.

Explaining his impulse for writing the play, Harris says, "I'm interested in a wider idea of canonical blackness and black entertainment. I'm not really drawn to writing the 'righteous black struggle play,' about black people who are suffering or fighting oppression. We see a lot of the same tropes in black theatre: stories about the people who led the march, the people who were brave and went out and changed the world." Almost in spite of himself, he laughs: "But, like...that's not fun! Also, I know a lot more people who missed the march instead of actually going. So I wanted to put that onstage. The characters in *Everybody Black* are both really wrong and really right, and they have no entitlement to righteousness or sincerity. That's more interesting to me, and I think it's an aspect of theatre we don't see as much."

As Harris imagines him, the black historian—flawed as he is—has one key advantage. Just like he feels no responsibility to serve up the Truth of Blackness, he also feels no responsibility to frame The Black Experience as a noble struggle against injustice. As a result, his portrayals of blackness are strikingly less solemn. Instead, they're full of joy and bombast, chipper defiance and unapologetic hyperbole—and the characters he envisions are hardly heroic. As it turns out, that becomes a sticking point for the actors enlisted to bring these people to life.

The actors argue that the historian is too careless with stereotypes—even worse, he's made them look foolish. What they want sounds pretty simple: they just want the record to be historically accurate. And yet, the black historian argues, is anything really "historically accurate"? "On some level," muses Harris, "the difference between recording history and writing theatre is so, so flimsy. All we're looking at when we read a play is the manipulation of words for a specific effect, and when we read a historical text it's the same thing."

"I think a driving question for me," Harris goes on to say, "is what *is* the truth in this play?" *Everybody Black* ostensibly starts as a play about Black History—but it ultimately grapples with the notion that all writing about history fundamentally reveals more about the person shaping the story than it does the story itself. Why do we return to narratives that frame the black experience as a monolith? Is struggle against oppression really the defining characteristic of blackness?

According to Harris, the challenge of Black History—or really any history—is that it erases nuance. The richness and complexity of a first-hand experience can be diminished by time and distance. But for Harris, finding a personal way to look at the past is essential. "Whatever I think I know," he says, "there were real people before me who were super complicated, and probably in a lot of pain but also had a lot of joy, and also were probably fucked up and did a lot of hurtful, terrible things.... For me to give anyone the benefit of agency and the benefit of humanity in my writing, I have to see that they were just making choices, and they were complicated and selfish and great and horrible and hurtful—and I think that's beautiful."

—Jenni Page-White

3

BIOGRAPHY

Dave Harris is a poet and playwright from West Philly. He is the Tow Playwright-in-Residence at Roundabout Theatre Company. His plays include *Everybody Black* (Actors Theatre of Louisville's 2019 Humana Festival), *Exception To the Rule* (Roundabout Underground), *White History* (Manhattan Theatre Club's Ted Snowden Reading Series, Victory Gardens Theater's IGNITION Festival), *Incendiary* (Goodman Theatre's New Stages Festival, NNPN/The Kennedy Center's MFA Playwrights' Workshop), *Tambo & Bones* (Black Swan Lab at Oregon Shakespeare Festival, Ojai Playwrights Conference, SPACE on Ryder Farm), and *Watch Me* (The Ground Floor at Berkeley Rep), among others. Select honors include: the 2019 Ollie New Play Award, the Lorraine Hansberry Playwriting Award and Mark Twain Prize for Comic Playwriting from The Kennedy Center, the 2018 Venturous Playwright Fellowship from The Lark, a Cave Canem Poetry Fellowship, and being named a semifinalist for the Relentless Award. His first full-length collection of poetry, *Patricide*, was published in May 2019 from Button Poetry. Harris received his BA from Yale University and is a third-year MFA playwright at the University of California, San Diego.

ACKNOWLEDGMENTS

Everybody Black premiered at the Humana Festival of New American Plays in March 2019. It was directed by Awoye Timpo with the following cast:

> J. Cameron Barnett
> Ashley N. Hildreth
> Galen Ryan Kane
> Sharina Martin
> NSangou Njikam
> Christina Acosta Robinson

and the following production staff:

Scenic Designer	Kristen Robinson
Costume Designer	Oana Botez
Lighting Designer	Reza Behjat
Sound Designer	Christian Frederickson
Media Designer	Philip Allgeier
Original Music by	Luqman Brown
Movement Director	Safiyyah Rasool
Stage Manager	Alex Hajjar
Assistant Stage Manager	Jessica Kay Potter
Dramaturg	Jenni Page-White
Casting	Erica Jensen, Calleri Casting
Dialect Coach	Joniece Abbott-Pratt
Properties Director	Mark Walston
Directing Assistant	Janelle Renee Dunn
Understudy for Galen Ryan Kane	Rasell Holt
Assistant Dramaturg	Susan Yassky
Rehearsal Room Assistant	Sharifa Yasmin
Stage Management Apprentice	Annalise Fosnight

CHARACTERS

There are more than thirty characters in this play. You'll meet them.

Seven to nine actors should be enough to cover all of them. But do whatchu gotta do.

SETTING

The canon, or the mind of one person who has the power to write history.

NOTE

The only characters for whom gender is specific are AUNT JEMIMA (F) and UNCLE BEN (M). Feel free to adjust character pronouns accordingly. Otherwise, regardless of how they are referred to in the text, anyone can play anyone.

Or rather, ANYONE BLACK can play anyone.

Every actor, including BLACK HISTORIAN, should play multiple roles.

I like the dreams of the future
better than the history of the past.
—Thomas Jefferson

History is the version of the past
that people have decided to agree upon.
—Napoleon Bonaparte

Fuck outta here.
—Harriet Tubman

Ashley N. Hildreth and J. Cameron Barnett
in *Everybody Black*

43rd Humana Festival of New American Plays
Actors Theatre of Louisville, 2019
Photo by Jonathan Roberts

EVERYBODY BLACK

BLACK HISTORY

Black.

Enter BLACK HISTORIAN.

BLACK HISTORIAN. Hi.

I'm Black.

I'm also a historian.

I'm a Black Historian.

And I would like to welcome you to…THE CANON.

You see, I, Black Historian, have dedicated my life to the study
of theater and popular entertainment.

And there's this thing that happens in theaters nowadays
where the playwright feels so overwhelmed by THE CRAFT!

That he decides he must not only write a play, but he must also write a play
wherein he, or a surrogate for him, is a character in that play.

Someone did it first. I'm sure they're famous now.

But the Black playwright appears onstage and explains some concept,
rather didactically, to the audience.

Instead of letting the audience just enjoy the drama.

He feels he must come out and pronounce his genius to the world.

That'll become bored soon I imagine. Save that for the talkback, am I right?

…

Anywho, I promise you that I am not that person.

So here's what happened:

This group of white historians with lots and lots of money offered to
commission me

to write the definitive version of The Black Experience™.

An absurd request made slightly less absurd with a checkbook.

They asked me to write the definitive version of The Black Experience™
and they offered to publish it. But what's more!

They were going to publish it and then put that published piece into a time
capsule, and then put that time capsule onto a rocketship, and BLAST IT
INTO SPACE!

So that on the fateful day in the future, when the aliens finally arrive to our galaxy,

they'll read my words and they will understand the TRUTH about Blackness™.

…

And I thought long and hard about this request.

How can I speak THE TRUTH?

How do we chronicle the pain of yesterday in a way that makes sense today?

And these white historians were like: "We want the full history."

"We want the boats! We want the chains! We want the whips and the Negro spirituals!

We want the crack rocks and the marches!

We want the bloods and the crips!

We want the drive-bys and the police brutality!

We want the struggle, the pain, the neverending fight for FREEDOM!"

And I thought long and hard. I thought I thought I thought.

And I looked at their check.

And I said…

…

…

CHA-CHING!

And so I got to work.

But there's one thing the white historians didn't account for.

The white historians did. not. realize. that…

…

…

I

AM

ABSOLUTELY

MAD!

> (BLACK HISTORIAN *bursts into wicked, echoing laughter.*
> *The sound of a Negro spiritual startles* BLACK HISTORIAN.
> *It fills the space.*
> *Something like that one from the movie* Glory *where Morgan Freeman sings at some dramatic moment.*
> *I don't remember what it's called or any of the words besides:*)

SPIRITUAL SINGER. (*Singing.*) *Oh my lordddddddddd. Lord. Lord. Lord. Oh my lordddddddddd. Lord. Lord. Lord.*

BLACK HISTORIAN. (*To the music.*) CUT THAT SHIT OUT!

(*The song abruptly stops.*

BLACK HISTORIAN bursts into wicked laughter again.)

You see, I'm a wicked man and I know nothing of history.

People assume all the time that cuz I'm a Black Historian,

I'm the ambassador to Negrohood.

Truthfully I've never even met a Black person. Not a single one.

I only know two Black people: me and my reflection. Ok?

The Race Problem. HAAAAAA.

Well guess what?

I got a big ol' check from some white folk who think I know history.

I don't know history; I wasn't there! I just be making shit up about Black people.

But that don't matter. Y'all paying me.

Watch:

(*BLACK HISTORIAN becomes a wild conductor.*

BLACK HISTORIAN waves their hands and creates a song.

Spinning history like a DJ.

It sounds like a spiritual jazz trap snap Motown classical symphony.

It's epic. Dramatic. The opening credits to a wild imagination.

The music continues on its own.

BLACK HISTORIAN pulls out a snack that would be sold at the theater's concession stand.)

Oh, at some point you might be like what the hell is actually happening here?

Well that's how I feel whenever I read a history book.

History doesn't apologize for itself. Why should I?

Toodle loo!

(*BLACK HISTORIAN SNAPS AND IS GONE.*

We are transported into their mind somehow.

Or rather, the mind of the play.

Through the lens of a camera? Or the sound of pages turning?

Either way, some spectacle happens here that makes us go like damn the rules of this world are CRAZY.

But when it's over, we are transported into a sitcom house.

*Note: in this large cast of characters, the actor playing BLACK HISTORIAN may appear as any role. You never know. Though when they appear, they might at some point turn to the audience and wink wink, or something that says "Hey y'all it's me!")

HOUSE OF GOOD LOVIN'

An R&B song plays, the type of song you'd hear at a Black family reunion.

Think: Freddie Jackson's "Jam Tonight."

This is the theme to the timeless Black sitcom:

"House of Good Lovin'."

THEME SONG. (*Singing.*) *Family's not always easy.*

But for sure, we gonna keep on riding.

Hmmm.

> (*As the theme song progresses, the stage begins to light up with single spotlights, mimicking the intro sections of TV shows.*
>
> *Each character is given a moment as the theme song plays.*
>
> *Think: the intro to* The Cosby Show.
>
> *The first spotlight shines on* EUGENE, *the playfully overweight father of the family. He stands with his arms crossed, stern, disapproving, but tender. He grooves slightly to the music.*)

Times been hard; always are.

> (*Spotlight on* BEVERLY, *the mother, smiling and warm.*
>
> *She dances like she's at church.*)

And that's why we stick together!

Hey!

> (*Spotlight on* DIANA, *the teenage daughter.*
>
> *She dances a little seductively, but not too much for basic cable.*)

With my lord (with my lord).

Do them chores (do them chores).

Everything gonna be alright.

> (*Spotlight on* MAMALICIOUS, *the matriarch.*
>
> *She goes wild like she at the club but knowing damn well she like 65 years old.*)

It's our house (it's our house).

Yes our house (yes our house).

It's the House of Good Lovin'.

It's our house (it's our house).

Yes our house (yes our house).

It's the House of Good Lovin'.

(*As the song ends,* EUGENE, DIANA, BEVERLY *and* MAMALICIOUS *come together as a family, like they always do at the end of the opening theme.*

Fade to black.

The TV show resumes. Homely intro music plays.

The stage is set in a sitcom living room.

EUGENE *enters carrying his mail.*)

EUGENE. Let's see here...Bills. Bills. Bills.

PAYCHECK!

(EUGENE *dances.*

The sound of AUDIENCE laughter.

EUGENE *sings.*)

I just got my pay-check.

I just got my pay-check.

What am I gon buy-next?

Imma buy some chick-en.

(*AUDIENCE laughter.*)

And then I'm gon go swimm-in.

Get me some hot wom-en.

BEVERLY. (*Offstage.*) You gon do what with who?

(*Enter* BEVERLY *from the offstage kitchen holding a spatula.*

The AUDIENCE ooo's like he's in trouble when she enters.)

EUGENE. Uhh what?

BEVERLY. Mhmm. I heard you Eugene. You said you gon get you some hot women.

EUGENE. I ain't say that.

BEVERLY. Honey. I seen you without clothes on. Hot women?

Only thing you need is a hot shower.

(*AUDIENCE laughter.*)

EUGENE. Hey now, back in my day I used to be surrounded by the females. Had them flocking to me like a fire hydrant in July. Yup. Papa was a rolling stone.

BEVERLY. Yeah, and now you just a roll.

(*AUDIENCE laughter.*)

EUGENE. Speaking of rolls, woman where is my dinner?

BEVERLY. (*Threatening with the spatula.*) Boy whatchu say to me?

EUGENE. I SAID...will dinner be ready soon, my loving wife Beverly.

BEVERLY. That's what I thought. You lucky I loves you.

(*She exits back to the kitchen.*)

EUGENE. (*Under his breath.*) And you better hurry up wit my got damn food woman.

BEVERLY. (*Offstage.*) Whatchu say?

EUGENE. (*Louder.*) I said I loves you too!

Just like I loves my paycheck!

(*On the word paycheck, enter* DIANA.

She is dressed a bit too revealing for her father's tastes.

AUDIENCE ooo's and whistles as she enters.

EUGENE *stops dead in his tracks.*)

DIANA. Hi Daddy.

EUGENE. Dontchu hi daddy me.

Diana what the hell are you wearing?

DIANA. What?

EUGENE. You know exactly what I'm talkin bout.

DIANA. Daddy stop being ridiculous; I'm not wearing anything.

EUGENE. Uh huh, that's the problem.

(*AUDIENCE laughter.*)

DIANA. It's called a Bando, obvi.

It's retro. All the pretty girls are wearing it.

EUGENE. Well you ain't pretty.

(*AUDIENCE laughter.*)

Coming out here lookin like some kinda Rhiyonce Minaj.

DIANA. (*Deeply hurt.*) You don't think I'm pretty?

EUGENE. Hell no.

…

Uh I ain't mean that, I meant…

You're beautiful.

(*AUDIENCE "awwww."*)

But you go outside wearing that bando and Imma whoop you wit the ugly stick.

I got one too. Right next to my Vaseline.

You gon give me a heart attack on my payday.

DIANA. Speaking of payday…

EUGENE. Oooo I knew you wanted something.

Whatchu want? Money to buy a Barbie?

DIANA. No silly! I'm going on a date!

EUGENE. A DATE!

> (EUGENE *has a heart attack and faints to the floor.*
> *AUDIENCE LAUGHTER.*)

DIANA. Daddy, not again!

MAMALICIOUS. (*Offstage.*) What's this I hear about a date?

> (*Enter* MAMALICIOUS, *still in her nightgown.*
> *AUDIENCE erupts in cheers when she enters.*
> MAMALICIOUS *pats her wig.*)

DIANA. It's nothing Mamalicious.

MAMALICIOUS. Naww honeychild. I been up and down every block from here to Crenshaw

so believe me. I can tell when you tryna get on up like James Brown,

ain't that right?

> (*She sings "ain't that right?" to no one in particular. It's her*
> *catchphrase.*)

DIANA. You wouldn't understand.

MAMALICIOUS. Why not?

DIANA. Because you're old.

MAMALICIOUS. Old! Oh I'm old?

Well lemme tell you sumthin: I'm rubber, and you're glue

And if you talk back to me one more time, Imma beat that ass.

Now you gon tell me what's happenin.

DIANA. It's a boy!

MAMALICIOUS. I knew it!

> (*Flustered,* DIANA *falls on the couch.*)

DIANA. There's a boy named RayKwonShon, who I really like and I just want him to like me too, but I'm worried because he's only into girls like Rachel who dress up and make twerk videos and I don't have a twerk video, but then he asked me out so I went and bought this outfit so I could look hot, and now I don't have money for the date

AND I DON'T KNOW WHAT TO DOOOOO—

> (MAMALICIOUS *winds up and slaps the mess out of* DIANA.
> *AUDIENCE laughter.*)

MAMALICIOUS. Honeychild you need to get a grip!

Ain't no man in the world worth changing yourself for.

You perfect just the way Gawd made you, wit that tight little behind of yours.

Sometimes you gotta fight for it, but lemme tell you: any woman can get any man.

(*Doorbell rings.*)

DIANA. That's him!

Mamalicious what do I do?

MAMALICIOUS. Answer the door is what you do.

(DIANA *answers the door.*

Enter RAYKWONSHON, *in a sleeveless white tee and a du-rag.*

Probably with a pencil beard.

His vibe is hot and dangerous with nice arms.

MAMALICIOUS *is taken aback by* RAYKWONSHON.)

MAMALICIOUS. Oh my.

RAYKWONSHON. (*To* DIANA.) What's good?

DIANA. Hey…

(DIANA *gazes at him awkwardly.*

MAMALICIOUS *moves to* RAYKWONSHON *and throws* DIANA *out of the way.*)

MAMALICIOUS. Well well well, who's this sexy young milk dud we got here?

I'm Mamalicious. But you can call me tomorrow morning.

RAYKWONSHON. What's good? I'm RayKwonShon. I like dangerous things, but I also have an emotional side hidden beneath my dark exterior.

MAMALICIOUS. Mmm I love a man with inner trauma and nice arms.

(*She meows at him and then snaps her teeth.*)

DIANA. Ahem?

MAMALICIOUS. (*To* DIANA.) Oh didn't I tell you honey?

Any woman can get any man!

Ain't that right!!!!

DIANA. Mamalicious!

MAMALICIOUS. I might be old, but I can still get it right get it tight.

(*To* RAYKWONSHON.)

You ever been with an older woman?

RAYKWONSHON. No.

MAMALICIOUS. You ready to make a change?

RAYKWONSHON. Uh oh.

(*She grabs* RAYKWONSHON *and stuffs him into her bosom.*)

MAMALICIOUS. Awww sookie sookie now!

(*AUDIENCE laughter.*)

DIANA. Back off! RayKwonShon is mine!

(DIANA *pushes* MAMALICIOUS *out of the way and kisses* RAYKWONSHON *passionately.*

AUDIENCE ooo's and whistles.

EUGENE *senses a man in the house and sits up.*

He has a shotgun somehow.)

EUGENE. AY! GET THEM THERE HANDS OFF MY DAUGHTER!

(RAYKWONSHON *screams.*

EUGENE *begins to chase* RAYKWONSHON *in circles around the room.*

AUDIENCE ERUPTS.

BEVERLY *reenters.*)

BEVERLY. Oh lawd Jesus. Oh lawd why. Whyyyyyyyy.

DIANA. DADDY NO! I LOVE HIM!

MAMALICIOUS. Eugene you want backup? I'll pin him between my legs.

(MAMALICIOUS *joins the chase.*

BEVERLY *fans herself with a frying pan.*

DIANA *cries.*

AUDIENCE applauds furiously.

Pleasant outro music plays.

The sitcom is over.)

DAT AIN'T ME

Enter LOST NIGGA.

LOST NIGGA. Hi.

My name is Lost Nigga.

And you might be wondering why I go by the name Lost Nigga.

Well.

I go by Lost Nigga because I am frequently lost when watching the world around me.

For example, I turn on the television and watch all the big shows, the movies, and I think…

DAT AIN'T ME!

And then I turn on the news and see stories, the world is just so crazy these days, and I think…

DAT AIN'T ME!

And then I go to the theaters and they tell their stories and talk about the issues and social justice and whatnot, and I think…

DAT AIN'T ME!

And then I myself decided to write an autobiographical story where I was the main character and some folks put it up on a small stage with a modest budget and we sold out and got an extended run and people gave me hugs and I watched my own show on closing night, and I thought…

DAT AIN'T ME!

And I was so upset, so lost, that I slit my own wrists in the bathroom in the lobby. And I looked down at all the blood. I had so much blood in me. Who knew? I didn't know. I just looked down at the blood and I thought…

IS DAT ME?

(*A pause?*)

And then I was dead.

And I met my creator in heaven.

And they looked at me and told me what my name was. My real name.

And so I looked in the mirror.

And I said the name out loud.

Said my true name.

And I thought…

…

WHO DA FUCK IS DAT?

(LOST NIGGA *is gone.*
The sound of picks on stone.
The sound of labor.)

WORK

Enter SLAVE.

Enter BLACK MILLENNIAL.

BLACK MILLENNIAL. Yo. I've had a hard day.

SLAVE. Yo tell me about it.

BLACK MILLENNIAL. Man where do I start. Can you believe today, this girl Becca grabbed my hair?

SLAVE. No she didn't.

BLACK MILLENNIAL. Yes she did. I turned around and I was like girl you better not.

And then I'm sitting in class right, and the teacher called me by the name of the only other Black student in the room.

SLAVE. Stop it.

BLACK MILLENNIAL. And I said oh my lorddd.

And then, on the way home, a cop followed me, pulled me over, and then tried to shoot me.

SLAVE. He tried to shoot you?

BLACK MILLENNIAL. He tried to shoot me! But, I ducked so, you know, I'm alive I guess.

SLAVE. Dat's wild. Like yo, my day was crazy too! Like you won't believe it. Get this: I woke up this morning on the plantation at the crack of dawn.

BLACK MILLENNIAL. Damnnnn.

SLAVE. And it was like, it was like, it was like at least 105 degrees.

And then I had to start picking cotton.

BLACK MILLENNIAL. Whaaat?

SLAVE. Yup. And then guess what.

BLACK MILLENNIAL. What?

SLAVE. Massa started whipping me for making eye contact with him.

BLACK MILLENNIAL. Stop playin!

SLAVE. Mhm. I had a hard day too man.

BLACK MILLENNIAL. That's real. That's so real.

Like I came home from school and I had to comfort my sister

because no one asked her to the prom

because America doesn't value Black beauty.

SLAVE. Yep, you right true true.

Like I came home, and I had to comfort my sister

cuz she was pregnant wit massa's child.

So like that's all fine and good, but my day was harder.

BLACK MILLENNIAL. I mean that's bad and all.

My uncle's on crack kinda casually. You ever seen someone on crack?

It's rough, yo.

SLAVE. I feel you I feel you,

but also don't tell me shit.

BLACK MILLENNIAL. I mean I can talk. Like you don't know my life.

You not out here tryna pay tuition on $7 an hour.

SLAVE. Nigga I can't read.

BLACK MILLENNIAL. Nigga schools ain't teaching kids how to read now neither.

SLAVE. Bro. Bro. They will literally cut out my tongue if I even look at a book!

BLACK MILLENNIAL. Homie! They give us standardized tests just to reinforce the fact we ain't learning what they want us to learn.

Like how you gon give us a test that we meant to fail? Huh? HUH?

SLAVE. Nigga I'm a slave.

BLACK MILLENNIAL. Bruh, bruh, I get that. I do. But look here: there is a 1 in 3 chance that I am incarcerated. Because I'm Black.

SLAVE. Oh 1 in 3? 1 in 3?

BLACK MILLENNIAL. 1 in 3!

SLAVE. NIGGA THERE IS A 3 IN 3 CHANCE I DIE IN SERVITUDE!

BLACK MILLENNIAL. Well if you hate it so much, why don't you run up North?

SLAVE. Nigga how you gon tell me to run up North?

BLACK MILLENNIAL. I'm just saying, Harriet Tubman did it.

SLAVE. Oh Harriet?! OH HARRIET! Niggas always wanna bring up Harriet.

Well if it's like that, then why don't you go be Barack Obama!

BLACK MILLENNIAL. Man I would love to be Barack! You think I don't wanna be Barack?

If I could find me a Michelle...

SLAVE. IT'S YO FAULT! You ain't working hard enough!

BLACK MILLENNIAL. You ain't working hard enough!

SLAVE. Bitch! You hate America so much, maybe *you* should run North.

BLACK MILLENNIAL. To Canada?

SLAVE. Yeah.

BLACK MILLENNIAL. Nigga naw. Canada real cold this time of year. And Canada don't like Black people neither!

SLAVE. MOTHAFUCKA. THEY AIN'T EVEN GIVE US BREAKFAST THIS MORNING.

BLACK MILLENNIAL. GIVE? I CAN'T AFFORD BREAKFAST! NOT NO PANCAKES! NOT NO WAFFLES!

SLAVE. WHAT THE FUCK IS A WAFFLE!

(*Some vaguely "African" sounding music.*

Enter HOTEP THE ANCESTOR *dressed in a Black Panther Pan African Ankh Leather Headband Dashiki from Kmart.*)

HOTEP THE ANCESTOR. Cool it now, my peoples.

(BLACK MILLENNIAL *and* SLAVE *turn to* HOTEP THE ANCESTOR.)

BLACK MILLENNIAL & SLAVE. Nigga!

HOTEP THE ANCESTOR. This right here is an example of the white man working to keep my brothas my sistas my queens from recognizing they dreams, nahmean?

BLACK MILLENNIAL. Whatchu talking about?

HOTEP THE ANCESTOR. Y'all don't gotta fight. Y'all just gotta open your mind's eye and rise up against the tyranny of the white man.

Let me take it from here.

(HOTEP THE ANCESTOR *raises a Black Power fist.*)

HOTEP THE ANCESTOR. Kujichagulia, my brothas.

(SLAVE *and* BLACK MILLENNIAL *disappear.*)

HOTEP THE ANCESTOR

HOTEP THE ANCESTOR. Hi.

My name is Hotep the Ancestor.

(HOTEP THE ANCESTOR *raises a Black Power fist.*)

Ashanti Ja Rule.

I'm here to teach lessons that weren't ever taught in the history books.

Cuz my people not woke yet.

Woke to the fact that we are kings and queens.

Cuz all Black people were kings and queens in the country of Africa.

Yup.

My ancestors had shea butter instead of sweat.

That is, before the white man.

Before the white man came and tainted our nubian skin.

Cuz when we was back in the motherland,

all Black people had diamonds and ruby chains. Did y'all know that?

Getting fanned by banana leaves n shit.

And every nigga had like 14 beautiful black women.

And when I read those historical facts in a pamphlet from the guy who sells bootleg DVDs at the barbershop, it changed my life. I was like damn…

I wanna get fanned by 14 beautiful black women.

Why didn't no one teach me this in the history books?

Had to learn like 23 different versions of Shakespeare

but couldn't no one teach me about no jollof?

And that's when I got mad. And said I'm not gonna take it anymore.

So I got real mad.

And I grew out my hair.

And I changed my name from Jonathan Smith to Black African Power X.

And then I was woke. And I decided I was gonna go back to the motherland.

Nothing was gonna stop me.

And so I went to the coast of America and looked out over the middle passage.

And I could smell the shores of Africa across the water.

And then I remembered I don't know how to swim.

…

So now I'm sellin bootleg DVDs at the barbershop.

Y'all wanna buy any DVDs? They'll aid you in your quest to open your third
eye!

Nah?

It's all good.

I'm gon get there eventually.

     (HOTEP THE ANCESTOR *raises a Black Power fist.*)

Labelle Sade, my queens.

     (HOTEP THE ANCESTOR *is gone.*)

WORD ON THE STREET

Fancy relationship talk show lights and music.

Enter DANDELIAH JONES, *talk show host.*

DANDELIAH JONES. Hello and welcome back to *WORD ON THE STREET.*
I'm your host Dandeliah Jones.
And we're here to ask the tough questions of our world.
My guests today are Trevor and Mona, two average-looking African Americans who,
beneath that plain exterior are hiding troubling truths:
Trevor and Mona can't stop dating white people.
Please welcome Trevor and Mona!
> (*Music!*
> *Enter* TREVOR *and* MONA.)

Hello, hello.
How are you today?

TREVOR. Good, yeah I'm good.

MONA. Glad to be here.

DANDELIAH JONES. Thank you for joining us to share your story.
I know this can be a little touch and go, and I just want you to know that I am here for you.

TREVOR. Thank you!

MONA. Mhm.

DANDELIAH JONES. So I guess, where to begin.
I just, ya know, it's 2019.
It's 2019, and you two are still dating white people.

TREVOR. UGH. I know! Right!

MONA. God! I know. I know!

DANDELIAH JONES. Ya know?

TREVOR. I do, I do know!

MONA. Right! Ugh.

DANDELIAH JONES. It's just, it's 2019. Ya know? Like 400 years later and...

TREVOR. UGH. I know.

MONA. I know!

TREVOR. It's like, we're already in the frying pan.

MONA. America is the frying pan.

TREVOR. America is the frying pan.

And I see the fire. Like right there. And I'm like oop, yup, in the fire now. Just walked right on into the fire.

MONA. Right!

TREVOR. Right?!

DANDELIAH JONES. Right. So, ya know, I don't know, how come you guys keep dating white people.

TREVOR. I KNOW!

MONA. I actually swore off white people. It was my New Year's Resolution. After getting over Peter...Woof.

And I swore. I am not going back, no.

It was like when I tried to go vegan.

It was amazing!

I had more energy. I was thinking clearer. I started jogging.

And then, whaddya know, six weeks later I'm at a steakhouse with Jesse!

DANDELIAH JONES. Are you attracted to Black people?

TREVOR. Black. Is. Beautiful.

DANDELIAH JONES. Have you dated Black people?

MONA. I joined Blackpeoplemeet.com.

DANDELIAH JONES. And it never works out?

TREVOR. Eh what does "working out" even mean?

MONA. I think I date white people because I know it won't work out.

TREVOR. Oh that's a theory! See I'm currently with a white who I think I'm really into, on a deeper level, but then she doesn't know what paprika is and I'm like Oh God.

MONA. I know!

DANDELIAH JONES. It's just perplexing to me.

(*Intense investigative talk show music.*)

You know, as a talk show host, I see so many people with unhealthy patterns that they can't seem to break. Even when they are aware of the pattern.

TREVOR. Yup yup.

MONA. I know those people.

DANDELIAH JONES. And I think about history, how white people ultimately turn out so disappointing, all the terrible things white people have done, still do, rape, colonize, brutalize, red line, micro-aggress, macro-aggress, / fetishize, demonize, pollute, genocide,

TREVOR. Oh yeah that one.

MONA. One hundo.

DANDELIAH JONES. Incarcerate, appropriate, defenestrate, dominate, and it makes me sad.

It makes me sad for the world. But mostly: it makes me sad for YOU.

TREVOR. Well gee I don't know about—

DANDELIAH JONES. And I wonder how, equipped with that knowledge, how you can consider, CONSIDER, dating, marrying, swiping right, or hell even FUCKING a white person! When you know everything they've done and will continue to do. How!? How?!?!

(*A long awkward pause.*)

TREVOR. (*Awkward. To* MONA.) Sounds like somebody's single…

MONA. (*To* TREVOR.) Woof!

DANDELIAH JONES. What if you just stopped dating white people!?!

MONA. I mean gosh there's just so many of them.

TREVOR. Like you'd have to try really really hard to not ever date a white person.

DANDELIAH JONES. Well most white folks do a great job of never dating a Black person.

TREVOR. Not with us they don't.

MONA. I know that's right!

(TREVOR *and* MONA *high-five.*)

DANDELIAH JONES. I just don't understand why you would choose to love a white person

WHEN I HAVEN'T HAD SEX IN 4 YEARS.

TREVOR. Ya know…love is weird. Like it feels like the right choice and the wrong choice all the time. I knew I was in love with my partner because I would fall in and out of love every day. Why just yesterday morning it happened six different times. I watched the way she was cutting her pancakes and I thought, I absolutely despise you. And then she squeezed toothpaste onto my toothbrush and I thought, you're the only person I've ever known.

DANDELIAH JONES. …that's beautiful.

TREVOR. Yeah, I guess it is.

…

That doesn't explain the shake though.

DANDELIAH JONES. The shake?

TREVOR. This weird thing happens where whenever a white person touches me, I, like, can't stop doing the Harlem Shake.

DANDELIAH JONES. What?

TREVOR. Uncontrollably.

MONA. OH MY GOD I THOUGHT THAT WAS JUST ME.

DANDELIAH JONES. You're telling me that whenever a white person touches you you start...doing the Harlem Shake?

MONA. Yes! Well not exactly. This weird thing happens where, I'm with a white person, and next thing you know I'm just doing incredible amounts of emotional labor.

TREVOR. Oh my god, I know.

MONA. I know!

DANDELIAH JONES. That's...that's not normal.

Whoa. Let's unpack this.

I'm gonna show you some photos and I want you to just.

Control yourselves. Just as a test.

MONA. Sure.

TREVOR. Alright.

 (DANDELIAH JONES *holds up a photo of a famous Black person.*)

MONA. Oh my god I love them.

TREVOR. So talented!

MONA. And like really pushes the line between artist and activist.

TREVOR. Ugh yes. Yes!

 (DANDELIAH JONES *holds up a photo of a famous white person.*

 A moment.

 TREVOR *shudders.*

 MONA *taps her knee.*)

DANDELIAH JONES. How do you feel?

TREVOR. (*Clearly not good.*) I'm good.

MONA. (*Holding it together.*) Mhmmm.

 (DANDELIAH JONES *holds up a photo of a famous Black person.*)

TREVOR. WOW. They were so good in that thing.

MONA. Oh my god yes! Fabulous!

 (DANDELIAH JONES *holds up a photo of a famous white person.*

 [Maybe the Artistic Director of the theater?]

 A moment.

 TREVOR*'s neck twitches like Michael Jackson in* "Thriller.")

MONA. (*Cracking.*) Mhmm...mhm...

TREVOR. Yep.

 (DANDELIAH JONES *holds up a photo of a famous white person.*

 A moment.

TREVOR *is lightly body rolling in his chair.*)
TREVOR. Uhhhh......Uhhhhhh...
MONA. (*Fighting herself hard.*) I'm good. I'm good.
(DANDELIAH JONES *holds up a photo of a famous white person.*
A moment.
TREVOR *JUMPS OUT OF HIS SEAT!*)
TREVOR. AHHHHHHHHHH! IT'S HAPPENING!
MONA. I'M LOSING CONTROL!
(TREVOR *begins to do the Harlem Shake.*)
MONA. (*Petting the famous white person photo and doing emotional labor.*)
Shhhhh. I know baby I know.
You can let it out.
TREVOR. I CAN TEACH YOU HOW TO DOUGIE!
(TREVOR *is breakdancing.*
DANDELIAH JONES *screams and rips the photo in half.*)
MONA. Peter! Peter I just wanna help you become your best self!
DANDELIAH JONES. SNAP OUT OF IT!
(DANDELIAH JONES *slaps* MONA.
That slap was mostly for her, if we're being real.
The spell is broken.
MONA *turns to* TREVOR.)
MONA. Whoa...It...it happens to you too?
TREVOR. I thought I was the only one. It...it feels so good to not be alone.
MONA. I feel so seen by you, Trevor.
(MONA *touches* TREVOR.
TREVOR *looks at* MONA.
They share a moment.
Are they going to date?
DANDELIAH *holds two halves of a photo in her hand.*
Some sexy R&B music plays.
The show fades to commercial.)

EVERY BLACK FATHER EVER

Enter EVERY BLACK FATHER EVER.
He is dressed like a professor and has a British accent.
He speaks to the audience like an infomercial.

EVERY BLACK FATHER EVER. Hi.

I'm Every Black Father Ever.

What's important for you to know is that I am here.

I am here and I am not with my children.

My children, yes, it seems they grew up without me.

Pity.

Indeed, it can be hard to be Every Black Father Ever.

There are many reasons why Every Black Father Ever moved on, without his children.

Mass incarceration took many of us.

As did poverty, generational violence, the Fermi paradox, and so forth.

And yet, within that, it turns out that an overwhelming number of Black fathers are actually present in the home, and play a more active role in the home than fathers of other races.

They've done studies. Har har.

Still, it seems, we cannot escape the narrative that Black men don't take care of their children.

Wild!

I, of course, did not take care of my children.

But not because of any stereotype, silly.

I simply did not want to be there and so I was not.

Yes I left before my child's first words, and never looked back.

Toodle loo!

Since then I've lived a rather wonderful life.

I've become a professor at Oxford.

I've slept with 17 and a half different people.

I've read the dictionary in nine different languages.

I've written the dictionary in four.

I've killed six men and gone on three drive-bys.

I cruised through Los Angeles in a purple Cadillac.

Bottle of Hennessey in my left hand and a breast of chicken in my right.

I know what you're wondering:

With both of my hands full, how am I driving?

Well the answer is quite simple. I'm driving with my penis!

And since the fatal mistake of doing the act that leads to one becoming a father,

my penis is perpetually covered in latex.

Even right now, under these khakis, I'm wearing six condoms

because one can never be too careful out here in these streets.

Quite effective I might add; I can barely even remember what my son looks like!

He could appear before me and I wouldn't even—

> (EVERY BLACK FATHER EVER *notices something. A presence.*)

...

...

David.

...

David Harris.

Is...that you?

This is your father talking.

I know you're out there.

> (*No response.*)

I know you're listening somewhere out there.

I know you just want to know where you come from.

David! DAVID!

> (EVERY BLACK FATHER EVER *runs off in the direction of the presence.*)

uh what?

BLACK HISTORIAN *runs on after* EVERY BLACK FATHER EVER.
BLACK HISTORIAN. uh what?
"David Harris."
That was weird.
…
I don't know who that is, but that ain't in my time capsule.
Back to my show y'all!
(BLACK HISTORIAN *conducts.*)

BATTLE RAP

BATTLE RAP intro music!

Enter as many people as possible.

They form a semi-circle.

In the middle of the semi-circle is MISTER BOOP BOOP BLOCKA*, the host of today's rap battle.*

MISTER BOOP BOOP BLOCKA *holds a microphone.*

MISTER BOOP BOOP BLOCKA. Ch-ch-ch-chyeah. What's good and welcome back to Absolute Battle League

where we pit the fiercest wordsmiths against one another

in a fight to find the best battle rappers of our generation.

I'm your host Mister Boop Boop Blocka!

(Airhorns! Gun sounds!)

Let's get this thang started.

Today we got a newcomer,

STRUGGLE RAPPER,

versus the previous champ,

I GOT MONEY.

Rapper on my right introduce yourself.

(STRUGGLE RAPPER *appears.*)

STRUGGLE RAPPER. Yo yo yo. I'm Struggle Rapper. Straight out the trap. Out of the frying pan into the fire. Allegory of the cave gang.

Handling my business for the streets. Free my nigga Tre and my nigga Wiley. Let's get it.

MISTER BOOP BOOP BLOCKA. Alright alriiiigghhttt. Rapper to my left. Tell them who you is.

(I GOT MONEY *appears.*)

I GOT MONEY. YEOO! It's ya boi. I Got Money. Forward flex record labels. Mo money no problem.

Whatchu know about that ay I know all about that! (*Rapper laugh.*)

MISTER BOOP BOOP BLOCKA. Let's get it.

I GOT MONEY won the coin toss and chose STRUGGLE RAPPER to go first. Round one. Struggle Rapper…spit that shit.

(Rap battle begins.

Rappers spit acapella and transition between flowing and talking.

Think SMACK: Ultimate Rap League. *Crowd reactions are a must.)*

STRUGGLE RAPPER. Aight y'all. I need you to hold it down and listen to these words.

>   *(To make it easier, rhymes are highlighted in **bold**.)*
> *Struggle Rapper here. / Speaking truth is my **game**.*
> *Teachers said I wouldn't make it. / Like my shit was **so lame**.*
> *I said nah / you need to know about **the life***
> *I gotta rap my pain, / so you can know about **the strife***
>
> *Cuz your life / ain't as **hard as mine***
> *Sold ya soul / now ya **heart is mine***
> *You know / I go **harder, crime***
> *If I lose / I'm a **martyr, fine!***

CROWD. Wooo.

STRUGGLE RAPPER. *Struggle Rapper / The **streets is my church**.*
*Pen game crazy / Make the **people berserk**.*
*You niggas leave us hanging / then **yo soul converts**.*
*Till I take the mic / and I **show you work**.*
Now let me tell you about the struggle.

>   (STRUGGLE RAPPER *TAKES A DEEP BREATH AND*
>   *IS SUDDENLY VERY ANGRY.*)
> *I USED TO BAG COCAINE / WIT **MY TITTIES OUT!***

MISTER BOOP BOOP BLOCKA. OH SHIT!

STRUGGLE RAPPER. *ON MY FEET SO LONG THAT / **IT GIMME GOUT!***
*BEEN **THROUGH THE SHIT**, YOU A BITCH / I GOT **BIGGA CLOUT!***
*JOHN PATRICK SHANLEY COULDN'T EVEN / **GIMME DOUBT!***

CROWD. OHHHHHHHHHHHHHHHHHH!

STRUGGLE RAPPER. *DON'T TALK ABOUT MONEY TO ME / THIS IS **STRUGGLE RAP!***
*TOUCH ME, IMMA GET SHIT POPPIN / **BUBBLE WRAP!***
*I'M TWICE AS REAL AS YOU / THAT'S A **DOUBLE FACT***
*MONEY CAN'T SAVE YO SOUL / now you in **trouble mac**.*
That's round one.

>   (*AIRHORNS!*
>   *Crowd is like damn.*)

MISTER BOOP BOOP BLOCKA. Oh shit! That's real talk.

Homie three months behind on the rent and ain't paying any time soon!
I Got Money: it's on you.

I GOT MONEY. Y'all can hear me? Well check it.

*Fuck yo broke ass / I move like **Kings Do***
*Sip lean, fresh nigga wit purple / **Mace Windu***
*I'm rich bitch / Got rubies and **gems too***
*I heard you work at Target / yo ass in aisle **ten, boo**.*
CROWD. GOT EEEEMMM!
I GOT MONEY. *Really think you gon win? / Cocaine, you **sharin sniffs?***
*I ride limousines / you make **bail by hailin Lyft**.*
*Versace nigga / I can **tell you wearin thrift**.*
*I said Fix My Suit Quickly! / my **tailor Taylor Swift**.*

*Gas bill high / I **blast heaters***
*You ol' dusty nigga / **rags, beaters***
*I got **fat stacks** / hitchu wit a **back slap***
*You don't got life insurance / no Geico, **Aflac***
CROWD. DAMMNNNN.
MISTER BOOP BOOP BLOCKA. That's real shit ay run that back.
I GOT MONEY. *I said I got **fat stacks** / hitchu wit a **back slap***
*You don't got life insurance / no Geico, **Aflac***

*Boy I got **cash racks** / you got **back rashes***
*And yo head game the **trashest** / you can't even **boast hun***
*You boutta get jacked by a beanstalk / I **fe fi fo fum***
*I **creep high blow sumthin** / bitch better **go run***
*Cuz I'm blowing power puffs / I MoJo **Jo son***
CROWD. HOOOOOOOOOOOOO MY GOD!
I GOT MONEY. This nigga dead! Money!
        (*Airhorns!!*)
MISTER BOOP BOOP BLOCKA. ABSOLUTE BATTLE LEAGUE IT'S GOING DOWN.
STRUGGLE RAPPER. It's not enough.
I GOT MONEY. I already won.
STRUGGLE RAPPER. How you gonna Mojo Jo a nigga; that bar don't even make sense!
I GOT MONEY. Fuck you.
STRUGGLE RAPPER. Eat my ass.
I GOT MONEY. You wish I would.
STRUGGLE RAPPER. I BEEN FAKING MY ORGASMS FOR THE LAST 3 YEARS!

I GOT MONEY. BITCH WHAT!

CROWD. OHHHHHHH SHIT!

MISTER BOOP BOOP BLOCKA. AIGHT Y'ALL LET'S NOT GET IN ANY FIGHTS HERE.

Struggle Rapper you got more?

STRUGGLE RAPPER. Oh I got more.

I GOT MONEY. (*Mocking.*) I got more.

STRUGGLE RAPPER. I'm ending this once and for all.

I SAID YO!

　　　　　(STRUGGLE RAPPER *IS ABOUT TO GO OFF.*)

*You can't match what I been through / my **written's are stickin.***

*Yo rhymes is unseasoned / like a **white woman's chicken.***

CROWD. OOOOOOOHHHH OHHH SHIT OH SHIT!

STRUGGLE RAPPER. Nah let me rap!

*You can't match what I been through / my **written's are stickin.***

Yo rhymes is unseasoned /

STRUGGLE RAPPER & CROWD. *Like a **white woman's chicken.***

STRUGGLE RAPPER. *I said it I meant it / I know you **like what I'm spittin***

*Survived the best of times, the worst of times / I out-**write Charles Dickens!***

MISTER BOOP BOOP BLOCKA. GO OFF NIGGA!

I GOT MONEY. Aight that's enough.

STRUGGLE RAPPER. Nah I ain't done yet!

*You got nothin left / so I hit you wit a **right hook***

*Call me out my name / you get Kunta Kinte's **right foot***

Knife stook / Cash who? Cash you?

*Nigga please I go nuts / like **cashews***

I GOT MONEY. Chill I got a peanut allergy.

STRUGGLE RAPPER. *Creep up on ya block in my used / **Honda!***

*Running this show wit my Rhimes: / **Shonda!***

*Two guns, both magic: / Cosmo, **Wanda!***

*Leave ya head bowed, arms crossed: / **Wakanda!***

MISTER BOOP BOOP BLOCKA. (*AD LIB AD LIB!*)

STRUGGLE RAPPER. *AHHHH YOU MAKE ME SO MAD / NIGGA I GRAB **THE TOASTA***

*NOT WASHING YO DIRTY DISHES / I **GOTTA ROAST YA***

*MARRIAGE BE HARD SOMETIMES / A **ROLLA COASTA***

*BUT I'M A MAGICAL NEGRO / **WINGARDIUM LEVIOSA**!*

MISTER BOOP BOOP BLOCKA & CROWD. THAT'S A SLYTHERIN ASS NIGGA!

YOOOOOOOOOOOO, OHHHHHHHH, WHAT, STOP, IT'S TOO MUCH IT'S TOO MUCH!

IT'S TOO MUCH FIRE!

> (*AIRHORNS! A FAKE EXPLOSION!*
> STRUGGLE RAPPER *has won the crowd and the battle.*
> MISTER BOOP BOOP BLOCKA *turns to* I GOT MONEY.
> I GOT MONEY *doesn't know what to do.*
> I GOT MONEY *is scrambling.*)

I GOT MONEY. Umm. Ummm. Uhhh. Uhhh.

> (*Struggling.*)

SpongeBob, on ya streets… / …I am ready.

Big guns, aim good… / …iron steady

CROWD & MISTER BOOP BOOP BLOCKA. BOOOOOOO! BOOOOOOOOO! YOU SUCK NIGGA!

I GOT MONEY. Wait wait wait wait. Um.

> (*Suddenly confident.*)

I DON'T GIVE A FUCK ABOUT YO STRUGGLE / **I Got Money.**

YO BARS DON'T MATTER / cuz cuz **I Got Money.**

I DON'T CARE THAT YOU'RE BROKE / since **I Got Money.**

THE ONLY REASON YOU HERE / is because…**You. Want. Money!**

> (*Silence.*
> *Everyone turns to* STRUGGLE RAPPER.
> I GOT MONEY *is like yeah what.*
> *The crowd closes in and looks between* STRUGGLE RAPPER *and* I GOT MONEY.
> *They continue to react, but now they whisper.*)

STRUGGLE RAPPER. Are you satisfied?

I GOT MONEY. I got money!

STRUGGLE RAPPER. Babe. Come on. You lost.

I GOT MONEY. I. Got. Money.

STRUGGLE RAPPER. We got bills to pay.

I GOT MONEY. I…got—

STRUGGLE RAPPER. Sure, if that would make you come home. You won. You're the best rapper in the world.

Alright?

Our kids miss you.

CROWD. damnnnnnn

I GOT MONEY. I got money?

STRUGGLE RAPPER. And…and I miss you…

CROWD. awwwwwww.

I GOT MONEY. …i got money…

STRUGGLE RAPPER. Shh I know, babe, I know. I don't like sleeping alone either.

Are you ready?

(STRUGGLE RAPPER *holds out their hand.*)

I GOT MONEY. Wait.

(I GOT MONEY *turns to* MISTER BOOP BOOP BLOCKA *and takes the mic.*

I GOT MONEY *looks at* STRUGGLE RAPPER.)

We don't got money.

(STRUGGLE RAPPER *beams and gives* I GOT MONEY *a deep thug kiss.*

Airhorns!!

I GOT MONEY *takes* STRUGGLE RAPPER's *hand and they leave to work on their marriage.*

Black love y'all.)

COLORED PEOPLE TIME

Enter THE NIGGA WHO MISSED THE MARCH.

Dressed in an all-black afro fist comb leather jacket Black Lives Matter get-up.

THE NIGGA WHO MISSED THE MARCH. Hi.

I'm the nigga who missed the march.

And I'm here to tell you what had happened.

What had happened was, I had heard from some people

that there was gonna be an event. People was gonna gather and march

on the White House to be like "Stop racism!"

And I was like "Oh word?"

And they was all like yeah we gon ride up and let The Man know what's what.

Cuz we ain't gonna take it no more.

And I was like "Word."

And they was like if it gotta come to violence, we gon do what we gotta do.

Is you wit me?

And I was like "Word."

Errybody made signs and was gonna wear all black.

And it was about to be this big event. National news.

SWAT teams n shit, cops and pepper spray.

And then what had happened was, the day of, it was like,

raining.

And so naturally, I assumed that the event would get

cancelled because of inclement weather.

Like we can postpone the function to a time that's more convenient, right.

Right? I'm making sense, right? Cuz I ain't tryna get wet.

I don't got no rain boots.

So me, making acute presumptions as I am prone to do, I stayed in bed.

Cuz like, it's raining y'all.

Come to find out, I'm getting text messages talkin bout where you at.

Where I'm at? I'm sleep nigga.

And they poppin off like nigga you missed the march, nigga they arresting us, nigga they breaking Darnell's arms.

And I'm like "Oh word?"

And they like it's yo fault cuz you wasn't there to help.

And I'm like no I was not. Shiitttt. I like my arms. I ain't tryna get em broke.

Ain't nobody tell you to march on the White House. They strapped.

And it's raining!

Y'all must've lost yo damn, talkin bout come march in the rain and get yo ass beat to end racism.

Fuck outta here.

Niggas been dying for like a thousand million years. I don't got time to be marching for everyone.

So Imma march my ass to my bed.

I ain't saying I fucks with racism.

But like. I think, personally, I'm more valuable here.

Y'all have fun.

> (*BOOM!*
> *RIOTS!*
> *MUSIC!*
> THE NIGGA WHO MISSED THE MARCH *is gone.*
> *Then!*)

EVERY BLACK MOTHER EVER

Enter EVERY BLACK MOTHER EVER.

She carries a burlap sack and has an inexplicable dramatic Southern accent.

EVERY BLACK MOTHER EVER. Hi.

I'm Every Black Mother Ever.

And I'm here to tell stories about my chilren.

(*She pulls a Black doll out of her burlap sack.*)

This here is my son. Isn't he perfect?

He got stars for eyes, and skin the color of hot cocoa. Look!

He's the best basketball player his high school ever seent.

They say he the next Kobe, my baby. He's gonna get outta here.

He's gonna get out of the hood. Go to college and then the NBA!

That's what I say.

I says go on! Get out of here and make something of yourself!

You let the world know that you my son and nothing can stop—

(*BANG!*

The Black doll is somehow flung.)

NOOOOOOO! NOT MY BABY! DAMN YOU GANG VIOLENCE!

(*She pulls out another doll.*)

This here is my daughter.

She can't do no wrong.

She got skin the color of midnight mahogany oak.

She never done a drug in her life. Not the weed. Not the reefer.

Comes home every night and works the soup kitchen on the weekends. Mhm.

She on track to cure cancer by the age of 19...so long as she makes it out of the hood.

And that's what I say. I say get out of these projects and go live your dreams. Reach for the stars—

(*BANG!*)

NOOOOOO! WHYYYYYYYYYY! DAMN YOU POLICE BRUTALITY! YOU VILLAIN! FIE!

(*She pulls out another doll.*)

Y'all see my lil other son? Ain't he something? He got skin like sweet caramel fudge brown sugar synonym synonym synonym synonym.

And when he makes it out the hood, he's gonna be an astronaut lawyer judge
rapper athlete synonym synonym synonym synonym—

    (*BANG!*)

NOT AGAIN!!!!! DAMN YOU...POLICE BRUTALITY...AGAIN! WHO COULD
HAVE FORESEEN THIS DRAMATIC TURN IN THE ARC OF MY LIFE!

    (*She pulls out two golden statues.*)

These my other other two kids. They names is Oscar and Tony.

They got skin bright as gold.

And they are going to get out of here.

They took a lot of work to raise, but they got dreams of being stars once
they escape their fate!

    (*BANG! BANG!*

    EVERY BLACK MOTHER EVER's *awards are flung.*

    EVERY BLACK MOTHER EVER *does not react.*

    EVERY BLACK MOTHER EVER *notices something. A presence.*)

...

David.

David Harris is that you?!?

This is your mother talking.

I know you're out there.

I know you're just looking for answers.

...

DAVID!

    (EVERY BLACK MOTHER EVER *runs off in the direction of the
presence.*)

huh?

BLACK HISTORIAN *runs on after* EVERY BLACK MOTHER EVER.

BLACK HISTORIAN. Trippin. They trippin.

Nah honey. This is my White Historian Sponsored Definitive Black Experience Time Capsule For The Aliens In Space. Ok?

LET'S GET IT!

(*BOOM. MUSIC.*

SIMILAR TO THE MUSIC THAT BLACK HISTORIAN *CONJURED AT THE TOP.*

BLACK HISTORIAN *IS JAMMING TO THE CREATION.*

Then.

A mob of ACTORS *marches onto the stage and stops the show.*)

STILL NOT ME

ALL THE ACTORS, *in various costumes from the play, and* BLACK HISTORIAN.

ACTORS. WE NOT HAPPY.

BLACK HISTORIAN. You're not happy?

ACTOR 1. NOPE.

ACTOR 2. WE'RE NOT.

ACTOR 3. HELL TO THE NAW.

BLACK HISTORIAN. I'm confused.

What did I do wrong?

ACTOR 1. WHAT DID HE DO WRONG?

ACTOR 2. Oh he don't get it.

ACTOR 3. This is not what I signed up for.

BLACK HISTORIAN. How so?

ACTOR 1. I want real people!

ACTOR 2. Real stories!

ACTOR 3. Shit I can relate to!

BLACK HISTORIAN. Ok I'm lost.

ACTOR 1. I don't rap.

ACTOR 2. I don't sing.

ACTOR 3. And I definitely ain't no slave.

BLACK HISTORIAN. But there are rappers. And singers. And slaves!

ACTORS. BUT DAT AIN'T ME.

ACTOR 1. They gonna blast yo shit on a rocketship for the aliens in space and it's gonna be all wrong.

BLACK HISTORIAN. Wrong? How am I wrong!

ACTORS. THIS IS NOT OUR BLACK EXPERIENCE.

ACTOR 2. The fuck it ain't!

BLACK HISTORIAN. But you understand what I'm doing, right?

I'm a real historian wink wink.

I'm trying to use the constraints of history to imagine beyond the constraints of history—

ACTOR 3. SHUT YO MOUTH. I went to Juilliard. Aight.

(*Everyone is like what does that have to with any*—)

Which means I'm not tryna act a fool.

ACTOR 2. And you're making Black people look foolish!

BLACK HISTORIAN. Aren't we all fools in the grand scheme of things?

ACTOR 3. Fuck yo grand scheme.

You gonna put this in a time capsule and make people think it's me.

BUT DAT AIN'T ME.

DATS AN OFFENSIVE REPRESENTATIONS!

BLACK HISTORIAN. I mean it's satire—

ACTOR 3. I said what I said.

BLACK HISTORIAN. Oh so you mean to tell me you've never been part of a TV comedy about a Black family with an abundant matriarch? You've never bagged cocaine with your titties out? You've never been addicted to dating white people—

ACTORS. NO!

BLACK HISTORIAN. Really? Am I that far off?

ACTORS. YES!

ACTOR 1. I've never missed a march!

ACTORS. RIGHT!

ACTOR 2. And I've never used my Black pain to win an Oscar.

ACTORS. PREACH!

ACTOR 3. And I've never dated a white person.

ACTORS. COME ON NOW!

ACTOR 1. Wait what about that one dude you were with?

ACTOR 3. Man that was just some head.

ACTORS. ...

ACTOR 2. And I definitely wouldn't accept no money from some white historians!

ACTORS. NEVER!

ACTOR 1. I make art to uplift my people! Show the world that we can be better than what they say we are!

BLACK HISTORIAN. Well what do you want then?

ACTOR 2. I want to see my life reflected back to me onstage.

ACTORS. Hell yeah!

ACTOR 1. I want to see the struggle.

ACTORS. THE STRUGGLE!

ACTOR 2. I want to see the pain.

ACTORS. THE PAIN!

ACTOR 3. And the neverending fight for FREEDOM!

ACTORS. FREEDOM!

ACTOR 2. Ashanti Ja Rule!

BLACK HISTORIAN. So you're saying…you want to see the pain?

ACTOR 1. And then see myself overcoming that pain! Cuz that's what we do. We overcome the pain!

That's the history of Black people. Can't we do it?

ACTORS. YES WE CAN!

BLACK HISTORIAN. Oh no…

Ohhhhhhh no…

     (*Gasp.*)

What you're saying is you actually want the boats!

You want the chains!

You want the whips and the Negro spirituals!

You—YOU WANT A BLACK STRUGGLE PLAY!

ACTOR 3. WE WANT…

Yeah that sounds right.

BLACK HISTORIAN. You sound like the white historians.

ACTOR 1. No. Because they used history to tear us down. I'm saying you need to build us up.

ACTOR 2. I want to be a fully developed character who speaks truth to power.

ACTORS. Mhhhmmm!

ACTOR 3. I wanna be a historical hero, coming back to set the record straight.

Striving for justice and my humanity!

ACTOR 1. (*Catchphrase.*) Ain't that right!

BLACK HISTORIAN. Well don't you think that by using this strange, mysterious device of theater,

that we can reach for something even deeper,

perhaps universal,

if only we allow ourselves the freedom to IMAGINE beyond—

ACTOR 2. Excuse me. Um.

I think what we're all saying is that your imagination doesn't speak to my idea of myself

and thus we don't want to speak it.

Because this.

Every Black Mother Ever.

Mister Boop Boop Blocka.

Mamalicious.

This ain't it.

> (*A long pause.*)

BLACK HISTORIAN. Wow. Well. I guess now you've all enlightened me as to…The Black Experience™.

And my version of history needs to validate your Black experience.

Because oppression is the truth, and thus you want to see yourself oppressed onstage and then surviving through the power of your Black soul.

> (*The* ACTORS *confer.*)

ACTOR 2. YES.

ACTOR 1. SPEAK TRUTH TO POWER.

BLACK HISTORIAN. Right. Right!

ACTOR 1. And make it good!

BLACK HISTORIAN. Oh it'll be good. Really good. So good in fact that it'll feel like it could stand alone as its own piece. But it can't. I assure you it can't.

Because nothing can stand alone in the face OF HISTORY!

Oh. Also.

Here are your artist stipends.

> (BLACK HISTORIAN *hands them each an envelope.*
>
> *The* ACTORS *begin to leave.*)

Hey…um.

I have a bit of a confession to make. Can I tell you a secret I've never told anyone?

Ok. How should I put this. I…

I've never met another Black person before.

I haven't. You're the first ones.

I debated even saying anything at all. But, here we are.

I'm mostly just working from the voices I hear in my head.

ACTOR 3. Well you ain't hearing me nigga.

> (*The* ACTORS *are gone.*
>
> *As* BLACK HISTORIAN *imagines, the next scene begins to form.*)

BLACK HISTORIAN. Alright. The new truth. The Black truth. Oppression and overcoming it.

Because oppression is Black History.

And I am a Black Historian wink wink, and thus I must tell the truth.

Because that's what…

That's what my new Black friends want.

It must show...THE STRUGGLE. The Black Struggle™.

And be grounded in a fully realized world with fully developed characters.

And encapsulate all of history while also rebuking the errors of history.

Oh this is a lot. Hmmm.

Alright. Let's see here.

The perfect Black Struggle play!

How about we start with this:

> (*We are transported into their mind somehow.*
> *Or rather, the mind of the piece.*
> *Some spectacle happens here that makes us go like*
> *damn the rules of this world are...different from before.*
> *Actually, very different.*
> *Now we're just in a naturalist kitchen.*)

WHITE PEOPLE OWN THIS KITCHEN
AND TWO FULLY DEVELOPED BLACK CHARACTERS
NAMED AUNT JEMIMA AND UNCLE BEN
HAVE TO WORK IN IT AND SURVIVE
DESPITE HARSH REALITIES N SHIT

Lights click on.

AUNT JEMIMA *is bent over the counter dredging some chicken in flour and egg. The sound of oil popping on the stove.*

UNCLE BEN *is peeling carrots. He occasionally looks at* AUNT JEMIMA *working.*

The routine. It's just some Black folk doing their jobs I guess.

After a while:

UNCLE BEN. You doin it wrong.

AUNT JEMIMA. Whatchu say?

UNCLE BEN. I said you doin it wrong.

(UNCLE BEN *observes her chicken.*)

UNCLE BEN. See the chicken all bloody.

AUNT JEMIMA. It's supposed to be.

UNCLE BEN. Nah you can't be serving the white folk upstairs no bloody chicken.

AUNT JEMIMA. I ain't.

UNCLE BEN. You doin it wrong.

AUNT JEMIMA. Say that one more time and Imma pop you with this spatula. Think I'm playing.

UNCLE BEN. Miss Betsy ain't gonna be too pleased.

AUNT JEMIMA. You know what Miss Betsy had the nerve to tell me? Her sunburnt ass was like *"Aunt Jemima, can I tell you a secret?"* And I says *"Sure thing Miss Betsy."* And she gets all distraught. Damn near crying. She all like *"Aunt Jemima I don't think my husband loves me anymore."* And I'm like Lord have mercy. She says *"My husband goes off on these business trips and when he comes home, I always have dinner ready. The house is clean. I have his suits tailored. And he won't even look at me."* And I'm like heffer, did you forget who really takes care of this place? Who cooks and cleans and makes sure you can see your lily-white reflection in the spoon while you eating my soup? But that's none of my business so I kindly say... *"Well maybe he's cheating on you with Miss Martha!"* And she gets all angry, like *"Aunt Jemima how dare you! I am the most beautiful girl in the whole wide world."* So I get an idea. I tell her that she should go buy some lingerie and *make* him pay attention. So, check this out, she goes off to the shop and she buys herself...

A FRENCH MAID OUTFIT! With a little feather duster and everything!

She dressed up as a servant!

A servant! She up there pretending she's me!

    (AUNT JEMIMA *bursts out laughing.*)

She don't even know how to use it. She think it's a make-up brush. Tryna apply foundation with a feather duster. You believe that? ...You not even listening.

UNCLE BEN. I'm listening.

AUNT JEMIMA. No you ain't. You prolly fantasizing about Miss Betsy in a French Maid outfit right now.

UNCLE BEN. Did it come wit the fishnet stockings too?

AUNT JEMIMA. Uncle Ben if you don't cut it out. I'm tryna tell you a story.

UNCLE BEN. Well then get to the point.

AUNT JEMIMA. The point is...the point is...I don't know what the point is.

UNCLE BEN. Of course you don't got a point. You never got a point.

Everything I say got a point.

Watch Imma tell a joke right now. You ready?

Knock knock.

AUNT JEMIMA. Who's there?

UNCLE BEN. Silence.

AUNT JEMIMA. Silence who?

    (*Silence.*)

See that ain't even funny.

UNCLE BEN. You know you wanna laugh. And that's the point.

    (*Silence.*)

AUNT JEMIMA. You really think Miss Betsy the most beautiful woman in the world?

UNCLE BEN. Do I think she the most beautiful woman in the world...You know what I see when I close my eyes? I see a mountain. Tallest mountain ever. You wouldn't believe how tall it is. And you know what it's made out of?

AUNT JEMIMA. What?

UNCLE BEN. Potatoes. And I gotta skin all them potatoes to reach the top. And the mountain is shrinking. And just when I get to the top, I see that there's more mountains. One is made of rice. So I gotta wash all the rice. Then I gotta slice all the onions. And I keep on doing this. And I keep on doing that. And I keep on keeping on.

AUNT JEMIMA. And Miss Betsy at the top of the mountain waiting for you?

UNCLE BEN. Nah.

AUNT JEMIMA. What's at the top of the mountain?

UNCLE BEN. A Cadillac.

AUNT JEMIMA. A Cadillac?! Whatchu know about cars?

UNCLE BEN. I don't know. I never drove one.

AUNT JEMIMA. So whatchu know about Cadillacs?

UNCLE BEN. I know I want one.

AUNT JEMIMA. Whatchu gonna do with it?

UNCLE BEN. Nothing. I'm not gonna touch it. Not even gonna look at it. Imma just make other people look at it. And they ain't gonna forget who it belongs to. They ain't gonna forget...I'm done with the carrots.

AUNT JEMIMA. Get started on that lettuce.

> (UNCLE BEN *gets started on that lettuce.*)

I know you think she beautiful.

UNCLE BEN. Miss Betsy?

AUNT JEMIMA. You think you slick, but the walls is thin.

UNCLE BEN. Whatchu talking about?

AUNT JEMIMA. You be whispering her name while you sleep. While you dreaming.

UNCLE BEN. No I don't.

AUNT JEMIMA. The walls is thin.

UNCLE BEN. How you know I'm not having a nightmare?

AUNT JEMIMA. Cuz you whisper my name when you having a nightmare. Not my fault you loud. I can hear you whispering her name at other times too.

...

Don't play dumb.

> (AUNT JEMIMA *makes a phallic masturbatory gesture with her spatula.*)

UNCLE BEN. Hey now whatchu doing?

AUNT JEMIMA. Oh Miss Betsy.

Keep going Miss Betsy.

UNCLE BEN. I don't know whatchu talking about.

AUNT JEMIMA. Mmm you got soft hands Miss Betsy.

> (AUNT JEMIMA *laughs and continues more vigorously.*
> *If* UNCLE BEN *could blush, he'd be red as a stop sign.*)

UNCLE BEN. There are things—

AUNT JEMIMA. I likes it when you do me right there.

UNCLE BEN. Stop it now—

AUNT JEMIMA. Yo husband ain't never gonna find out.

UNCLE BEN. I SAID STOP IT! Alright! Now lookie here. There are things that I, that men need to do in the private comfort of their rooms that you ain't s'posed to be listening to.

AUNT JEMIMA. It ain't my fault you loud. Sound like you playing pattycake on yo ding-a-ling.

UNCLE BEN. Hush up woman.

AUNT JEMIMA. You know all them paintings they got upstairs? In their galleries. They got portraits of these old French women. And you know what? They all fat. They huge. They like planets. Don't none of them got manicured nails or waxed coochees. They all fat and desirable. Ain't none of them Black, but ain't none of them look like Miss Betsy neither.

UNCLE BEN. Woman have you lost your mind?

AUNT JEMIMA. Cut the goddamn lettuce.

> (*They work in silence.*)

UNCLE BEN. Did I do something wrong?

AUNT JEMIMA. Did you do something wrong.

…

Ain't no men in none of them paintings neither.

UNCLE BEN. Yeah but who you think painted them?

> (*Back to silence. The sound of metal on metal, metal on food. Things cooking.*
>
> UNCLE BEN *takes a bite out of a piece of* AUNT JEMIMA'*s chicken.*)

AUNT JEMIMA. Put that chicken down.

UNCLE BEN. What?

AUNT JEMIMA. I said put that chicken down now!

> (*She takes it out of his hands.*)

AUNT JEMIMA. You ain't even ask.

UNCLE BEN. Lemme have a piece of chicken.

AUNT JEMIMA. No.

UNCLE BEN. How you gonna keep the chicken this close to me but not let me touch it?

AUNT JEMIMA. Cuz it ain't for you.

UNCLE BEN. It ain't for you neither.

AUNT JEMIMA. That don't change nothing.

UNCLE BEN. I'm hungry.

AUNT JEMIMA. And?

UNCLE BEN. And when I'm hungry I gots to eat.

> (*He lunges for the chicken.* AUNT JEMIMA *smacks him with the spatula.*)

UNCLE BEN. Ow.

AUNT JEMIMA. I said no.

UNCLE BEN. Woman why you so serious over a drumstick?

AUNT JEMIMA. I said no.

UNCLE BEN. Imma have to call Boss Man down here and tell him you burning his chicken.

AUNT JEMIMA. And what else he gonna do to me?

UNCLE BEN. What's that mean?

> (*Silence.*)

Hold on now Aunt Jemima what does that—

AUNT JEMIMA. Ain't nothing.

I shouldn't have said...

You ain't the only man around here that got fantasies is all. Boss Man been making passes at me for as long as we known each other. Some words here. Then some touching. What am I gonna do, you know? I got a job to do. Just words and touching. Not like a man's thoughts can hurt you, you know?

UNCLE BEN. Did he...? If he...you know what I would do to him if he—

AUNT JEMIMA. That's all that matters to you? See why's that the first thing that always comes into y'all's heads... And you be out here thinking the same thoughts as him too. I just know it. I know it.

> (*Silence.* AUNT JEMIMA *is cooking. She hasn't looked at* UNCLE BEN. *Suddenly,* UNCLE BEN *has an idea. He takes an entire container of salt and dumps it in one of the dishes.*)

Hey whatchu—

> (*He begins destroying the meal however he can. He spits in the soup.*)

What the hell?

UNCLE BEN. He thinks he can get away with it. He thinks we'll just take it. Nah. Not like this. Not like this. We gonna rise up!

AUNT JEMIMA. What do you think you're doing!

> (*He rubs his armpits with the lettuce. He puts his feet in the bread.*)

UNCLE BEN. They wanna make us take their shit; they can take mine too!

AUNT JEMIMA. Stop it Uncle Ben.

UNCLE BEN. Nah come on. Break some shit. Make them lick the scraps from our toes.

AUNT JEMIMA. No.

UNCLE BEN. They think they can just do what they want with you. With my Jemima. They done messed with the wrong cook now.

AUNT JEMIMA. No.

UNCLE BEN. Come on and help me destroy this place. We gonna poison their food.

AUNT JEMIMA. No Ben, Ben—

(UNCLE BEN *pulls down his pants and tries to pee on the chicken.*)

No hey hey AHHHHHHHHHHHHHHHHHHHHHHHHHHHHH!

(AUNT JEMIMA*'s scream has stopped* UNCLE BEN *from peeing on the chicken.*)

AHHHHHHHH. Do you know how long I worked on this meal?

UNCLE BEN. I'm helping you. We'll poison Miss Betsy. And Boss Man. We'll make them feel what we feel.

AUNT JEMIMA. No no no see but I never said that.

UNCLE BEN. So you tellin me that you not angry?

AUNT JEMIMA. Do you know how long I worked on this meal?

UNCLE BEN. A meal you not gonna eat.

AUNT JEMIMA. But it is mine all the same. Mine. My recipe. I cooked this. I made this, not for you to come and piss all over it.

UNCLE BEN. I'm trying to help you.

AUNT JEMIMA. You know what pisses me off? You have always looked the same. On the box. Always. Your image has never changed. I used to be fat like those French women. I used to take up the whole room. And then time went on and they said *be smaller* and *act pleasant*. So they made me skinny. And painted a smile on my face. Gave me wide hips, unreasonable breasts. Then they came for my hair. Bleached my teeth white and my skin brighter. And you? Uncle Ben. You have always been the same. White haired, broad shouldered, barely smiling. They have changed me over and over while you got to sit there and watch. And you still think you got the right to what's me and what's mine.

(UNCLE BEN *sits back on his stool.* AUNT JEMIMA *begins picking up the kitchen.*)

UNCLE BEN. Uh…whatchu want from me then?

AUNT JEMIMA. Uh whatchu want from me whatchu want from me. ...
I don't know if I give a fuck about you.
But I tell you one thing. Mhm.
There's a lesson in all this.
> (*Cue dramatic music.*)
Cuz I done survived this world. Over and over.
And no matter what this world throws at me, I'm gonna survive it again.
Because that's the history of my soul.
Like my mother's mother's mother, ain't nothing on this here Earth more powerful than me.
I'm not perfect but I'm pretty good.
And all the wrong in all the lands gonna try to take me out.
And they will all fail.
As I overcome my oppression.
Cuz I am strong and Black
and can't nothing break my back.
Fate doomed me to this dreadful estate
but Imma rise above it and finish my plate
and on that high road one day, Lord one day, I will escape.
To the sweet by and by.
With or without you.
Now you gonna help me cut this lettuce or not.
Miss Betsy's hungry.
> (UNCLE BEN *and* AUNT JEMIMA *resume cooking for their masters.*
> *Some old-time music plays them out.*
> AUNT JEMIMA *and* UNCLE BEN *fade.*
> *Then flashes of light.*
> *Like cameras.*
> *A press conference.*)

THE FIRST BLACK PRESIDENT Y'ALL

Enter BARACK OBAMA *in a suit.*

BARACK OBAMA. Hi.

I'm Barack Obama.

Uhhh my fellow Americans.

I stand here today to address something.

Something that has plagued my campaign.

Some folks been spreading lies and rumors about me.

Saying that I am not an American.

Saying that because of the color of my skin, I cannot possibly be a product of this nation.

And as President, sometimes I don't get the luxury of truth and honesty.

I don't get to say "Ya know, that hurts."

I don't get to slap people. Not in America.

I can drop a bomb on the Middle East.

I can send a jet to Syria.

I can pardon a turkey.

But as President, I cannot slap a muhfucka who needs to be slapped.

So it's time to say what needs to be said.

…

Let me be clear: I was in fact born in Africa.

2Pac is still alive.

We ball together on weekends and smoke all the weed.

I am currently high as a kite. Tripping off that OG kush. That good good.

…

Also. I hate Christmas. Michelle hates Christmas.

I am an atheist. I don't believe in God because I killed him with a drone strike.

I have more swag than all you crackers. Ritz, saltine, and wheat thin.

And America needs to know

    (*Suddenly enraged.*)

THAT I AM THE PRESIDENT! I WILL ALWAYS BE THE PRESIDENT!

THERE ARE NO OTHER PRESIDENTS!

THE BEATLES ARE OVERRATED! ALL MY NIGGAS BANG! GANG GANG GANG—

    (*The mob of* ACTORS *is back.*)

ACTOR 1. You fuckin up again!

BLACK HISTORIAN. What?

ACTOR 1. Barack Obama ain't say that.

BLACK HISTORIAN. But he needed to!

ACTORS. You fuckin up!

ACTOR 1. Barack Obama still alive.

You can't fuck with someone's history if they still alive.

BLACK HISTORIAN. But just imagine if he did say ALL MY NIGGAS BANG—

ACTORS. Nah! Dat ain't real!

BLACK HISTORIAN. NONE OF THIS IS REAL!

ACTORS. EXACTLY!

BLACK HISTORIAN. I tried it your way. I gave you a Black struggle kitchen sink story.

And frankly, I was bored!

ACTORS. (*Gasp.*)

BLACK HISTORIAN. Oh come on! You thought that was fun?!

ACTOR 1. I thought that was truthful! Reminds me of my mama working in that kitchen.

That was truthful.

ACTOR 3. And I want that truthful shit.

ACTOR 2. You're a Black Historian. You gotta be truthful and historically accurate.

BLACK HISTORIAN. BUT NOTHING IS HISTORICALLY ACCURATE!

ACTOR 1. Excuse me my brotha, but I know the history of my people.

My people are strong.

ACTOR 2. My people are brave.

ACTOR 3. My people are smart.

ACTOR 2. My people are kings and queens.

ACTOR 3. My people are beautiful.

ACTOR 1. My people are joyful.

ACTOR 2. My people are brilliant.

BLACK HISTORIAN. You're just naming adjectives right now.

ACTOR 1. We're trying to tell you!

The world, the government, the news, the history books, they all told us we were nothing.

I am more than that.

BLACK HISTORIAN. And how do you expect me to tell you who you are?

ACTOR 1. Well you can tell them who we are.

Because they, because white people took history and twisted it to make it seem like we are wrong for existing. And I want you to fix that by saying that WE ARE GREAT!

BLACK HISTORIAN. BUT YOU'RE NOT GREAT!

And neither am I!

All of this is a story.

Black History is a story. American History is a story.

And it is not my job to affirm your puny little existence with my stories!

ACTORS. NIGGA YOU CRAZY!

BLACK HISTORIAN. I'M ABSOLUTELY MAD.

Let me tell you how a story works:

You take a group of characters.

For the sake of the argument, let's call them: Black.

Everybody Black wink wink.

They're living their lives. Just kidding, no they're not.

Because that's a boring story.

WE NEED A CONFLICT. WE NEED A PLOT DEVICE.

Oh! I know!

RACISM. OH LAWDY GEEZUS.

Character. Conflict. Racism.

Character. Conflict. Racism.

Story. History. Story. History.

Slavery. Civil Rights. Genocide. Police Brutality.

Generational Poverty. Inner-City School Systems.

And eventually, it all becomes cliché!

Because you tell the same story over and over

and there is no difference between

history-making and storytelling

and there's this whole mythology of suffering,

but none of us really know what that suffering was like...we just...

even though the effects of that suffering are still with us but...what was I saying?

...

I was saying what's real! That's what!

AND I AM TRYING TO CREATE SOMETHING NEW SOMETHING BEYOND YOUR TRUTH!

To think, my first Black friends have no imagination.

…

You're looking at me like I have the answers but where did I even come from?

Huh? Ya know?

And another thing!

At least I'm acknowledging that YEAH I wanna get paid.

But you're here too which means YOU!

You also wanna get paid!

So the White Historians gonna blast my shit up into space.

And you're gonna be in it! And some alien is gonna receive it.

And they'll do whatever they want and think whatever they think.

Because I am not responsible for you.

Or my ancestors. Or the generations that will come long after I am dead.

Because they are not real; they only exist in whatever way I imagine them.

And the only thing…YEAH! The only thing that is real…

Is this artist stipend that I am paying you!

Because I know you are not trying to live on some pitiful, broke nigga truth either.

> (BLACK HISTORIAN *pulls out more envelopes.*)

Well?

> (BLACK HISTORIAN *waits. And waits.*
>
> *The* ACTORS *take their envelopes.*)

Yay!

Now if you'll get back into your places, we need to end on a message for the aliens in space.

This is my favorite part y'all.

> (BLACK HISTORIAN *is in control again.*
>
> *The* ACTORS *get into their places.*
>
> *Someone gets* BLACK HISTORIAN *a stool and a microphone.*
>
> *Maybe a fur shawl and a piano.*
>
> BLACK HISTORIAN *sits.*
>
> *A spotlight on* BLACK HISTORIAN.)

THE BLACK EXPERIENCE™

A piano plays a few notes underscoring the text.
BLACK HISTORIAN *is going to sing a jazz standard.*
BLACK HISTORIAN *is a diva with a crowd, and loving every second of it.*
BLACK HISTORIAN. Hi.
You might remember me.
I'm Black Historian.
I'm the orchestrator of this whole shebang.
I've made this project. For you.
Creatures from another dimension.
To explain the meaning of our Black lives.
They say you can tell the history of the world through the history of song.
Well. I'd like to sing a tune for you, if you don't mind.
>   *(The song begins slow.*
>   *Think: Ella Fitzgerald "Easy to Love" or Nancy Wilson "Guess Who I*
>   *Saw Today.")*
I know too well that time
Just keeps on passing by
And yes I've always known you see
That lies are what built history

Some people came before, and surely now hereafter
So I must ask: does anything I say or do
even matter?

...

A five, six, seven, eight!
>   *(The beat drops!*
>   *A big musical number.*
>   *Music comes in and the* ACTORS *dance onstage, all mic'd up.*
>   *They're all wearing matching outfits.*
>   *Something celebratory. Maybe gold sequins.*
>   *They have choreo and are killing it.*
>   *Musically, think big. Gloria Gaynor or Whitney.*
>   *Like that moment in "I Will Survive" when the beat comes in.)*
BLACK HISTORIAN. Ow! Come on y'all!

Hey! Hey!

BLACK HISTORIAN. *I'm thinkin bout the past*   **CHORUS.** *Oooooo!*
and all that it beheld.

Can't tell what's real or fake I'm screaming what   *Oooooo!*
the hell.

Will the world ever change; only time will tell.   *Oooooo!*

But if I'm gonna get paid then might as well.   *Oooooo!*

BLACK HISTORIAN. Sing it!

CHORUS. *There's so much we can't know.*

There's so much we can't know.

There's so much we can't

So much we can't

So much we can't know.

BLACK HISTORIAN. Shamone!

CHORUS. *There's so much we can't know.*

There's so much we can't know.

There's so much we can't

So much we can't

So much – YEAH YEAH YEAHHH!

BLACK HISTORIAN. How can anyone work their way through the mess that is history?

It was all written by someone else!

And that complicates everything.

Watch:

ACTOR 1. Your favorite dead hero changed the world for the better!

ACTOR 2. Your favorite dead hero cheated on his wife 23 different times!

ACTOR 3. Your favorite dead hero gave their child inherited traumas that they would have to unpack for the rest of their lives!

BLACK HISTORIAN. All those things could be true.

CHORUS. *I don't know!!*

BLACK HISTORIAN. And I don't either!

CHORUS. *There's so much we*   **BLACK HISTORIAN.** *Might as well*
can't know.   *imagine.*

There's so much we can't know.   *Might as well imagine.*

There's so much we can't   *Make some shit up.*

So much we can't   *Make it funny.*

So much we can't know.   *Bet they will give you some money.*

BLACK HISTORIAN & CHORUS. *Oh oh oh OHHHHHHHHHHHHHH!*
Let's take it to church now come on!
> (*Music changes.*
> *Gospel choir.*)

GOSPEL SINGER. *Oh happy day!*
CHORUS. *Oh happy day.*
GOSPEL SINGER. *Oh happy day!*
CHORUS. *Oh happy day.*
GOSPEL SINGER. *I'm getting paid!*
CHORUS. *I'm getting paid.*
GOSPEL SINGER. *I'm getting paid!*
CHORUS. *I'm getting paid.*
GOSPEL SINGER. *I'M GETTING PAIIIIDDDDDDDDDDDDD!*
BLACK HISTORIAN. REMIX!
> (*Music changes.*
> *A segue.*)

CHORUS. *Paid. Paid. Paid. Paid. / Get it.*
> (*Hip hop. Trap.*
> *Something that goes hard.*)

RAPPER. *None of this matters / you niggas can't **delay me***
*You know I went hard / these muhfuckas better **pay me***
*Photo in the history books / nigga I **say cheese***
*Black as shit / and I do it on the **daily***
ANOTHER RAPPER. *It **amazes me** / history was written so **lazily***
*It's **hazy see** / never deprive me of my **agency***
*The **rage in me** / put on a good show, **paying me***
*Look at the future / like BOYYY DON'T **PLAY WIT ME***
BLACK HISTORIAN. (*Call.*) *I had a dream!*
CHORUS. (*Response.*) What!
BLACK HISTORIAN. *I made a scheme!*
CHORUS. What!
BLACK HISTORIAN. *Yo stories they bore me I give em new sheen!*
CHORUS. Ha!
BLACK HISTORIAN. *They say I'm mean.*
CHORUS. Ha!
BLACK HISTORIAN. *Say I'm obscene.*
CHORUS. Ha!

BLACK HISTORIAN. *Well say what you want long as I get the green.*

CHORUS. OHH!

> *(DANCE BREAK.*
>
> *STEP. TAP. SOUL TRAIN. HOLY SPIRIT. VOGUE.*
>
> *WHATEVER THE CURRENT DANCE CRAZE IS.*
>
> BLACK HISTORIAN *HAS A SAXOPHONE SOLO. OR A GUITAR SOLO.*
>
> CHORUS *begins doing that criss-cross dance from "Lip Gloss."*
>
> *At some point,* BLACK HISTORIAN *steps out of the routine.)*

CHORUS. *(Diminuendo into whispers.) Everybody Black. Black Black Black.*
Everybody Black. Black Black Black.
Everybody Black. Black Black Black.

> *(It continues, underscoring* BLACK HISTORIAN.*)*

BLACK HISTORIAN. Now I told you. I said it I said I'm absolutely mad.

And what I meant by that was:

I am bound to no one.

I studied the canon.

What some people called THE TRUTH.

And it was so played out.

So I'm making it up as I go.

How can you ever know what your ancestors felt?

Ya can't! And ya never will.

Your quest is a failure.

That's what I'm here to tell you, aliens.

Your quest to understand us is a failure.

Everything is just a story. It's a choice. And ya learn from it and change.

Or ya don't.

And then you die.

You die.

You die.

You die.

CHORUS. *(Diminuendo into whispers.) Who came before you? Everybody*
Black.

*They died, and you here, now ain't that a **fact**.*

*Who came before you? Everybody **Black**.*

*They died, and you here, now ain't that a **fact**.*

> *(It continues.)*

BLACK HISTORIAN. And it won't matter.

No one will remember your name.

And all you'll get in return is a silly little story.

Because at the end of the day, that's what you are. And will always be.

Until the end of time.

A silly, silly little story.

> (*Everyone stops.*)

BLACK HISTORIAN. *I don't know the truth.*

And neither do you.

Neither do youuuuuuuuuuuuuuuuuuuu.

Yeahheeahheaheeehhhhhh

CHORUS. *Hmmmmmmm.*

Mmmmmmmm.

Hmmmmmmm.

> (*Or some dramatic ass vocal run.*)

BLACK HISTORIAN. There. That's my time capsule.

> (BLACK HISTORIAN *disappears into history.*
>
> *End of song.*)

BLAST YO SHIT INTO SPACE

COUNTDOWN. Ten.

Nine.

Eight.

Seven.

Six.

Five.

Four.

Three.

Two.

One.

Blast off.

    (*WE TRAVEL LIGHT-YEARS AWAY!*)

FACTS?

SPACE!

We're in space, ok?

Time passes. Some years in the future. A century at least.

An astronaut arrives.

The astronaut takes off their helmet.

It's DAVID HARRIS.

DAVID HARRIS. Hi.

I'm David Harris.

And I'm the Black playwright.

And history is this great conversation across time, and I just feel like I need to come up

and explain a concept for everyone—

BLACK HISTORIAN. (*Offstage.*) OH THIS MUHFUCKA! SEE I TOLD Y'ALL I WASN'T THAT PERSON!

DAVID HARRIS. SHUT UP.

It's just the past was calling my name and so I had to try to—

BLACK HISTORIAN. (*Offstage.*) UH HUH, YEAH OK, BRANDEN JACOBS-JENKINS DID THAT ALREADY!

DAVID HARRIS. OH MY GOD SHUT THE FUCK UP.

...

Hi.

I'm David Harris.

And I think about Black History all the time.

And it's full of so much great, funny, painful, absurd, truly consequential shit.

And yet still, all of that pain birthed something so utterly...beautiful.

...

Nah that's corny.

I guess, I think about Black History the same way I think about my parents meeting.

Actually yeah that might be a better...I don't know history that well.

But I have this.

> (*Enter* EVERY BLACK FATHER EVER.
>
> *Enter* EVERY BLACK MOTHER EVER.
>
> *They begin to act out how* DAVID HARRIS's *parents met in a melodramatic, reductive manner.*)

My mother and father met in community college in Los Angeles.

She'd cook. Pancakes for breakfast; brown rice for dinner.

He'd get the paycheck.

He'd get super possessive because my mom was hot. Obviously.

They'd get into arguments about who was smarter.

One day, my mom caught my dad checking out this white girl, and she got real mad.

And he was like if it's there Imma look. That was a weird moment, probably.

My mom was mad political. She wanted to go to all the rallies and protests.

My dad usually slept in.

My dad had dreams of being really rich and famous. Like, a rapper maybe.

But of course, that was never going to happen.

My mom just wanted to be the smartest person in the room. Life always got in the way.

She was like a walking tragedy you wouldn't believe it.

They had some sex.

And then I popped out like "hey…"

Then they started getting into lots of fights. These awful, terrible fights.

They were both working really hard to raise a baby in South Central L.A.

But neither of them could tell how hard the other was working.

I'm sure one of them was actually working harder…

But when it was real good, they'd lie on each other and watch the planes fly over Compton.

And when it got bad, my dad would, um…

And everyone was poor. Not everyone. A lot of people.

And crime. And drugs. And police.

Because slavery.

And because choices.

But they were in love.

> (EVERY BLACK FATHER EVER *and* EVERY BLACK MOTHER EVER *strike a pose that is bursting with love.*)

And one day, my mom made my dad really, really angry.

And he took his anger out the way he thought he should take his anger out.

Because that's what his history taught him to do.

And also, because that's the choice he made.

> (EVERY BLACK FATHER EVER *does something physically violent toward* EVERY BLACK MOTHER EVER.)

And it happened over and over again.

Until one day, my mom called the cops. And then we moved down south.

And my dad moved to London. I think?

I don't know what he did next.

...

This all happened when I was like twelve months old by the way,

so it's hard to really get it right, I'm just sort of piecing together different little...

But I didn't know whether to blame my history or to blame my parents.

And so I blamed myself.

I could hardly focus on anything,

I was just stuck in school studying a bunch of white history so that I could become the exception to the rule; it was incendiary.

And I had no control over anything except what I could imagine.

And I hated myself for being the cause of my parents leaving each other.

Because I definitely was not worth that. And I dedicated my life to redeeming that fact by writing down everything and trying to turn it into something... something ... ...

> (EVERY BLACK FATHER EVER *and* EVERY BLACK MOTHER EVER *return to that bursting love pose.*)

They're both dead now. My parents.

So now, they are Black History.

> (*With that, the stage begins to flood with still images of Black History.*
> *And by Black History, I mean our parents.*
> *Photos of Black parents and their children.*
> *Single parents. Couples.*
> *The parents of the cast.*
> *Dozens of images.*
> *Black History.*
> *Black History.*
> *Black History.*
> *All here. A time capsule.*)

DAVID HARRIS. Black History.

That's it. That's all it is.

And somehow. I'm alive.

Is that redemption?

> (*And with that, the photos are gone.*)

And so the point of that story was to make you feel something.

…No, that's not right.

The point was that some people build fences to keep people out, while others build fences to keep people in… That's not…

The point is that our dreams will dry up, like a raisin in the sun…

…

No.

The point is that…

That it's ok.

It's ok.

We'll never be worth the pain that got us here.

> (DAVID HARRIS *turns around to see his parents in love.*
>
> *DAVID HARRIS,*
> EVERY BLACK FATHER EVER,
> *and* EVERY BLACK MOTHER EVER.
> *Black History.*
>
> *DAVID HARRIS looks up for a moment.*
> *A bright light shines down from above.*
> *Some footsteps.*
> DAVID HARRIS *and the stage begin to glow green.*
> *Enter an* ALIEN.
> *The* ALIEN *looks at* DAVID HARRIS.
> *The* ALIEN *speaks.*)

ALIEN. Hi.

> (*A flash of light.*)

End of Play

THE THIN PLACE
by Lucas Hnath

ABOUT *THE THIN PLACE*

> *This article first ran in the* Limelight Guide to the 43rd Humana Festival of New American Plays, *published by Actors Theatre of Louisville, and is based on conversations with the playwright before rehearsals for the Humana Festival production began.*

Everyone who ever died is here, just in a different part of here. And if you listen, *really listen*, you can hear them—in the thin places—the places where the line between our world and some other world is very, very thin. "It's sort of like if you were to imagine an octopus in an aquarium, pressed up against glass...except that there's no glass, and no octopus," explains Hilda, the woman who begins to reveal her story in Lucas Hnath's eerie new play. What is it that Hilda might have felt on the back of her neck, alone in dark rooms with candles burning low? If she were to open her eyes, tightly closed in terror, would someone be there? When Hilda meets Linda, a professional psychic, *The Thin Place* ventures into the sphere of séances and mediums who channel ghostly visitations.

While writing a play that ponders such supernatural experiences, time to investigate with collaborators has been central to Hnath's process. "This is how I often build plays," he observes. "There's a subject that I want to explore, and I'll get actors together in a room. I'll have written scraps of moments, exchanges, bits of dialogue—but I won't have the whole play yet, not by a long shot." His initial opportunity to work on *The Thin Place* was a Creativity Fund workshop at New Dramatists, where Hnath is a resident playwright. "I gathered four actors, including Emily Cass McDonnell, who plays Hilda," he recalls. "I asked them to describe their experiences with psychics and the paranormal, and did a lot of listening at first, as people talked and shared stories." And when Actors Theatre partnered with the Colorado New Play Festival for another workshop, Hnath asked the cast to tell him scary tales. "Actors throw me off in a useful way, bringing voices into the room that I can't control, that aren't from my own head," notes the playwright.

Another key resource during the play's evolution has been director Les Waters, who reunited with Hnath for this Humana Festival premiere. "We're so familiar that we just give each other a look and we know what it means," says Hnath of the trust with which he and Waters negotiate their roles in a rehearsal room. "I'm very rigorous and careful about the logic of the play, and the structure of it, and Les is very comfortable with the stuff that's nebulous and murkier—he gets the weird logic of emotion. So I can lean into my efforts to figure out the rational logic, and part of his job is to throw a wrench into that, to pull me in the other direction." Commissioned by Actors Theatre during Waters's tenure as artistic director, *The Thin Place* was imagined specifically for the intimate Victor Jory Theatre. "I wrote it in conversation with that space," Hnath remarks. "This is a play that wants to feel like we're sitting around a character who's telling a story."

When it comes to divulging what happens as *The Thin Place* unfolds, though, the playwright is cautious not to reveal too much, preferring that the audience embark with few expectations. "With material that gets into the uncanny, in order to really enter that space, you can't have a life raft to take you back to shore. I have to be able to put you out to sea," Hnath asserts. He likens this reticence to the way he approached discussing his 2014 play *The Christians*. "I refused to answer questions about my own beliefs, because *The Christians* wants to throw you into the middle of an unresolvable argument. This play is not dissimilar; if you go into it thinking about the context in which it was written, it gives you an easy 'out,' rather than the more unsettling space that I want to get to with it." So in *The Thin Place*, even characters and relationships are hovering in the in-between, difficult to pin down. The kind of experience Hnath is aiming for requires maintaining, in his words, "a delicate state where nothing can be too concrete."

Hnath's extraordinary ability to put an audience out to sea stems from a creative process that involves asking himself questions from every conceivable angle—a practice reflected in the dialectical richness of his plays. While writing *The Thin Place*, one of the questions he's been mulling relates to rational thought itself, and why we're compelled to depart from it. Sometimes there's a short distance between being a flexible thinker and one too open to influence. For example, Hnath cites his reading about the Spiritualist movement in late nineteenth- and early twentieth-century America; this popular fascination with communicating with the dead attracted both abolitionists and advocates for women's suffrage—people whose political leanings were as adventurous as their metaphysical ones. But although a certain susceptibility of the imagination can have benefits, "There's a real vulnerability there," Hnath reflects. "Can you have such an open mind that your brain falls out? Where's the line between staying receptive to what you don't know, and keeping the critical faculties you need to see the world clearly?" This tension between the value of being persuadable and the necessity of shrewd perception is just one of the puzzles in Hnath's riveting new play.

—Amy Wegener

BIOGRAPHY

Lucas Hnath's plays include *A Doll's House, Part 2* (eight Tony Award nominations, including Best Play), *Hillary and Clinton, Dana H.*, *Red Speedo, The Christians, A Public Reading of an Unproduced Screenplay About the Death of Walt Disney, Isaac's Eye*, and *Death Tax*. He has been produced on Broadway at the John Golden Theatre and Off-Broadway at New York Theatre Workshop, Playwrights Horizons, Soho Rep, and Ensemble Studio Theatre. His plays have been produced nationally and internationally, with premieres at the Humana Festival of New American Plays, Goodman Theatre, Center Theatre Group, Victory Gardens Theater, and South Coast Repertory. He has been a resident playwright at New Dramatists since 2011. *Awards:* Steinberg Playwright Award, Guggenheim Fellowship, Whiting Award, two Steinberg/ATCA New Play Award Citations, Outer Critics Circle Award for Best New Play, an Obie Award, and the Windham-Campbell Prize.

ACKNOWLEDGMENTS

The Thin Place premiered at the Humana Festival of New American Plays in March 2019. It was directed by Les Waters with the following cast:

HILDA...Emily Cass McDonnell
LINDA.. Robin Bartlett
JERRY...Triney Sandoval
SYLVIA...Kelly McAndrew

and the following production staff:

Scenic Designer..Kristen Robinson
Costume Designer...Oana Botez
Lighting Designer...Reza Behjat
Sound Designer..................................... Christian Frederickson
Illusion Designer.. Steve Cuiffo
Production Stage Manager........................... Paul Mills Holmes
Dramaturg ....Amy Wegener
Casting...Taylor Williams
Dialect Coach..Rachel Hillmer
Properties Director...Mark Walston
Production Assistant .... Michael Donnay
Directing Assistant .... Emily Moler
Assistant Dramaturg.. Susan Yassky
Stage Management Apprentice............................Lizzy Gordon

The Thin Place was commissioned by Actors Theatre of Louisville. The commission was generously underwritten by Elizabeth Rounsavall and Caroline Martinson as part of the Les Waters New Works Fund.

The Thin Place was a recipient of an Edgerton Foundation New Play Award. The play was developed at the Colorado New Play Festival, Steamboat Springs, Colo., June 2018. *The Thin Place* benefited from a week-long residency at New Dramatists with support through the Jerry A. Tishman Playwrights Creativity Fund.

CHARACTERS

Hilda
Linda
Jerry
Sylvia

NOTE

This script is the version of *The Thin Place* that was produced in the 2019 Humana Festival, prior to its Off-Broadway run at Playwrights Horizons. Companies wishing to produce the play should acquire the most updated script.

dedicated to
Les Waters
and to the memory of
Ricky Jay

Robin Bartlett and Emily Cass McDonnell
in *The Thin Place*

43rd Humana Festival of New American Plays
Actors Theatre of Louisville, 2019
Photo by Jonathan Roberts

THE THIN PLACE

hilda & linda

There's really not much on stage. Two chairs, that's all. When the play begins, Hilda enters. She's in her late 30s. She's carrying a mug of tea. She sits in one of the chairs. The house lights don't dim. They won't dim. Not for some time. She considers the audience. Sips her tea. She's really looking at one audience member in particular. She's staring. And after a bit of that, she finally says to that audience member...

HILDA. I'm sorry it's just the funniest thing but
you look just like my grandmother —

you do.
Oh I wish I had a picture of her — I'd show you.

— and it's so funny because I was just thinking about her the other day
and about this thing she'd do with me when I was little,

this thing where she'd sit with me on the floor — down on the carpet —
she'd have me
face her
straight on —
And she'd take her little notepad
and she'd write down a word in it — She
wouldn't show me the word — she'd just
hold the notepad close to her chest,

and she would tell me that she was going to try to send that word
into my mind.

She'd say: *all you have to do is listen,*
and when you listen,
you're going to listen
not with your ears,
but with this part here,
just behind your eyes,
just behind and just a little above
your eyes.

She'd say: *Do you understand?*

I'd nod my head.

And then she'd look at me,
and she'd say *I'm sending the word to you.*

And I'd say a word,

and she'd say *no.*

She'd say: *you're not listening.*
And I'd try to listen.

I'd say another word,
and she'd say, no, don't guess.
Just listen.
Just…

… and she'd pick these just completely random words,
words you could never guess.
Like — I don't know — kumquat
or spiral
or… trapezoid.
Because, she didn't want it to be by accident,
because, she wanted to know that I really could
hear her thoughts.

My mother walked in on us doing this once.
Oh she got so upset — she yelled at her,
she yelled: *what are you doing bringing that*
demonic activity into our house,
bringing demonic spirits into our home,
teaching my daughter these
— I don't know — *demonic things*, you know.

I mean she never even liked grandma all that much —
and eventually — eventually she would tell my grandmother
no more, no more,
you're not allowed to come into this house,
you're not allowed to see my daughter,
you're not allowed — this and that.

But before all of that, before she was "banished,"
we did — we got very good at it.
Our little game.

Could sometimes even get almost a whole sentence.
And it was — it was just the funniest — and I have no idea if it was real —
was I really hearing her thoughts in the space
just behind and a little above my eye?

Or was it something else.
Did I just get good at guessing,
guessing the *kinds* of words and thoughts and — ?
were we really just getting to know each other,
getting to know each other really
really well?

now my grandmother — she said
that what she was doing was — and my mother
really would <u>not</u> have liked <u>this</u> —
was that what she was doing was getting me ready
for the day she died.

And that if we got really really good at hearing each other's thoughts like this,
then when my grandmother died, someday,
she would still be able to talk to me.
She'd be able to send words to me from beyond the grave.
Just like you know how you pick up a phone and say *hi how are you* —

hope you're well —

trapezoid —
          (*Laughs.*)

...

But you know, the thing about these little games I
played with my grandmother — those little...
they sort of opened up a door
for me — a door
to this
"other place," this — I don't know what to call it —
this...
thin place(?)

This place where the line between this world
and some other world is
very
thin(?)

Like it's sort of like if you were to imagine an octopus

in an aquarium

pressed up against glass,

... except that there's no glass

and no octopus.

...

...

Not long after my mother told her to go away,
not long after "the rift,"
as we called it,
grandma did die.
It was a stroke,
I think.

Now, have I heard from her since?

Sometimes I'd go up into my bedroom,
after my mother was asleep —
I'd take a candle,
I'd turn off the lights,
and I'd close my eyes,
and I'd open up the
eye that's inside my head — the eye just behind here —
and I'd open it, and I'd ask for grandma.
I'd ask, "grandma?
hello?
are you there?"
And I'd hear things, sure.
And I'd sometimes even feel things,
soft things,
on the back of my neck.
And I'd smell smoke because the candle had gone out.
and I'd just scare myself silly,
because I'd have my eyes closed
and I'd be so scared of what would happen if I opened them?
Who'd be there?

Would someone be there, staring back at me?
And would it be grandma,
or something else?
And I'd just sit there in the dark until…
until I'd fall asleep,
just too scared to open my eyes until morning.

    … but, I don't know.

It's because of my interest in this sort of thing that I met Linda.

I first met Linda at the start of last year, just a few months after my mother had gone missing...

died — ? gone missing — ?

(*Shrugs.*)

Linda was a psychic —

a real professional psychic.

And I just thought that was so exciting, because I'd

always had an interest in this sort of thing

but I really didn't know anything about it.

I first met Linda at something called a "sitting"

which is something that's sort of like what I did alone in my room as a kid,

but it's done by someone who really knows what they're doing.

And it takes place at a house, like someone's nice house,

and there's a bunch of people there, gathered together

in the living room, and there's candles and there's incense burning,

And Linda walks into the room, and it begins...

Linda enters. She's in her 60s. She wears a brightly colored muumuu. She sits next to Hilda. When Linda talks she addresses the audience. She has a British accent — more working class than posh. Her affect is flat, blunt, no nonsense, sort of rote, and maybe just slightly bored with it all.

LINDA. Now let's get one thing straight:
There is no death.
When you die you merely pass on
to something else.

What I do is like a radio antenna.
I pick up on things, I hear things.
I tune my dial, and all these voices just start coming at me —
I don't know what I'm going to get.

The spirits — all they want
is to have their voices heard.
It's like they're in a place where there are just a few telephones,
and so they're all crowded 'round
tryin' to use the phone all at once.
And I'm the telephone.
Imagine how frustrating it would be to be in a place where
you just have a few phones
and you put in your call an' no one answers.
So remember, I can't do what I do without you.
Don't be afraid to speak up —
if you think the voice I'm hearing is for you, you have to let me know
otherwise I move on and your grandad or your mum or whoever it is
is sad no one picked up, and I look like an idiot.

… While I wait for the spirits to show up,
I'll tell you a funny story:

I was in an airport a year or two ago and a spirit starts talking to me —
I can't help it, this kind of thing just happens to me —
and he's telling me that his wife is sitting over at Gate 9 —
that he loved her very much in life and that
he has a message for her.

And I think to myself: well, shit — there is no way
that I am going to go up to some poor
stranger and tell her that the spirit of her dead husband
has a message for her —

But the spirit is begging me, *please please please,*
so I say alright, what's the message.
And he tells me to tell her:
the money is in the attic.

So I walk over to this woman, and there she is
mindin' her own business, doin' a crossword puzzle,
and I ask her, *I'm sorry but I think your husband*
is telling me something from the other side:
He would like you to know that the money is in the attic.

And she starts laughing like you wouldn't believe,
and I'm wondering what's going on — and after she's done
havin' her laugh, she explains to me that her husband —
when he was in the hospital dying from
cancer of the bowel — I think it was —
he thought it would be a fun joke to try to get as many mediums as he could
to tell his wife "the money's in the attic."
I was the fourth one who fell for it!
Can you believe it!

But most spirits — they are sincere.
They just want to say hello.
Sometimes they want to remind you of somethin' you might have forgot,
Sometimes there's a warnin'.
Sometimes — oh now here it comes.

Come at me like a wave.
        (*To audience.*)
— give me a second
        (*She's listening to voices that only she can hear — voices that seem to*
        be coming at her from somewhere behind her head.)

...

...

Alright.

...

There's a spirit with the name Andy,
Andrew — Andrea —
    (*To the spirit.*)
             sorry dear you have to speak up — can't hear you —
        Alex…
Seems I'm talking to a young man named Alex.
HILDA. (*To audience.*) … and I remember that when she
said the name Alex,
that a woman in the far back corner of the room
raised her hand. And Linda
asked the woman if Alex was her child,
and she said yes.
LINDA. — now if I'm hearin' it correctly, Alex is telling me that
he only recently passed over, is that right?
HILDA. And she said yes
LINDA. Yes, he says he sees you from the other side.
That's what he's telling me — he says:
I see you mum.
I see you cryin.
I see you cryin yourself to sleep every night.
He says — He says you have a picture of him
by your bed — is that right.
He says he sees you before you go to sleep,
sees you kiss his picture goodnight
And he wants you to know that he feels it on his cheek —
feels it all the way through to the other world —
when you kiss that picture that's by the bed on the left nightstand —
makes him feel like you're right there beside him.

        — now say that again please, Alex —

He says: *I'm very happy,*
I'm very happy on the other side —
I wish you could see how wonderful it is here,
I have friends and there's family here, and
I've even got my dog with me —
Did Alex have a dog growing up?

No?

No dog —

> Alex, your mum's tellin' me you didn't have a dog —
> who's this dog with you?
>
> ...

He says the dog's name is Henry.

Who is Henry.

You don't know a dog named 'Henry' —

Was there a cat named — ? No.

Who is Henry what does that name mean — Alex is telling me about a 'Henry.'

...

HILDA. And then the mother thought about it for a little bit, and she remembered that there was a next-door neighbor dog, and that his name was Henry—

LINDA.

> Oh, you liked that dog didn't you, Alex.

Oh yes, yes he did, he says that he used to play with Henry

through the fence, in the yard, through a hole in the fence —

And when Henry was put down that made Alex very sad.

But now Henry is there with him, in the world beyond this one,

and Henry's his best friend there,

and there's no fence to divide them anymore,

and that they go and they play together, runnin' about,

hours on end.

> ...
>
> ...

Now he's talkin' to me about the cause of death —

the spirits do that sometimes, recount the details of their passings.

> ...

was a terrible accident,

Alex is telling me it was a drowning.

HILDA. But the mother said no,

she said it wasn't a drowning.

She said it was a car accident—

LINDA. Alex keeps talking about drowning —

felt my lungs filling up,

couldn't breathe, felt it gurgling —

> Alex, your mum tells me it was a car accident.
> Why are you talking about drowning?

couldn't breathe, feeling of water,

feeling of — Oh I see, he's telling me that his

lungs were punctured in the accident —

look at the autopsy report —

his lungs were punctured and that's why he felt like he was drowning.

But he wants you to know that it wasn't your fault.

You know that, right. But you sometimes feel it was.

But he wants to know that you know that it wasn't your fault.

And he wants you to know that where he is, there's no more pain —

no more broken bones, no more bruises,

no more scars —

the scar that he had right here, right under his chin,

that he got when he was very little, when the ceiling lamp fell on his head —

Even that's gone.

> ...

> — alright, Alex — I'll tell her —

He wants you to — when you get home

look in your top dresser drawer.

He doesn't want to tell me what's in there,

he wants it to be a surprise, a surprise just for you and him,

and you'll know what it means when you see it.

Alex is telling me that when you see it you will feel peace.

He's saying *mummy you'll feel peace, it will all be alright.*

That little sore spot that you feel in your soul

it will start to fade away when you see what's in that drawer.

See, my love, all he really wants is for you to be happy, you understand that.

HILDA. Linda talked to a lot of spirits that night —
most everyone heard from someone — except
when she got to me, she looked at me
for a long time — just sort of...
looked at me
LINDA. ...

...

...

I'm sorry dearie — what's your name?
HILDA. Hilda
LINDA. Hilda, yes...

yes, I'm very sorry, Hilda, but
I've not got anything for you tonight —
I'm not hearing from anyone.
HILDA. It was strange I guess that everyone received messages
except for me.

... But then before I went home, Linda stopped me,
and she touched me on the arm,
and she said
LINDA. I feel terrible about
not having anything for you — Doesn't normally
happen, but sometimes it does. So
I would like very much to make it up to you.
Here's my private number. Please call me, and
I'll have you come by my place some time. Alright?
HILDA. And that's how Linda and I started spending time with each other.

And I just — I just found her so endlessly interesting.

I'd never met anybody like her.

I often thought I wanted to be her,

but I could never be her, so the best I could do is be near her,

all the time, and we'd just have these long talks and dinners

where she'd tell me about her childhood in England,

and about how her family didn't have money,

and how she had 13 brothers and sisters and none of them liked each other,

and how they were always fighting, like violent fighting

with rocks and sticks.

And I remember she also told me about how

ever since she was a child

she's had this strange sickness, where

she would just out of nowhere get these sudden attacks on her lungs

that felt like knives inside of her, and that no one could explain it,

no doctor knew what it was

LINDA. oh it still happens to me to this day, no idea why

HILDA. and she'd tell me the most interesting stories about how

there was always a lot of death around her when she was growing up,

and how these terrible deaths became just a normal thing —

LINDA. — had this one aunt and uncle who had the most terrible marriage.

Aunt Doris and Uncle John.

Oh the way they'd just scream at each other —

screaming like bloody murder, could hear them from a mile away.

She'd always be threatening that if he didn't make more money,

she'd go off and get her own job.

She'd tell him,

I don't need you, John —

you're as useless as a spare prick at a wedding.

And he'd scream back at her,

Shut yer evil yammering gob you foul mouthed cunt — ha ha ha —

and they'd just go back and forth — just the most horrible people.

But then she did get herself a job, and it just infuriated John.

And to make matters worse they had only one car between 'em,

and the job Doris had got herself was way out in Sleaford —

that's nearly a 70-minute drive from where we lived —

and she'd told John well he was going to have to
find some other way to get around
as she needed the car for her new job.

Now Uncle John was never the most stable person,
and we had gone in and out of worrying about him.
He did on more than one occasion threaten to top himself —
but who hasn't done that when emotions get the best of them —
and we — well — we just figured that Auntie Doris is no
walk in the park either, so — but truth be told
I don't think anyone quite anticipated how much Doris
getting herself a job would upset him.

I think John took a lot of pride in his ability to provide for Doris,
and he was probably afraid that Doris would leave him if
she found she could do better by herself.
Also you can't underestimate just pure hatred.
John hated Doris,
and he wanted her to feel just as awful about life
as he felt every single day.

So what he did was he fashioned himself a noose, a good strong noose
made out of cable, put the noose round his neck, and
tied the other end to the underside of their car.
She had no idea, no idea at all that he was under the car, waiting,
noose around his neck and piss drunk out of his mind.

And when she went off that morning for her
first day of work at her new job —
well — you can imagine what happened —
dragging poor John all the way to Sleaford —
but no, she didn't actually make it to Sleaford —
someone stopped her well before she got to work.
But Uncle John he was pretty well mangled — not entirely dead, yet,
but definitely mangled when she stopped the car to see
what the fuss was about.

You'd have thought that what happened would have scarred us,
but to be honest, this sort of thing was always happening in my family.
Life was so hard that you never quite felt it.

You know what I mean, Hilda?

> *(Linda takes Hilda's hand and strokes it gently...)*

I have a feeling you do.

That's what I like about you.

HILDA. ... I started to feel so comfortable with Linda that I started to
tell her more about myself, just like she'd told me about herself.

I didn't tell her everything, because I wasn't sure that
would be a good idea —
my mother would always tell me when I was little,
Hilda you tell people too much —
some things you keep to yourself, some things you don't say out loud
because if you do, people won't want to be around you —
and this was always
a lesson I could never seem to learn — but Linda seemed different,
and so I did — I did tell her about my
grandmother and the little games we'd play,
and about the things I'd do in my bedroom,
late at night with all the lights turned off.
I'd tell her about the voices that I thought I could hear,
about how when I'd pass by the abortion clinic I could hear the sound
of all the crying babies that had died there, or about how sad it made me
that — even though there were some things I could hear —
I could never quite seem to reach my grandmother
even though we practiced it,
and how what I really wanted to do was what Linda did —

but Linda never really liked talking about her work — she
sort of went out of her way to avoid it, so every time
I'd bring it up she'd say
LINDA. oh I don't want to talk about work, I'm resting now,
let's just enjoy each other's company.
HILDA. I just thought it was strange that there was this thing she could do
that was really something special, and that she did this thing
with other people, all the time, but never with me.
And it started to make me wonder
was there something wrong with me?

I even once suggested that maybe sometime we just try
seeing what happened if we lit a few candles,
and sat together in the dark — to see what would happen
if we just, you know, called on the spirits, just once, just for —

LINDA. (_Very stern._) Hilda.

HILDA. …

LINDA. No.

HILDA. … But I think she could tell that it was really bothering me
and that it wasn't something that was going away,
and so one evening she sat me down,
and she said

LINDA. Alright Hilda —

I'm going to tell you some things that I don't tell many people,
but you're special —
and I think we're at a threshold,
and if I don't tell you, then we can't be
as close as I would like us to be.

But Hilda, I want you to know
that once I tell you about what it is
that I really do, there's no going back,
there's no unhearing what I'm about to say.

Would you like to know?

HILDA. Yes.

I would like to know.

the unveiling

LINDA. well you <u>do</u> understand, don't you,
that what I do is sort of a trick.

Right?

Nothing to it, really.
It's more about listening than anything else.

I always start with names —
I just say whatever names jump into my head, an' I keep sayin' names
until someone in the room claims a name as being important to them.

Why — you remember that woman from that first sitting you went to — ?
that poor mother who lost her child in — what was it — a car accident?
I was saying some names and I saw her head nod
when I said the name 'Alex,' and that told me
that the name Alex meant something to her — what it meant — I'd no idea,

so now my job is to just ask questions,
but ask them in a way that doesn't sound like I'm asking questions,
because I don't want her to feel like I'm trying to get anything from her.

So I simply said to her *Alex was yours wasn't he,*
and she said "yes Alex was my child."

— now I'd imagine if you asked her afterwards, she'd tell you it was me who
told her that Alex was her child, but I didn't — no, I just said Alex was hers
and it was her that told me the rest.

But really, who said what doesn't matter,
the point is, now we're having ourselves a conversation —
we've opened a door — and she's one step closer
to getting what she really wants
which is just to hear that her dead loved one misses her
or is happy in the afterlife, or doesn't blame her for his death —
something like that —

but before that can happen she needs to
feel like I'm <u>really</u> talking to her son's spirit,
and so I just need to say a few things that I couldn't possibly know.

So I just say a couple thoughts or pictures that pop into my head — I

think I remember saying something about a dog
and something about the name Henry,
and I think I made a little guess that turned out to be wrong —
I said Alex had a dog growing up and she told me he didn't.

But instead of backing off it,
I very gently push on her,
because between those two things one of 'em's got to mean something,
an' so I keep repeating —
dog and Henry, dog and Henry, this means something,
tell me what it means —
until she puts it together for me — And what do you know,
it turns out there was a neighbor dog that the boy liked —
And the mum even told me that the dog's name was Henry —
and who knows, maybe it was,
but maybe it wasn't and she was just agreeing with me to agree with me...

... but of course I do get people who just want to say 'no,' people
who — even though they've gone through the trouble of coming
to see me, payin' me money — ha ha — they
just sit there and no matter what I say to them,
they just come back at me with
'no.'
'No.'
No, Ms. Linda I don't know anyone named Bill,
and, no the image of a blue and white vase with a long crack along the edge
doesn't mean anything to me at all
— and they're just not working with me at all —
maybe they even want to prove me wrong.

So I just say,
        that's alright, dearie —
        I want you to write all of this down,
        because it does — it does mean something —
        but it's not going to make sense until
        later. Not until the time is right.

And 9 times out of 10, I swear to you, I get those 'no people' callin' me back

because they've walked into their flat, and they
see the vase that their grandfather gave them,
and it's not in the position it was when they last noticed it,
and what do you know —
it's got a crack in it — ! and they go and they make all sorts of just —
just the most <u>wonderful</u> meaning out of it.
Because that's just how the mind works,
it will make what meaning it wants to make — just you try an' stop it.
You can't.

HILDA. And honestly, I'm not sure how I felt about everything she was telling me. I mean, yes, at first, I guess I did feel disappointed, but then after awhile I started to feel something else… something —

LINDA. You compare what I do to this so-called psychotherapy where

you have these people who have been in psychotherapy for five, seven years

over a decade in some cases if you can believe it,

and what do they get out of it?

All I end up hearing about is

how little they've got out of the whole thing.

But take some little pudgy girl with greasy hair —

and she's lost her father, and her father never said a kind word to her

and I can see plain as day what's happening —

so when I tell her

that her father is so very proud of her,

and loves her so very much,

and that he thinks she has become such a beautiful woman —

the sight of — the tears streaming down her face —

the transformation that's happening,

right there in front of my eyes…

Because when you see someone living with so much pain,

How can you just let her —

Linda can't finish her sentence. She can't speak. She grabs her chair, her face contorts, and then she begins making a horrible sound — something between a wheeze and a low croak. This happens a couple of times, then it stops.

HILDA. ... I'd never seen Linda have one of her
"episodes" before, and of course, I felt really bad
seeing her like that,
so helpless,
so weak,

but part of me
also wondered if her having that attack
had anything to do with... you know —
her saying certain things about certain things
that maybe she shouldn't be saying...
like maybe there are certain things that it's just dangerous
to talk about...

and part of me also wondered if maybe there are things that
she wasn't telling me or that maybe
when she did the thing she called a trick,
not even Linda understood what was really happening,
because how could she *really* know
that a spirit wasn't actually talking through her
when she'd say names and talk about how people died —
how could she know for sure
where the thoughts were coming from?

I mean, she did say a lot of things to those people
that she could not have possibly known.

I don't know.
I just try to keep an open mind about these things.
My mother would always yell at me for that.
She'd say *Hilda* —
don't you know —
don't you know you can have such an open mind that your brain falls out.

HILDA. It was around this time though that I feel like
Linda and I actually became even closer, and
she introduced me to her friends,
and it was like — it was like I was part of some — I don't know —
inner circle. I'd never been part of anyone's inner circle.

I'd be invited to all of Linda's Sunday night get-togethers —
these little parties she threw with her friends,
where we'd meet at these really nice places, nice houses and apartments,
and there was always really good food,
and really nice wine, expensive stuff
where you could drink a lot without your head hurting too much,

and there'd be the most interesting people there —
like there was this guy who I think he was some kind of auctioneer
of things that were very expensive, or like architects or —
and of course there'd be Linda's cousin Jerry who
did something having to do
with politics, politicians — I don't know — They were always these
people with job descriptions
that you would ask them what they did
and they would tell you but somehow by the end you felt
like you knew even less than before you asked —

But it was fun — and they all told really fun stories,
and I just liked to listen.

And I especially liked that no one ever really
asked me many questions about myself —
nobody really paid much attention to me because I
wasn't like them and I didn't know people or have stories to tell —

I don't go to those parties anymore, no, I don't see those people anymore.

But the last one I went to — the last one was actually
a party to celebrate Linda getting her visa —
There had been a problem —
and we all thought that maybe she'd have to leave the country —
but then it all got figured out and — so we had a Sunday night party —

That night was just me and Linda, and Linda's cousin Jerry,

and this woman Sylvia who Linda was in some way close with,

I don't know exactly how — just that I know that Sylvia gave Linda money.

Like they had some sort of arrangement where Sylvia paid for Linda's rent(?).

... Anyway, that was the last night I ever saw Linda.

linda's party

... a good bit of laughter comes from offstage, and Linda laughs too, and Sylvia and Jerry walk on stage — Sylvia with wine glasses, Jerry with wine bottle and corkscrew, mid-chat, having a real great time —

JERRY. well, so that reminds me of this thing I saw when I was in Japan

LINDA. now when were you in Japan,/ Jerry — ?

JERRY. oh you know back during the uh —

the <u>fallow</u> period/ as I call it — back during the —

LINDA. yes yes Jerry's fallow period —

JERRY. I was/ living in Takayama —

SYLVIA. Is everyone drinking?/ Does everyone need a — ?

LINDA. oh right oh right after that thing with/ — yes Sylvia I think we're fine

JERRY. right, and my friend Randy/ invited me to this thing, this —

SYLVIA. oh I <u>know</u> Randy —

JERRY. I don't know what to call it exactly —

it was sort of a party and sort of a performance —

where everyone gathered together in a room,

/about the size of the room we're in right now,

and it's filled with candles, like about 50 candles

LINDA. (*Whispered.*) oh now don't you look fetching Sylvia —

SYLVIA. what — ? no

LINDA. yes

JERRY. forget it no one's listening/ to me

HILDA. I'm listen/ing

LINDA. we're listening — room filled with candles, in Japan, go on —

JERRY. so then at a certain point someone steps forward

and begins to tell a story,

a ghost story, and at the end of the story

the uh teller extinguishes the candle —

and then another person steps forward

and tells another story, and tries to make their story

even scarier than the last, and when they're done,

they extinguish another candle, and —

SYLVIA. for every candle?/ Jesus sounds like torture

JERRY. /uh-huh

LINDA. 50/ candles!

JERRY. oh it goes on for hours really,

until there's just one candle left,

and then the last person tries to tell the scariest story of the night,

and once it's told, the last candle gets blown out,

and then everyone's just left in total darkness.

LINDA. ... well so what was the last story?

JERRY. uhhh/hhhh —

SYLVIA. better have been worth it —

JERRY. you know I don't remember —

SYLVIA. well there you go —

JERRY. it's on the tip of my brain — this is going to/ drive me crazy —

LINDA. you'll remember and you'll tell/ us and —

JERRY. (*The wine is uncorked; Jerry, offering.*) there we go —
Hilda, may I — ?

HILDA. oh alright —

LINDA. (*Adjusts herself.*) I would like to raise a little toast to my dear
dear cousin Jerry — my American cousin — oh I remember
when I first met little Jerry so many years ago — you were this tall — this
tall — ! and now — ha ha — you're my savior

JERRY. naw —

LINDA. saved me from being carted off back to England, and for that
I'll be forever grateful.

JERRY. No I'm just happy that I could finally be useful to someone in this
world —

LINDA. more than useful, more than —

SYLVIA. To Linda.

LINDA. Oh!

SYLVIA. right — ? To Linda,
who I consider both a friend —
a very close friend — a friend I wish I saw more of
but I know she's in demand so I'll take what I can get —
And, To the Linda who I consider a
mentor, um,
because you have — you've taught me so much
about life, and priorities,
and — especially after my divorce — um
helping through a really hard time,
and I will never forget that.
So thank you.
And I'm happy you're here —

JERRY. yes. To Linda.

To Linda — yay — cheers/ cheers —

HILDA. cheers

SYLVIA. Jerry — cheers —

LINDA. cheers.

(*Full beat to drink.*)

... oh this is very good, Sylvia

JERRY. /oh yeah —

SYLVIA. well unfortunately I'm worried now I didn't buy enough wine —

JERRY. /naw we're fine —

SYLVIA. (*To Linda.*) didn't know that you'd be bringing your uh
friend, I didn't/ — just feel a little embarrassed that I —

LINDA. it's fine — you're a wonderful host — thank you for —

JERRY. So Linda —

LINDA. /yes

JERRY. how does it feel being an American

LINDA. well I'm not —

JERRY. one step closer —

LINDA. honestly... ?

It feels fucking wonderful — it does —

no really, I love America.

I love this country. I do.

Much prefer it to dreary England,

dreary England with its dreary weather,

and dreary people,

dreary history,

always looking back — I'll tell you what I so love about

all of you — In America,

you look forward.

In America you all really believe — deep down —

you believe that you can be whatever

you want to be, and that just strikes me as the most wonderful

thing — well and you know this is the birthplace

of what I do — all of the great spiritualists/ —

all Americans.

JERRY. really, huh.

LINDA. And I won't lie,

I'm treated better in America — I'm

better at my job in America — seriously —

JERRY. it's the accent, isn't it

LINDA. It is — It is! I have such authority here that I didn't have there.

There I always had to work so hard at it, but here —

here I open my mouth and everyone listens. I'm wise — !

like an old sage from another land —

SYLVIA. Well you better like it here, because

you don't really have another option —

LINDA. /ha ha ha — !

JERRY. Sylvia!

SYLVIA. what!

LINDA. you're being naughty, Sylvia — Don't make me bend you over

SYLVIA. yes please

LINDA. no, but it is true — they did run me out of the country

JERRY. well... I wouldn't/ put it that way

LINDA. criminal charges pending — no other way to put it — ha ha! No, what I blame is the E.U. — the fucking — excuse me —

the fucking European Union — what with all of their

rules — their little rules about what a medium can and can't do —

regulations, mandatory disclaimers — well I'm not going to do it.

It ruins the experience to start off a reading by saying

I'm not real. I'm just entertainment. I have no powers —

It ruins the mood is what it —

JERRY. is there more wine?

SYLVIA. what do you/ want?

JERRY. no no no, you sit, I'll/ get it

SYLVIA. but what do/ you — ?

JERRY. Linda — ?

LINDA. white,/ thank you

SYLVIA. down the stairs, to the left, in the second fridge —

JERRY. the second

SYLVIA. smaller —

JERRY. yep.

　　　(*Jerry exits.*)

SYLVIA. ... so how <u>did</u> you manage to get your visa?

LINDA. How?

SYLVIA. — last time I talked to you — they had denied your application — In fact, didn't you call me because you thought you were going to need some money — ?

LINDA. yes,/ yes well —

SYLVIA. and then I never heard anything else, and —

LINDA. they did deny it at first —

SYLVIA. /why?

LINDA. because apparently the occupation of "psychic" sounds not very legitimate to the people who grant visas — and it's so hard to talk about what I do —

SYLVIA. so did you — ?

LINDA. no, Jerry sorted it/ out —

(*Jerry re-enters with another bottle of wine.*)

JERRY. what did I sort out —

LINDA. the visa —

SYLVIA. how — ?

JERRY. I made some calls and —

LINDA. you know he's got special/ connections because of his work with the—

JERRY. it's nothing all that interesting

LINDA. and then he got me a legitimate job working with one of his/ people, on one of this —

JERRY. Linda Linda Linda Linda

LINDA. oh well now shit — ! was I not supposed to talk/ about that

JERRY. I'd prefer you didn't

LINDA. oh but can't I just tell <u>them</u>, Jerry. Please can I — they won't tell anyone — you won't tell anyone

SYLVIA. tell what?

JERRY. Okay, let's just — you know — none of this leaves this room —

SYLVIA. *oh*

JERRY. not because anything "illegal" is happening, or — just — see now we're making it worse by being mysterious/ about it

LINDA. you were the one being/ mysterious

JERRY. No — it's just that — so one of my clients is a candidate —

SYLVIA. running for office — ?

JERRY. running for office who has been struggling — who is — he's a terrific guy — just
not so good in public —
LINDA. that's an understatement —
JERRY. well what it was was that he lacked confidence,
and I got to thinking, and it just sorta hit me that —
I mean if you look at it from the right angle — what Linda does
and what I need this guy to do — they're not so far apart, they're
not so — they're really kinda related, in a way.
And I thought — well, Linda needs a legit-sounding job for the visa,
and what the hell, let's give it shot — what's there to lose —
SYLVIA. Who is it — ?
LINDA. Sylvia, he can't tell you <u>that</u> —
JERRY. someone in one of the 50 states/ — ha ha ha ha
SYLVIA. would I know the person — ?
LINDA. stop asking questions — it's making Jerry/ uncomfortable —
SYLVIA. okay but so you help this guy — what, how/ — you
LINDA. well you know when Jerry first showed me a tape of the guy —
you remember I said — I said he just wasn't very convincing —
the words he was saying were very nice, but it was like with everything he
said he was tiptoeing his way around — so worried about saying the wrong
thing — When I do what I do, I can't be worrying about that —
I have to not care so much about being exactly right.

So I worked with him, taught little things he could do,
body language, non-verbal cues, ways of inflecting his voice
to help people have an easier time agreeing with him —
but more than anything it's about an attitude —
an attitude of:
hey, I'm right,
and if you agree with me you're right.
And those who don't, they're wrong, it's their loss —
So that the particular words he's saying don't even matter all that much —
it's all about how you're saying it,
how you're presenting yourself, saying
follow me.

Come with me.

SYLVIA. You know who did that, don't you.

LINDA. Who?

SYLVIA. Hitler.

LINDA. Oh…

SYLVIA. he did, he hired a popular mind reader of the time —

JERRY. /what!?! — noooo —

SYLVIA. it's true —

LINDA. /oh for the love of —

SYLVIA. Hitler hired a mind reader because he saw that the guy was so good at controlling crowds, manipulating their minds —

JERRY. /no one's manipulating anyone —

SYLVIA. in his act he had these very commanding hand gestures
and Hitler was impressed with all of that —
It's where Hitler got all his hand gestures from — !

LINDA. 's the one thing I find irritating about you Americans —

SYLVIA. /what

LINDA. — your obsession with Hitler —

SYLVIA. /I'm just saying that —

LINDA. you are all obsessed — when in doubt 'Hitler' — whenever you want to prove your point you just shout out 'Hitler'/ — it's a sickness —

JERRY. I just want to be clear, everyone: the person
that Linda and I are working with
is not Hitler —
he is not — let's just be clear —

LINDA. oh no no no, he's very nice, very
sweet fellow — not even close to Hitler — isn't that funny:
you could not pick a more
un-Hitler kind of person —
and the funny thing is, that's sort of his problem.

JERRY. right/ right right — ha ha

LINDA. 'f you ask me he could stand to have a little more of — not — not in the killing-of-innocent-people/ sort of way — of course — ha ha —

JERRY. oh no no no no no no

LINDA. but just in the um

the um — well again it comes back to
confidence — in the area of just feeling:
I'm right and I'm amazing and I know what's best —
because if you don't have that, you can't lead — And
isn't that how it always goes — the nice people just don't have that
thing that would make anyone want to trust them with their lives
and their safety...
SYLVIA. ...
LINDA. what.

What, you have a look on your face, you have a —
SYLVIA. nothing

I don't know.

Just isn't it a little dishonest, isn't it a little —
LINDA. /in what way dishonest?
SYLVIA. I don't want to use the word manipulative —
JERRY. well but it's not —
SYLVIA. it's just kind of depressing though, isn't it — ?
JERRY. see, this is exactly why we don't talk about this, Linda
LINDA. /I know, I know
SYLVIA. How do you even feel about this candidate — ?
LINDA. I told you/ I like him
SYLVIA. and you support his ideas
LINDA. he has very good ideas
SYLVIA. like what, for example — ?
LINDA. I'm not going to sit here and — You'd vote for him.
He's in that party that you vote with —
SYLVIA. okay, well, I mean, <u>that</u> at least is a good thing,/ I guess, but —
LINDA. I mean Jerry and I wouldn't be helping out one of those other
ones —
SYLVIA. but still
LINDA. but/ still what?
SYLVIA. just sort of feels like it opens the door to something
LINDA. /opening a door to what?
SYLVIA. you know whatever tricks/ Linda's teaching him — it's

kind of like 'mind control' isn't it?

LINDA. tricks — what tricks — ?

JERRY. I mean, I get it Sylvia — we all want to think that the best idea wins, but I'm sorry to say that's just not how it works.

Because no matter how good or smart your ideas are,

the bad ones — the bad ideas, the bad voices —

those are always going to be louder,

well, because honestly they're just more interesting.

And the scary voices — oh the scary ones, they're like a car wreck —

you can't help but stare at the wreckage.

And so — I'm sorry — but in light of all of that

we have to do whatever we can

to make the good — albeit boring — voices louder —

that's all — It's called being persuasive.

SYLVIA. ... Well okay, I —

LINDA. Jerry can I have some more of that —

/thank you.

JERRY. So, Sylvia. Linda was telling me that you've been traveling the world this past month.

SYLVIA. yes, I have been —

JERRY. Where all did you go — ?

SYLVIA. it was amazing it was amazing —

I — wow — where to begin —

I was in Norway for two weeks,

and Norway — none of you have/ been, right?

JERRY. no, I haven't

HILDA. no

SYLVIA. it's really, amazing — it's a country

where I think they got a lot of things really right,

and where the level of equality,

and their sense of compassionate justice

is really something — there's a lot we could learn from them —

JERRY. /yeah wow

SYLVIA. I mean I could go on about the Norwegian prison system

for hours...

but I won't — ha ha — ! but um…

then I made a brief stop in Spain —

JERRY. in

SYLVIA. Barcelona —

JERRY. oh nice

SYLVIA. just a couple of days, visited a friend, did a little shopping, and —

but the highlight of the trip was when I was in Denmark and
I met this woman, and I mean, she was the most amazing woman —
she was 63, she swam a mile every day — her arms were — you wouldn't
believe it, I mean just incredible, and she lives in this shack on the edge of
the forest, owns almost nothing, like the bare minimum of what you need
to survive, and guess how much she's worth — ?

JERRY. Hmmmmm.

SYLVIA. 70 million —

JERRY. /oh

SYLVIA. easily — most of it family money, you know —
but she only lives off of like a 1,000 dollars a year, if that,
and anything she doesn't need to keep a roof over her head
and food on the table, she gives away.
All of it. Sends it off to other parts of the world where
people have nothing, where children are starving, where there's terrible
suffering — and every day we would spend hours talking,
and she told me — she was like it's very simple:
she believed that any money that isn't spent on
the absolute necessities of survival
is money that has a child's blood on it.

And I have to say I found it very difficult to argue with/ that

JERRY. I could argue with that.

LINDA. so could I —

SYLVIA. I don't know I don't know — really got me to thinking

JERRY. of living in a shack?

SYLVIA. I am strongly considering

JERRY. /nooooo

SYLVIA. end of next year, I really think I might make a big life change,

I might move into a more modest place
and live on a lot less than I live on now — I mean
this is a — what — two-hundred-dollar wine glass?
There are two-dollar wine glasses that'll do the job just fine,
and the difference is money that could feed a starving child in some place
like Haiti

JERRY. well —

LINDA. no, now this is the other thing that really irritates me about you
Americans: there's the Hitler thing,
and then there's this guilt you all seem to have —

SYLVIA. /guilt?

LINDA. yes, guilt for all of your success, and
for having/ done so well —

JERRY. it's not untrue —

LINDA. of course it's true — and I see it — see this guilt
sneaking into your country, its politics —
it's very insidious — and all because, for some reason,
you're not okay getting everything you want —
so you beat yourself up,

self-flagellation

SYLVIA. wanting to help someone isn't a bad thing —

JERRY. no, of/ course not

LINDA. no, this goes far beyond that — I can hear in your voice this —

JERRY. if I can just weigh in —

LINDA. /please do

JERRY. here's the thing: just looking at the facts,
looking at the numbers, on the whole, suffering in the world
is really very rare — I mean, the kind of suffering that
you're talking about — it's
actually decreased so much — even in just the past 50 years —
And not because people such as yourself
have deprived themselves and gone the 'martyr route' —

SYLVIA. not talking about being a martyr/ — I'm just —

JERRY. well, I mean, when/ you talk about —

SYLVIA. I just mean that I could give more

JERRY. maybe.

But even that — even throwing money that you can afford to throw
at the problem — even that — I mean there's the argument —
and I have this book you should read
I can send you a copy — that the money
you're putting out there — can actually make the problems worse —
destabilizing local economies, feeding corruption, hell,
that two-dollar wine glass — if you look at how that's made —
that alone probably causes more suffering/ in the world than the
198 dollars fixes —
SYLVIA. okay okay forget the wine glass
JERRY. truth is, the fact that things have gotten better
is due to all these very hard to understand,
very complicated, almost invisible movements
in the economy, in the world —
all of it way beyond anything one person can/ control —
SYLVIA. even a food bank, Jerry — you're saying even a food bank is —
JERRY. oh my god, food banks are the worst — !
SYLVIA. /how — ?!?
JERRY. food banks hurt local farmers and they
hurt the people who sell food —
No I'm sorry I tend to think that by-and-large
most charities are really only there
to make the people giving the money feel better about themselves —
and when you consider the fact that a lot of that money
can make things worse —
well, a lot of charity, if you really think about it, is actually pretty selfish
SYLVIA. that's crazy
JERRY. hey, just do a little reading —
SYLVIA. no, I'm sure I could go and read whatever
book it is you're going to send me
and I'm sure it says exactly what you're saying
with graphs and numbers and — But I'm
sure I could also find plenty of things to read
with different graphs and numbers
that say the opposite —

JERRY. I'm telling you which one is right

SYLVIA. and why would I believe you?

JERRY. I don't know, Sylvia — why do you believe anything?

SYLVIA. I don't know, Jerry — you're so smart — you tell me.

JERRY. Honestly, I just think it comes out of a need to feel important —
what you're believing here
sort of puts you at the center of everything,
and ignores reality, in favor making you feel/ like you're the —

SYLVIA. oh that is so fucking condescending

LINDA. Sylvia…

I'm getting an awful lot of negative energy from you tonight

SYLVIA. what does that mean

LINDA. it means you're being a real cunt.
Stop it. Alright?

SYLVIA. …

LINDA. Or if you've got something on your mind that you'd like to say to
me, then just spit it out, because —

SYLVIA. I think you take advantage of people.

LINDA. Alright.
How —

SYLVIA. all sorts of ways

LINDA. be specific

SYLVIA. with what you do —

LINDA. what I do, meaning — what do you mean "what I do"

SYLVIA. you know —

LINDA. my work as medium?

SYLVIA. It's just all of this meddling — meddling, meddling
with people's minds —

LINDA. what meddling — ! what/ is she talking about?

JERRY. naw I'm just gonna stay out of this —

SYLVIA. no, I do — I do I think that you're taking advantage —
when people are coming to you
at the worst times of their lives —
and you take their money and tell them lies —
and yeah you tell them lies to make them feel better,
and maybe it does, but you're still lying to people —

and I've been thinking about this for awhile now, and I think
what you do does a lot of harm —
LINDA. Harm? Sylvia, you have no idea what you're talking about —
why — you go take some little pudgy girl/ with
SYLVIA. yes yes with the greasy hair and the pimples on her face
and tears in her eyes and the dead father
who loves her very much, but what if —
what if, actually, her father didn't love her,
and what if he treated her badly — you don't know —
and you've gone and made her think that
her horrible childhood wasn't so horrible.
And maybe she <u>needs</u> to know that
actually he didn't love her and that that was
the reality, and to let her tell herself
that something was something that it wasn't —
doesn't that at a certain point
just gradually sort of take you away from yourself,
and away from what you see — ?
LINDA. but what that is, is that girl seeing through me
what she needs to see,
and far be it from me to tell her
that she's not seeing what she needs to see —
that — that would be cruel... hurtful...

Why — ! I don't even properly know
what I'm doing when I'm doing what I'm doing —
it's something that happens through me
SYLVIA. but you know, you/ <u>know</u> that it's not —
LINDA. I'm telling you, I know nothing.
I claim to know nothing
which probably makes me the most honest person in this room.
SYLVIA. ...
LINDA. But now let's talk about you, Sylvia.
You come at me, accusing me of taking advantage of people,
but you don't <u>really</u> believe that, do you.
No, what you're really trying to say to me
is that you think I take advantage of <u>you</u>.

Isn't that right?

SYLVIA. / Yeah, well...

LINDA. But have you ever stopped to think about the ways in which,
actually, you take advantage of me?

Do you ever stop to think about all of the late night calls,

all of the advice you're always asking for,

all of the emotional support that you need,

and how draining it must be to someone like me,

who is always trying to give so much to so many people.

Do you ever think about me and how I'm feeling,

do you even care?

Seriously Sylvia, sometimes I'm surprised by your total lack
of self-awareness.

　　　(*Sylvia walks off.*)

JERRY. …

HILDA. …

LINDA. I do find it very interesting how it's the so-called "victimized"
who are often the victimizers.

JERRY. …

LINDA. …

JERRY. …

LINDA. … alright alright, I'll go after her.

　　　(*Jerry and Hilda, alone.*)

JERRY. a little drama,

a little dinner and a show, right — ? ha ha ha...

HILDA. … yeah.

JERRY. …

HILDA. …

JERRY. How're ya' holdin' up there — can I get you anything?

HILDA. oh, no I'm fine

JERRY. great.

HILDA. …

JERRY. 'Hilda.'

What kind of name is that?

HILDA. Northern, of some kind.

JERRY. Right.

HILDA. (*Smiles.*) …

JERRY. You don't say much do you.

HILDA. Oh, I like to listen.

JERRY. You do. Yes. I can tell.

No, I like that about you, that you listen.

HILDA. (*Smiles.*) thanks.

JERRY. do you want any more — ?

HILDA. okay

    (*Pours her some more wine.*)

thanks.

JERRY. So what is it that you hear?

HILDA. Oh, I don't know — tonight, you mean?

JERRY. Sure.

HILDA. Oh. People. Talking. Having fun.

Having fun telling each other stories.

Having fun drinking.

JERRY. Yeah.

Yeah, that's about it.

Plus a little desperation

HILDA. ha ha — yeah, maybe

JERRY. yeah?

HILDA. Oh I don't know.

JERRY. We're all a lonely lot, aren't we.

HILDA. I suppose — What do you think they're doing in there?

JERRY. Oh who knows.

You know Linda. She and Sylvia,

they're always doing this dance.

HILDA. … dance?

JERRY. Oh I don't know.

What do I know. Hey — you know

we've hung out a little at Linda's get-togethers,

but really, I feel like I know next to nothing about you.

HILDA. Oh there's nothing to know

JERRY. I'm sure that's not true

HILDA. oh it is

JERRY. what is it that you do for work?

HILDA. Nothing special. I answer phones.

For a store.

JERRY. Oh

HILDA. yeah. See?

Not so interesting is it.

JERRY. No

HILDA. probably sorry you asked

JERRY. no, not at all. no no.

No — I have to admit.

I'd been asking Linda about you.

Asking her all sorts of — because you are kind of quiet,

kind of — So I ask her.

I ask her, hey, what's Hilda into.

What's she all about.

What's she doing with you and not me — ha ha ha —

just kidding, just — no she uh

She describes you as a very curious person.

HILDA. Oh that's nice

JERRY. yeah, she was um — I guess she was sort of kidding, joking,

she was "Hilda — why is she so..."

I don't know...

HILDA. what

JERRY. oh I don't know.

She just finds you endearing is all

HILDA. ...

JERRY. she says you tell these adorable stories about growing up, and your grandmother

HILDA. ...

JERRY. I just remembered it

HILDA. ...

JERRY. the uh — the story — the ghost

HILDA. Japan

JERRY. yes!

You want to hear it?

HILDA. Okay

JERRY. now how exactly did it go?

uhhhhh

there's a man.
And this man — he's a... terrible —
just a terrible, violent, angry human.
Nasty.

And he's married to this woman.
And they've been married for years,
and over the years, you know his wife sort of...
gradually changed —
you know, like people do, she...
she just sort of —
And the husband, he has these scissors,
this pair of really sharp scissors

> (*A SHRIEK OFFSTAGE!*
> *Followed by laughter.*
> *Linda and Sylvia re-enter, Linda's wearing a new dress.*)

JERRY. ladies ladies ladies

LINDA. Look at me — !!!
look at this dress — this wonderful dress Sylvia got me.
Does it look fetching? Ha ha —

JERRY. oh wow/ yeah

SYLVIA. bought it for her when I was in Barcelona

JERRY. very nice

LINDA. isn't it?

JERRY. Hey hey hey I remembered the scariest story in Japan —

LINDA. oh what is it

JERRY. so there's this man, and he's just this/ horrible —

SYLVIA. no, don't — I can't, it's too close to bedtime,/ I can't no, please, no—

LINDA. I want to hear it

SYLVIA. no, seriously, that's the kind of thing that when I'm in bed tonight
and the lights are turned out — that's the kind of thing that's
going to sneak back into my head —

JERRY. okay alright

LINDA. /boo

SYLVIA. no I'm just too susceptible — it's too easy for me to
get a thought in my head that sort of roots itself in there —

JERRY. right, yeah, no I know/ what you mean —

SYLVIA. Like there's this one thought, very recently,
that's wormed its way into my brain
and I swear I cannot get it out of there

JERRY. was it something about old Danish women's arms/ — I'm just
kidding, I'm just —

SYLVIA. ha ha ha ha —

nooooo, it was this thought about death

JERRY. oh, okay

LINDA. death — ?

JERRY. you know, Linda, that thing you're quickly/ approaching

LINDA. ha ha — fuck you — !

SYLVIA. no, I think I've figured out what happens when we die,
like what the experience is like —

JERRY. Oh okay

SYLVIA. no really, really —

do you wanna know, do you wanna know what it is?

JERRY. I guess(?)

SYLVIA. okay but I'm warning you, once I tell you,
you might not be able to get it out of your head

LINDA. oh this/ is exciting —

SYLVIA. okay, so,

I think
that we never experience the end.
Like of course we die, the body shuts off, blah blah blah —
but in the moments just before the brain goes dead —
it holds on to consciousness for as long as possible
and makes it feel like forever

JERRY. uh-huh

SYLVIA. like in a dream, you know how
a couple of minutes of being asleep in dreams
can feel like hours.

JERRY. Oh okay/ okay I see

SYLVIA. I think that's what happens to us when the brain shuts off —
that those final moments alive feel like they last forever, and what's happening
is that the brain is just sort of living inside of — cycling through —
whatever's in there when you die.

LINDA. Well that's very clever of you Sylvia

SYLVIA. well and here's the kicker.
Because, if that's what death is — and maybe it isn't — but maybe it is,
and if it is,
then that means you have to be very careful about
what kinds of thoughts you put in your head —
because
if you have dark and ugly thoughts in your head
and you walk outside
and you get hit by a car,
then those kinds of horrible thoughts are what you're going to live inside of
for the rest of
forever.

JERRY. Oh Jesus,/ that's — ha ha

SYLVIA. So that's why I've been trying very hard
to not let any negativity into my mind.

JERRY. well that's very — ha ha — that's very interesting/ Sylvia

LINDA. It is. I'm going to have to think about that more.

SYLVIA. hey — could you pass me some more of that — hey, you — Heidi
— ?

JERRY. Hilda

SYLVIA. huh — ?

JERRY. Hilda

SYLVIA. what did I say

JERRY. Heidi

SYLVIA. what did you say

JERRY. Hilda

HILDA. I have a story.

LINDA. I ever/ tell you Hilda tells the most
interesting stories —

SYLVIA. That's okay, I'll get it

JERRY. yes, yes you have

LINDA. is it one of the ones about your grandmother?

HILDA. no, this one's about the last time I ever saw my mother

LINDA. oh I don't know any about your mother —

HILDA. I know.

So, the last time I ever saw my mother —
was last Christmas.

Um.

I hadn't been to visit in awhile — hadn't been around much you know —
But it was Christmas, and Christmas that's what you do.
You pay a little visit.
You put in a little time.
You bring a gift, you drop it off,
you sit on the couch, you talk for about a half an hour,
and then you say, okay, well, nice to see you,
I have to go now, I have this thing I have to do — you've put in your time,
you're free to go.

But this time when I visited her…
She just looked bad.
She had this massive bruise down the side of her face.

And it was just really bad.

And…

At first I just said nothing.

I just stared at her…

but eventually I said something I don't remember what —
probably Merry Christmas,
because, well that's what you do and

and then I sort of asked what happened to her face

and she said she fell

and I asked 'when'

and she said she didn't remember.

And so that was
probably the first concerning thing of that afternoon.

and then inside the house,
the place was a mess.
Trash just everywhere
And the kitchen was like something out of a nightmare,
just horrible,
dirty and
and and there were these cans, open cans of
green beans and corn and and and
a cluster of the the silverfish by the sink faucet

and she seemed to be unaware of how disgusting it was.
She would — I actually saw her do this — she'd pick up a spoon and
she'd pick at the stuff in the cans —
have a little corn or —
the stuff was rotten, or it must've been,
it had been sitting there for days, I'm sure.

It was all so completely shocking.
The kind of shocking that just makes you mad at the person — mad at the
person with the bruised up face — which I know just sounds terrible and
maybe it is — but you look at that person and Jesus fucking Christ — get
yourself together. Life isn't *that* hard, is it?

And then when it's your mother
well that only intensifies the feeling of disgust because
really what you're thinking is — is that going to be me?
Am I going to someday completely lose all sense of
dignity?

So I really wasn't sure what to do. About my mother.
I mean you do what you can:
I did what cleaning I could, barely made a dent though —
what was I supposed to do move in with her, take care of her?
but that's not a real option, I mean, it's not like I'm a professional care taker.
Then do you hire someone? — well who has money for that — ? She doesn't.
I don't.

But then I thought to myself, you know there are other options,
public options, facilities, care-taking facilities —
not the type of thing she would have wanted per se,
not the type of thing she would ever agree to.
No, she would never want to leave her home.

But you know... there are scenarios in which it would be
out of anyone's control,
like, if, for example,

Like if a neighbor saw her walking around outside with her face like it was,
all bruised like it was — if a neighbor saw that, then
a neighbor would likely call Health and Human Services
and they would send someone to check on her,
and if that person from Health and Human Services
saw the house the way it was,
and her face the way it was,
they would have no choice — they would be legally obligated to take her in.

And so...

I decided that I would place a call,
tell them that I was her neighbor,
and tell them that I saw her,
out walking in the yard,
and that she seemed not well and that
her face was bruised.

I made the call.
It was easy.
For the most part.

And after I made the call,
I just waited.
Waited a week.

But I heard nothing.

So I called back.
Health and Human Services.
I got the case worker that I'd spoken with earlier,

and I knew that they wouldn't be able to say much to me
on account of they thought I was just the "neighbor,"
but they did say that
they thought everything would be fine

And I said, "so she's staying?"

And they told me that an examiner or something went,
and yes, the house was messy,
but they got to talk for a bit to her family
and since she had family around
they weren't too worried
and that's all they could really say,
and —

I mean, family?

Who was there? — I wasn't there —

and I said real casual like it was nothing,
"Oh so her family was at the house."

And the case worker said yes,
and thanked me for my concern,
and that was it.

...

Weird, right?

But I thought to myself "oh maybe there was some friend of hers around"
but she doesn't have any friends.

And so I called my mother.

She says hello.
I say hello back.

I ask how she's doing.

She says *oh just fine.*

And I'm trying to think,
so how do I ask what I want to ask?

Of course I don't want her to know that I called the Health and Human
Services on her,
and so —
so I say

"Hey Mom, I got a call from Health and Human Services and they said they
had to pay you a visit. What's that about? Is that true?"

And she said her neighbor had called them on her,
and that she was really upset about her neighbor doing that
and that she talked to the neighbor and the neighbor denied doing anything,
calling, and so on —

and I said "oh well, I just wanted to make sure everything was okay,
because that call got me worried."

And she said, "No, there's nothing to worry about."

...

And then I said,
I told her that there was just one more thing though
that I wanted to ask her about.
I said that the case worker said that when they visited
that there was
some 'family'
there,
and that that sounded odd
and I asked my mother
if that's true.
Was there somebody else there with her when
the Health and Human such and such person was paying the visit,
and
she said
yes.

And I asked,
who? Who exactly was there with her.

And there was silence.

And then very slowly she said

"would you like to talk to them?"

...

And I asked are they there with you now?

And she said yes.

And I said
sure.

And I could hear her put down the phone.

And it took a little while.
I could hear very faint
murmuring in the background,
it wasn't clear, it was
something like voices —

and after a little bit
I hear the phone pick up
and

I said, "hello?"

And there was silence.

And then a voice

on the other end —

I don't know if it was a man or a woman
I couldn't tell — I couldn't tell the age —

but the person said

"I know you."

That's what the person said to me —
the person said to me:

"I know you."

...

And I asked "Okay, and who are you?"

And the voice said again
exactly the same way:
"I know you."

And I asked again "Who is this?
Who are you? Are you a friend of my mother's?"

No answer.

And I said,
"I'm going to call the police. Alright? I'm calling the police."

And still no response.

And I said, "Put my mother back on the phone."

And the voice said,

"We're in the other place now."

...

And it said again

"We're in the
other place now."

And then the phone hung up.
And I called back,
and it was disconnected
or something.

I called the police.

They went to the house.

They called me back.

They said there was nobody in the house.

...

They put out a missing person's something-or-rather.
They did a search. They did all the things they do —
They put up posters in her neighborhood,
and local news alert and...

So.

Nothing.

Never turned up.

And that was almost a year ago.

> (*Silence in the room.*
> *Just silence.*
> *No one really knows what to say.*)

JERRY. wow Hilda.

um.

wow…

> (*… and more silence.*
> *Hilda's phone rings,* **loud***, startling everyone.*)
> *shriek, laughter, tension broken —*)

HILDA. Sorry, that's my phone

LINDA. oh that nearly gave us all a heart attack

JERRY. that was — ha ha — yes, that was quite a startle/ there.
Perfect timing.

SYLVIA. scared the living shit out of me.

HILDA. …

LINDA. …

> (*To Sylvia, re: wine.*)

Do you want to help me finish this — ?

SYLVIA. oh like you have to ask…

> (*Hilda is staring at her phone.*)

JERRY. … Hilda?

You alright?

HILDA. …

LINDA. Hilda —

HILDA. (*Holding out the phone as 'evidence.'*) that call.

That call was from my mother's house.

LINDA. …

JERRY. … huh.

You sure?

HILDA. (*Nods 'yes.'*)

…

JERRY. huh

LINDA. well now isn't that odd —

JERRY. and does anyone live there now?

HILDA. No.

No.

SYLVIA. So creepy —

JERRY. well...

LINDA. I think you should just give it a call back.

See what happens...

HILDA. ...

JERRY. You don't have to —

HILDA. okay.

(*Hilda dials, on speakerphone, holding it out so everyone can bear witness...*

...

Sound of a disconnected line.)

PHONE. *I'm sorry but this line has been disconnected —*

(*Hilda hangs up.*)

JERRY. ... It was probably some sort of random phone glitch.

Some sort of... I/ don't know

LINDA. I'm sorry but I'm very tired,

and I think it's time I turned in for bed.

But I want to thank you all for a —

(*Phone rings again.*)

HILDA. ...

(*Phone rings.*)

JERRY. ...

(*Phone rings.*)

HILDA. It's her.

(*Phone rings.*)

JERRY. Do you want to answer it?

(*Phone rings.*)

HILDA. ... alright.

(*Presses 'answer.'*)

PHONE. ...

HILDA. ...

PHONE. ...

HILDA. Hello... ?

Silence as everyone stares at the phone —

lights cut to black...

after the party

There's a period of darkness. Then we hear Hilda begin speaking. And as she speaks, a single red lightbulb begins to fade up. Much of the remainder of the play will be lit only with that one red lightbulb...

HILDA. after the party that night,

I was supposed to drive Linda home,

but when we got to the right turn that would take us there

... I took the left turn —

LINDA. where are you going, Hilda — ?

HILDA. because I had decided

that I was going to take us back to the house

where my mother lived.

LINDA. Hilda... where are you taking me?

HILDA. Because when I picked up that call from my mother's house —

there was definitely something there — it was very hard to hear —

but there was definitely some kind of — something was there

LINDA. I want you to take me home.

Right now.

HILDA. and Linda, she didn't want to go —

she complained it was too late,

that she was tired —

and she said that I'd behaved very badly at her party

and she was very mad at me,

and that maybe,

maybe we shouldn't be friends anymore.

But I thought that if there <u>was</u> something there at my mother's house,

then I thought we should see it

just to, you know, to <u>know</u>

that there are things in this world

that are more than just tricks,

more than just thoughts in your head —

there are real things in this world,

real

true

things

that cannot be explained —

We're here.

So, are you coming inside with me?

LINDA. …
HILDA. Come inside with me,
and I promise I'll take you home,
just come inside,
alright?
LINDA. (*Very quiet.*) … alright, Hilda.

HILDA. It was very very late at night

And because the doors were locked
and the house was all boarded up,
I had to go around to the back of the house
and break a window just to get in.

We climbed through the window —
there wasn't any power on in the house, so we
had to feel our way around.

This is it, I said.
This is the house I grew up in.

Hello?

Is anybody here?

I decided we should have a look around —
I took Linda by the hand,
I walked her from room to room…

I said,

>   this is the kitchen,
>   and this is the room where we'd eat our meals.
>
>   And through that little door you can go out to the backyard.
>   It's not much, just a narrow patch of dirt.
>
>   Here's the extra room where my grandmother stayed when she
>   lived with us.
>
>   And this is my mother's bedroom —
>
>   And this is the bathroom —
>   once I walked in and saw my mother
>   curled up on the floor. She was crying. She
>   thought she had a demon in her (?),
>   and she said *get it out of me, get it out,*
>   *you're my daughter and you have to fix me.*
>   And so I got down on the floor with her,
>   and she had me put my fingers in her mouth,
>   dig around, see if I could
>   help pull it out of her.
>   And I sort of felt like I felt something soft…
>   but I don't know.

And this — this is
my old room.

The door is closed.
That's odd.

I'm sort of scared to open it.
Should I open it?

I'm going to open it.

… I opened the door.

And

we walked in.

… And there was
nothing in there.

And there was definitely no one in the house.
At least, no one we could see…

I guess we can go now.

LINDA. No.

You're not ready to leave yet.

HILDA. …

LINDA. …

HILDA. … um, what do you mean?

LINDA. You made me come out here,

so that I would sit in this house with you, at god knows what hour.

You want to show me something, then show me something

I want you to call her —

HILDA. who —

LINDA. your mother. Call your mother,

like you used to call your grandmother.

HILDA. I don't want to.

LINDA. I don't care what you want.

HILDA. …

LINDA. …

HILDA. This is a bad idea

LINDA. You think you can do something I can't.

Then fine —

Prove it.

HILDA. …

LINDA. …

HILDA. I can't do it

with you here

LINDA. pretend I'm not —

HILDA. — can't do it with you watching me,

with you staring at me,

with your —

LINDA. I'll close my eyes then — how's that?

HILDA. …

LINDA. …

HILDA. …

LINDA. …

HILDA. take that sheet off the bed,

cover yourself in it,

don't move,

don't make a sound —

do you understand.

LINDA. ... alright

HILDA. ... Go stand over there.

LINDA. ... where

HILDA. over there — go stand over there,

and face the other way

LINDA. ...

There's a neatly folded sheet on the floor. Very neatly folded, as if it's just waiting for Linda to take it. She does so, just as Hilda has requested. Linda takes the sheet, walks over to a corner, and covers her entire body with the sheet.

HILDA. Alright.

shhhhhhhhh

now how does this go…

I breathe.

I breathe,

and I let my eyes go soft.

Focus on the light, the little bit of light there.

Focus on the dark around the light

because the senses need to be soft,

the outside senses — soft,

the inside senses — also soft,

but the inside senses by them-self they get sharp

very sharp

and I hum
just to myself
a single tone

      (*She starts giggling a little — a little tipsy? but then very serious.*)

okay.

Is anyone here?

Is anyone I know here.

…

…

is grandma here.

is mother here.

Is anyone here.

If you're here,
maybe you can do something?

Or say something

or... show yourself

just so I know you're there,

just so I know where you are

silence...

the single red light starts to flicker —
flickers and snaps...

some sort of presence is near...
some sort of... it's approaching, it's not in the room yet, but
we can feel it... approaching...

the red light flickers again...
any moment it seems it could go out for good...

it's so hard to see... it's very hard...
it's possible that objects are moving,
but maybe not...

it's possible that shadows are forming...
conspiring almost...

(*We hear a door open… on stage, but there are no doors on the stage, nothing that could make that sound*

… the sound of a door slowly opening

… followed by nothing…

… followed by stillness…

… silence…)

HILDA. hello… ?

silence...

HILDA. (*Speaking to the audience…*)

something had definitely entered the room…

> (*Linda begins wheezing — she's having an attack*
> *she runs away from her spot*
> *Hilda admonishes Linda.*)

>> Shhhhhhh.
>> Get back there.

> (*Linda returns to her spot.*)

… it was just… sitting with us…

>> sitting by Linda…

>>> I don't know if she could tell.

>> It stayed with her for awhile.

> I can't tell if it was just watching her

or if it was, in some way, feeding on her

> or…

>>> I wondered if I should do something.

>>> I wondered if I should try to ward it away,

>> but to be honest, I didn't want to attract its attention.

> If it was feeding on her, better that it feed on one person

instead of two.

... by now, Linda's wheezing has died down, her sheet-covered body lowers to the ground... assuming a rather pathetic-looking crouch under the sheet...

HILDA. And after some time, the thing left.

> (*THE DOOR THAT ISN'T THERE SLAMS SHUT.*
> *then nothing.*)

And we waited some more.

And at a certain point, I decided well I guess that's it
> (*The stage light flicks back on to full as the red light flicks off.*
> *Linda remains covered.*)

That was the last time I saw Linda.

I wasn't sure if I should try to call her.
I thought about trying to call her,
or trying to track her down.
But then I thought I shouldn't.

It's the thing that happens
when you show somebody something you
probably shouldn't have shown them.
And we all have these things, don't we(?), and we think about showing them,
but most people know enough to know to keep it to themselves.

So now she's gone.

Or I think.

Or

Because, sometimes what I think or what I wonder
is whether she's gone
or if I'm gone.

I don't know.

Maybe after that night I slipped through the crack,
maybe I'm on the other side,
maybe I'm in the other place now.

Isn't that something.
Now that would be — I'm sorry but —
> (*Catching the eye again of that audience member from the top of*
> *the play.*)

it's just the funniest thing

how much you look like my grandmother.

Oh I wish I had a picture I'd show you — I mean
It's just such a coincidence it must mean something, right? I mean
It just makes me wanna —
I really just wanna —
>   (... *fishes out a pad of paper from a side table*
>   *and she writes something down on the pad*
>   *and then Hilda starts laughing to herself as if from embarrassment...*
>   *then composes herself.*)

okay, just
just just —
all you have to do is listen
just
really listen

are you listening?

...

...

...

Do you hear the word I'm thinking of?
>   (*The audience member does not hear anything.*)

no like really listen

...

...

...

... you heard it didn't you.
>   (*The audience member actually hears a word that only they can*
>   *hear.*)

What word did you hear?
>   (*The audience member says the word they heard.*
>   *and Hilda just gets the biggest, happiest smile on her face.*)

Yeah,
that's it.

> *(Hilda turns the pad around to face the audience, and it's the word the audience member said...)*

That's—

That's just the funniest thing.

That's just the funniest —

Hilda is just so happy, so serenely blissfully happy.

And Linda — Linda who's been crouched this whole time under that sheet upstage —

Linda starts to rise, like she's about to do something, and the moment she stands fully, the sheet falls — Linda is gone.

A door slams.

Lights snap out.

The play is over.

THE CORPSE WASHER
adapted for the stage by
Ismail Khalidi and Naomi Wallace,
from the novel of the same name by
Sinan Antoon

ABOUT *THE CORPSE WASHER*

This article first ran in the Limelight Guide to the 43rd Humana Festival of New American Plays, *published by Actors Theatre of Louisville, and is based on conversations with the playwrights before rehearsals for the Humana Festival production began.*

Jawad, a young man coming of age in Baghdad, has spent his entire existence under the shadow of death. His father runs a Shi'ite Muslim *mghaysil* (or "wash house"), in which he cleans the bodies of the deceased to prepare them for burial. (It's believed in Islamic culture that this ritual helps departed souls enter the afterlife.) While the men in Jawad's family have carried on this honored profession for six generations, Jawad has other aspirations: he wants to be an artist. But in an Iraq beset by thirty years of military violence, dreams aren't achieved without cost. In *The Corpse Washer*, their adaptation of Sinan Antoon's award-winning novel of the same name, playwrights Ismail Khalidi and Naomi Wallace bring Jawad's story to the stage—creating a haunting portrait of a nation in which the borders between life and death grow increasingly blurred.

The Corpse Washer moves back and forth in time through Jawad's dreams and recollections, pulling us into his experience with a fluidity that mimics the flow of memory. We encounter him as an eager-to-please boy learning his father's trade, a rebellious adolescent discovering his passion for art, and a man struggling to channel his feelings of anger and loss into sculpture as his country crumbles around him. All the while, the harsh reality of war remains a constant. When teenaged Jawad recruits his brother, Ammoury, to convince their father to let him attend the Academy of Fine Arts, Ammoury's enlisted in another conflict, too—the Iran-Iraq War that spanned the 1980s. Jawad makes a new friend, Basim, at the Academy, and the two become close not only on campus, but also in an army bunker as soldiers during the Gulf War's aftermath. Jawad's relationship with his fiancée, Reem, unfolds amid the U.S.-imposed trade sanctions that crippled Iraqis' standard of living throughout the 1990s. And, in the wake of 2003's American invasion and subsequent occupation, Jawad faces an impossible choice. Will he leave his devastated homeland to pursue his creative ambitions abroad? Or, as the body count rises, is it his duty to take over the *mghaysil?*

For Khalidi and Wallace, retelling a story that chronicles the wars in Iraq from a civilian point of view felt like a rare and valuable opportunity. Although author Sinan Antoon emigrated from Iraq in 1991, he's written about his native land to critical acclaim throughout his career. Published in Arabic in 2010 and later translated into English by Antoon, the novel of *The Corpse Washer* became a *New York Times* bestseller and has been lauded for its humanizing portrayal of ordinary Iraqis' lives. "Iraq is a complex, sophisticated country with a rich history," says Khalidi. "In the book, Sinan captures over three decades of that history, but in a very personal and poignant way. There's not enough work in the American theatre about Iraq, especially not based in the perspectives of actual Iraqis. This story helps to fill that vacuum, and we wanted to honor that by building a bridge to the stage."

According to Wallace, delving into the world of *The Corpse Washer* was also an investigation of the U.S.'s complicated legacy in the Middle East. "There's an intimate connection between the people of Iraq and who we are as Americans," she reflects. "When you invade a country and destroy its civilian infrastructure, you exert tremendous force over that country's history and future. We talk a lot about 'American values.' As a writer, I'm interested in how those 'American values' unfold abroad." In addition, the viscerally poetic aspects of Jawad's journey spoke to Wallace as a theatre artist. As the years pass, Jawad's consciousness is increasingly inhabited by the ghosts of loved ones lost to the ongoing violence. For Wallace, this overlap between past and present, the realms of the living and the dead, seemed ripe for dramatic exploration. She explains: "The stage is a place where the past can be embodied; the dead can live, resurrected through the bodies of actors. On stage we can even put the living and the dead side by side, making it hard to tell sometimes who's alive and who isn't. Sinan does that beautifully in his book and this story really wants to be on the stage."

While the action of *The Corpse Washer* is grounded in Islamic custom and the landscape of war-torn Baghdad, Khalidi and Wallace emphasize that their adaptation can resonate with audiences of many backgrounds—and that fostering empathy for underrepresented narratives is a vital part of what theatre can accomplish. "Imagine what it's like to have conflict with your father, because he wants you to do something other than what's in your heart," says Wallace. "Or what it's like to not get to do what you want creatively because of war. Those are things a lot of us can connect to." Khalidi declares: "*The Corpse Washer* is about finding ways to maintain your dignity, your passion, and your humanity, even in the most inhumane of circumstances. Arabs and Muslims are human beings. Sadly we live in a country where that basic truth still needs to be pointed out (as does the fact that black, brown, native, and immigrant lives matter). Theatre is a great vehicle for exploring the depth of the underlying humanity of those folks whose histories (and futures) are systematically erased, ignored, or simply misunderstood."

—Hannah Rae Montgomery

BIOGRAPHIES

Ismail Khalidi's plays include *Truth Serum Blues* (Pangea World Theater, 2005), *Tennis in Nablus* (Alliance Theatre, 2010), *Foot* (Teatro Amal, 2016), *Sabra Falling* (Pangea World Theater, 2017), an adaptation of Ghassan Kanafani's *Returning to Haifa* (with Naomi Wallace, Finborough Theatre, 2018), and *Dead Are My People* (Noor Theatre, 2018). His writing has appeared in numerous anthologies as well as *The Nation, Mizna, Guernica, American Theatre, Remezcla, Kenyon Review, Al-Jazeera*, and *The Dramatist*. Khalidi co-edited (also with Naomi Wallace) *Inside/Outside: Six Plays from Palestine and the Diaspora* (TCG, 2015). Khalidi has received commissions from The Public Theater, Actors Theatre of Louisville, Noor Theatre, and Pangea World Theater. He holds an MFA from New York University's Tisch School of the Arts.

Naomi Wallace's plays—produced in the United States, the United Kingdom, and the Middle East—include *One Flea Spare, The Trestle at Pope Lick Creek, Things of Dry Hours, The Fever Chart, And I and Silence, Night is a Room*, and *Returning to Haifa* (adapted with Ismail Khalidi). In 2009, *One Flea Spare* was incorporated into the permanent repertoire of the French National Theatre, the Comédie-Française. Only two American playwrights have been added to the Comédie's repertoire in three hundred years. Awards include the MacArthur Fellowship, Susan Smith Blackburn Prize, Fellowship of Southern Writers Drama Award, Obie Award, the Horton Foote Prize, and Ubu Award (Italy). Wallace received the inaugural Windham-Campbell Prize in drama and an Arts and Letters Award in Literature.

Wallace is under commission by Headlong Theater in the United Kingdom, and she is writing the book for the new John Mellencamp musical.

Sinan Antoon is a poet, novelist, scholar, and translator. He has published four novels and two collections of poetry. His works have been translated into twelve languages. His translation of his own novel, *The Corpse Washer*, won the 2014 Saif Ghobash Prize for Literary Translation. Two of his novels were shortlisted for the Arabic Booker. His scholarly works include *The Poetics of the Obscene: Ibn al-Hajjaj and Sukhf*. He has published op-eds in *The Guardian* and *The New York Times*. His fourth novel, *The Book of Collateral Damage*, was released in English in 2019. He is an associate professor at New York University.

ACKNOWLEDGMENTS

The Corpse Washer premiered at the Humana Festival of New American Plays in March 2019. It was directed by Mark Brokaw with the following cast:

JAWAD KAZIM ....Arash Mokhtar
MAHDI/HAMMOUDY...Johann George
FATHER/UNCLE SABRI...................................J. Paul Nicholas
BASIM...Abraham Makany
MOTHER/GUARD ....Diana Simonzadeh
REEM ....Mehry Eslaminia
AL-FARTUSI/MAN ....Hassan Nazari-Robati
AMMOURY...Gus Cuddy

and the following production staff:

Scenic Designer.. Kimie Nishikawa
Costume Designer...Dina Abd El-Aziz
Lighting Designer.. Heather Gilbert
Sound Designer..Luqman Brown
Stage Manager..Stephen Horton
Dramaturg ....Hannah Rae Montgomery
Casting...Judy Bowman, CSA
Production Consultants..................................... Maia Directors
Properties Master ....Katelin Ashcraft
Directing Assistant ....Sharifa Yasmin
Assistant Dramaturg.. Alonna Ray
Stage Management Apprentice..............................Andie Burns

The Corpse Washer was commissioned by Actors Theatre of Louisville. The commission was generously underwritten by Jacqueline R. and Theodore S. Rosky as part of the Les Waters New Works Fund.

CHARACTERS

JAWAD KAZIM, from 12 to mid-30s
AMMOURY, Jawad's older brother
FATHER
MOTHER
BASIM, Jawad's friend
MAHDI/HAMMOUDY, attendant body washers
REEM, a young woman
UNCLE SABRI, Jawad's uncle, 50s
AL-FARTUSI/MAN, body collector, 40s

TIME

Before 1980s to 2010. Time is fluid, spanning the time before and during the Iran-Iraq War, as well as the first Gulf War and the second U.S. war against Iraq. Sometimes a step or a turn of character can indicate a day, a week, or years have suddenly passed.

PLACE

In both the real and imagined city of Baghdad, Iraq. In a wash house. A home. A street. Awake and asleep. And sometimes moving in that liminal, haunted space in-between. Spirits are just as real as the living.

The set is not realistic, but morphs from one space to the next on a dime.

We never see the statues or artwork Jawad creates. A chair can be used as a sculpture.

Arash Mokhtar
in *The Corpse Washer*

43rd Humana Festival of New American Plays
Actors Theatre of Louisville, 2019
Photo by Jonathan Roberts

THE CORPSE WASHER

PROLOGUE

The Present, 2008. JAWAD *is in the Mghaysil, the wash house.*

Copper bowls and jugs are neatly piled. A minimum of necessary things: a wooden stool, a water source, a bench.

JAWAD, *just off to the side, is about to light a cigarette. He's frustrated. He's had enough.*

MAHDI, *his assistant, enters, anxious.* MAHDI *hesitates a moment.*

MAHDI. Jawad.

JAWAD. Yes?

MAHDI. Fartusi is here with more bodies to wash.

JAWAD. I can't go back in there. I can't.

> (MAHDI *waits.*)

Is there something else?

MAHDI. My cousin called: They've bombed the graveyard.

JAWAD. The graveyard?

MAHDI. In Najaf.

> (JAWAD *takes in this news.*)

JAWAD. And my father's grave?

> (JAWAD *breaks off.*)

MAHDI. He said he'd call back. When it's safe. But there are craters. Some of the headstones are destroyed / and

JAWAD. (*Cuts him off.*) I understand.

> (JAWAD *is quiet for a moment, then:*)

Mahdi. You still think about getting out of here?

MAHDI. All the time. You?

> (*There is a KNOCK on a door.* MAHDI *leaves momentarily,* JAWAD *is just about to light his cigarette when* MAHDI *returns.*)

We need to get started.

JAWAD. Give me another minute.

> (MAHDI *exits. We hear the distant sound of jets. A dull explosion in the distance.* JAWAD *begins to hear voices from the past.*)

FATHER. Pay attention, my son.

BASIM. I don't want to be a king.

179

HAMMOUDY. He wanted you to do it.

AMMOURY. And the trenches get deeper.

MOTHER. I lost that ability.

REEM. Maybe it's you who's drowning.

BASIM. You think I suffered?

FATHER. I'm not asking you to touch them.

AL-FARTUSI. The dead are / everywhere.

MOTHER. You're selfish, / son.

FATHER. You will stay.

REEM. I'm old on the / inside

BASIM. He should shutter / this place.

AMMOURY. Don't fuck with / tradition, Shrimp.

AL-FARTUSI. If God won't knock you / down I will.

FATHER. Pay attention.

ALL. And learn.

SCENE ONE

JAWAD *now watches the past come alive. His* FATHER *is readying the wash house.*

The Past (1982). The sparse wash room of the Mghaysil. There is no body present.

When JAWAD's *father speaks, he is speaking to* JAWAD *as a boy, though* JAWAD *is still more adult than child.*

There is a KNOCK on a door.

HAMMOUDY. They're here. With another one.

FATHER. Thank you, Hammoudy. Just a few more minutes.

(*To* JAWAD *as a boy.*)

My son, you're twelve now. The same age that I was taught by my father. Now, the family will usually ask you about the fee, and you will say "Whatever you can manage, plus the cost of the shroud."

JAWAD. "Whatever you can manage…"

FATHER. "…Plus the cost of the shroud."

(HAMMOUDY *brings* FATHER *his white apron.*)

First I'll look carefully to see what the body needs. The dead will meet God, and the angels and the people of the afterlife, and must therefore be pure. Clean. First we put the lotus leaves in the water…

(HAMMOUDY *sprinkles lotus in a bowl of water.*)

Sprinkle the ground lotus on the head and wash the hair. The first time you touch the body/

JAWAD. I don't want to touch the body.

HAMMOUDY. Shhh.

FATHER. I'm not asking you to touch, Jawad.

HAMMOUDY. (*Whispers to* JAWAD.) You're trembling. Stop it.

FATHER. ...You will say, *In the name of God, most Merciful, most Compassionate. Oh, Lord, here is the body of your servant who believed in you.*

JAWAD. *Here is the body...*

HAMMOUDY. *You have taken his soul and separated the two.*

FATHER. And then each time you turn the body you say:

FATHER/HAMMOUDY. *Your forgiveness, Oh Lord. Your forgiveness.*

FATHER. Always begin with the right side of the body. The head, then the face, the neck, shoulder, arm, hand, chest and belly. Then again, on the other side. When you wash the private parts, do so without removing the cloth. Use cotton balls to stop any leaks.

JAWAD. This is how the Sunnis wash too?

FATHER. Not much difference between the Shia and the Sunni in washing. And a Christian or a Jew may also wash a Muslim if there are no Muslims at hand.

JAWAD. And the rich?

FATHER. The rich and the poor are buried the same. The important thing is to be

FATHER/JAWAD. Possessed of noble intentions.

FATHER. One day I won't be here and you will take care of God's work, and your mother.

JAWAD. Yes, Father.

FATHER. The last of the three washings is with water alone—and three parts to the shroud. But first rub the camphor on the forehead, nose, cheeks, palms, knees. And lastly, the branch from the palm tree.

FATHER/HAMMOUDY. *May God have mercy on his soul.*

(HAMMOUDY *snaps the branch.*)

HAMMOUDY. For when the body is in the coffin. To lessen the torture of the grave.

FATHER. When you finish school, you'll be ready to work beside me, like Hammoudy.

JAWAD. What if the dead man follows me home?

FATHER. Shame on you, Jawad. The soul rises to the sky, but the body remains.

HAMMOUDY. This will be your first dead body, huh? Scared?

JAWAD. No.

HAMMOUDY. You'll get used to it.

FATHER. Hammoudy, have them bring in the body.

(*To* JAWAD.)

Let's begin.

(HAMMOUDY *and his* FATHER *disappear as* JAWAD's MOTHER *appears.*)

MOTHER. Let me see your hands. Let me see if they're shaking?

JAWAD. Not anymore.

MOTHER. Impressive.

JAWAD. I hid them in my pockets and Father didn't see.

MOTHER. Smart. So what did you learn?

JAWAD. How to wrap the bands around the body.

MOTHER. What else?

JAWAD. That we live off dead people!

MOTHER. Jawad!

JAWAD. Father says this summer I'll only watch. (*Beat.*) Mother, if I have nightmares, I'm not going to tell anyone about them.

MOTHER. Smart boy! Shall we sleep on the roof tonight? The breeze will do us good. And if the sky is clear, I'll teach you about constellations. Named by astrologers right here in Baghdad, a thousand years ago.

JAWAD. Yes! And I'll teach you how to wrap the bands.

MOTHER. It's a deal.

JAWAD. Father says one day I will wash him too.

MOTHER. Yes. But not for a very, very long time.

JAWAD. Look. My hands still shake a little.

MOTHER. That's normal. It's your first day.

(*She takes his hand, then examines it carefully.*)

JAWAD. What?

MOTHER. How perfect the fingers, the thumb... Jawad, you are going to make your father proud.

SCENE TWO

C. 1980. UNCLE SABRI *appears with books and a soccer ball.*

SABRI *drops the ball and kicks it to* JAWAD.

UNCLE SABRI. Don't tell your father. About the ball.

JAWAD. Does he know you're here?

UNCLE SABRI. Not yet. But brothers can smell each other a mile off.

JAWAD. Do you smell like camphor too?

UNCLE SABRI. No, I smell like exile. And books. And football. Now kick the damn ball back to me.

JAWAD. Uncle Sabri, I'm gonna be a body washer.

UNCLE SABRI. Are you? Well, you have years to figure that out. In the meantime, *'O jogo bonito.'* The Beautiful game! Come on, boy, there's a Johan Cryff hiding in you. Or a Pelé, maybe? Kick.

(*He tries to get* JAWAD *to pass the ball back and forth but* JAWAD *is not quite as enthusiastic.*)

JAWAD. (*In one careful breath.*) Ammoury says he won't wash bodies and Father was upset 'cause Ammoury's his first son but now he says maybe it's better for Ammoury to study to be a doctor and so Father has decided that his second son, me, is his first choice to learn the trade.

UNCLE SABRI. Ah. But the land of the living is much more exciting! Take books, for instance.

JAWAD. What's a communist?

UNCLE SABRI. You even say "communist" the way your father does... Now pay attention. I have four books, see? You have none. I'll give you half of what I have. Now we both have two books. Equal. *That's* communism.

JAWAD. Father says some books can get you killed.

UNCLE SABRI. Just take the books.

(*He gives two books to* JAWAD.)

JAWAD. He says you carry books like that.

UNCLE SABRI. Ah, but it's not the books that kill. It's the semi-literate thugs in uniform who are scared of—

(*He breaks off.*)

In any case, these are completely harmless...in a dangerous sort of way. Take 'em.

(JAWAD *looks through the book.*)

JAWAD. (*Mispronounces.*) Gia-come-tti.

UNCLE SABRI. Giacometti.

JAWAD. Communist?

UNCLE SABRI. Just a man who could see through our flesh and bone! *For him to sculpt is to take the fat off of space.* Sartre said that.

JAWAD. They're so skinny... But their feet are big.

UNCLE SABRI. Good observation. If you won't be a football player or a communist, I suppose an artist will / do...

JAWAD. (*Engrossed in the book.*) The bodies look…burned. Why?

UNCLE SABRI. You'll tell me when you find out.

> (JAWAD *thinks, shakes his head "no," and gives* SABRI *back the two books.*)

JAWAD. Why don't you come back? To stay?

UNCLE SABRI. (*In a low voice, but playful too.*) Our president and me, well, we don't see eye to eye. Saddam and his Ba'thists are the running dogs of the CIA. Which is why I'm not really here! I slipped in under a different name, just for a few hours. To see you and your beautiful mother, and my beloved Iraq. I don't know when I'll see her next.

JAWAD. Mamma or Iraq?

UNCLE SABRI. Both. But I call when I can.

JAWAD. Why was Father interrogated when you phoned our house from Beirut last year?

UNCLE SABRI. I'm sorry, kid. I can't help myself when it comes to family.

JAWAD. Was Giacometti a Shia like us? Or a Sunni?

UNCLE SABRI. You look it up and tell me.

JAWAD. Will these books help me be a better washer?

UNCLE SABRI. Sure. Yes! And maybe *washing* will make you a better artist, too.

> (JAWAD *thinks about this, then takes the two books back from* SABRI.)

Attaboy! Just keep them under your bed: your father might not approve.

> (UNCLE SABRI *moves to leave.*)

JAWAD. Wait. Don't go yet!

UNCLE SABRI. *O jogo bonito!*

> (SABRI *disappears.* JAWAD *opens the book to study just as a young man enters, riding a nice bike.*
>
> *He is* JAWAD's *older brother,* AMMOURY. *A couple of years have passed.*
>
> AMMOURY *rides circles around* JAWAD.)

AMMOURY. What's the matter, little brother? Hiding in those books again?

JAWAD. (*Ignoring him.*) Leave me alone, Ammoury.

AMMOURY. Must be puberty. It can make you sick. Heartsick. Dick sick.

JAWAD. My teacher, Mr. Ismail, says my drawings are good, that I've got a strong hand/

AMMOURY. Jawad. Listen to me/

JAWAD. Why should I?

THE CORPSE WASHER

AMMOURY. 'Cause… I'm older and more handsome. Plus, I don't jerk off three times a day.

JAWAD. Mr. Ismail says that I'm talented. That I could be an artist if / I

AMMOURY. You keep working with Father.

JAWAD. Easy for you to say. Where'd you get that bike?

AMMOURY. Beautiful, isn't she? I paid half, Father paid for the rest.

JAWAD. Of course he did.

(*Mocks.*)

Father spoils you. "Oh my Ameer, my Ammoury, he's going to be a doctor one day blah blah blah."

AMMOURY. Shrimp. You do know that jealousy makes you impotent, right?

(JAWAD *jumps up and chases* AMMOURY *away on his bike.*)

SCENE THREE

JAWAD *with his* FATHER *at the wash house.* JAWAD *is sketching. His* FATHER *snatches the notebook from him and examines it.*

FATHER. Draw me if you like, sure, or Hammoudy but leave the dead in peace! The dead have their sanctity/

JAWAD. I wasn't drawing them… It's a sketch of the father who brought him to be washed/

FATHER. Don't lie, boy.

(FATHER *looks through the notebook.*)

Why do you draw these faces?

JAWAD. At night. When I can't sleep. I'm sorry.

FATHER. Not *when*, I asked you *why*?

JAWAD. I can't help it. My hands, they just / keep

FATHER. So your hands are to blame!? Maybe they have a mind of their own?

JAWAD. Sometimes I think they do.

FATHER. I know who's to blame. It's that renegade brother of mine. Writing you letters from Berlin, stuffed with nonsense about art! Before he got into your head, you were happy working with me.

JAWAD. I'm still happy working with you. It's just that I also like…to draw.

(FATHER *looks at a drawing of a face.*)

FATHER. I knew that man. Not well but. Well enough to see that you've got his eyebrows wrong. They were thicker.

JAWAD. Were they?

FATHER. Yes. Twice the size.

> (*While* FATHER *holds the notebook,* JAWAD *quickly sketches in thicker eyebrows.*)

More.

> (JAWAD *adds more.* FATHER *and* JAWAD *consider the portrait.*)

JAWAD. Yeah. You're right. That's it. That's him. When you look at them, Father, do you see what I see?

> (FATHER *closes the notebook.*)

FATHER. Tell me: you think the dead need your drawings?

JAWAD. Need them? Well no, I/

FATHER. You think the dead want you to draw the faces of their families when they themselves can no longer see?

JAWAD. Maybe not, but I/

FATHER. (*Gentle, firm.*) The dead need to be washed, Son. With full attention.

JAWAD. Yes, Father.

FATHER. The body will return to the earth from which it was made; the soul will face judgment; and we the living are reminded that our time on Earth is limited. Our opportunity to do good may end at any moment. Never forget that.

> (HAMMOUDY *enters.*)

HAMMOUDY. They've brought one. Accident at a petrochemical plant. Burned. I don't think his clothes can be removed.

> (FATHER *considers, then nods, agreeing.*)

FATHER. We'll only wash with water, then, and shroud him. Without rubbing him down.

HAMMOUDY. (*Whispering to* JAWAD.) If we try to rub him down, he'll fall apart in our hands.

FATHER. We must be delicate.

> (JAWAD *turns away.*)

Jawad. Don't turn away. Death is just a transition from one state of being to another, it is not an end.

> (HAMMOUDY *and* FATHER *prepare.* JAWAD *hangs back.*)

SCENE FOUR

> AMMOURY *appears, walking his bike. Time has passed (early 1980s).*

AMMOURY. No way is Father gonna let you go/

JAWAD. Don't start.

AMMOURY. To the Academy of Fine *Idiots.*

JAWAD. Arts!

AMMOURY. Idiots!

JAWAD. Ask him to let me go if I get the grades. Please.

AMMOURY. Enough. Here. It's yours.

(AMMOURY *gives* JAWAD *the bike.*)

JAWAD. But you love this bike!

AMMOURY. Yeah. But I can't take it to the front. Not gonna try to attack Iranian positions on my dirt bike am I!? Besides, it's too small for me now.

JAWAD. Is this a bribe so I stay at the wash house?

(JAWAD *examines the bike. He spins the wheel.*)

AMMOURY. Absolutely! But you're also good at washing. I'm not. I bet Father never told you 'bout that one time I went into the wash house and kept throwing up in a bucket? Yeah, as he's demonstrating the intricacies of his trade I'm chucking up. Man, he was ashamed.

JAWAD. He's never ashamed of you. With me it's different. I try to make him proud. Imitate his every move. Like how he ties his apron or how long he runs the water. The other day I found myself trying to clear my throat like he does.

AMMOURY. You mean like:

(AMMOURY *clears his throat.*)

JAWAD. No. Like this:

(JAWAD *clears his throat.*)

AMMOURY. Shit! That's it exactly!

JAWAD. But it's still not enough.

AMMOURY. You know what would help, Shrimp? If you got laid.

JAWAD. You're not getting laid.

AMMOURY. But I am engaged and when you're engaged well…

JAWAD. Yeah.

AMMOURY. My Wasan, she's a student of architecture. Knows where things fit.

JAWAD. (*Jealous.*) I hate you. Listen, please talk to Father about the Art Academy.

AMMOURY. Maybe… Maybe when you finish your exams, and *if* your grades are good enough.

JAWAD. Yesss!

AMMOURY. But on one condition, Shrimp.

JAWAD. Name it.

(*Elsewhere a man in a cleric's robe appears.* AL-FARTUSI *stares at* JAWAD *as he walks past him.* JAWAD *stares back. Only* JAWAD *sees the vision.*)

AMMOURY. That after the Academy you'll bust your ass so you can take over the wash house.

JAWAD. I promise. I'll wash bodies during the day and alter the course of art history at night!

AMMOURY. Good. 'Cause the mghaysil is tradition. Don't fuck with tradition.

AL-FARTUSI. Bodies must be cleaned and buried.

AMMOURY. You hear me?

AMMOURY/AL-FARTUSI. Don't fuck with tradition.

(MOTHER *enters holding a piece of paper. She waves the report card in the air.* AL-FARTUSI *disappears.*)

SCENE FIVE

MOTHER *is holding up* JAWAD's *degree. Time has passed.* AMMOURY *is about to leave for the front.*

MOTHER. Bravo, Jawad.

AMMOURY. I still don't understand how the hell he got better grades than I did? I bet you cheated.

MOTHER. Your father will be happy.

AMMOURY. Daddy's little boy.

JAWAD. I'm sending in my application to the Academy!

MOTHER. There's no rush, Jawad.

JAWAD. On Monday.

MOTHER. Why not wait a year or two, see if you change your mind?

JAWAD. I won't.   **AMMOURY.** He won't.

MOTHER. You don't need to go to university to draw.

JAWAD. I do. I don't know a thing about theory, or the 'why' of lines and form.

MOTHER. I found a way. Without the Academy. When I was young I drew. Hands... Nothing else.

(*The two boys stare at her for a beat.*)

AMMOURY. You drew?   **JAWAD.** You were an artist?

(*Their* MOTHER *just shrugs.*)

MOTHER. I could study people's hands without anyone knowing. Everyone just thought I was very modest and kept my eyes averted.

(*She demonstrates for them. They laugh.*)

JAWAD. You still have the drawings?

MOTHER. Threw them away. Long ago.

JAWAD/AMMOURY. Why?!

MOTHER. Well, I had to raise you two water buffaloes. I became a full-time zookeeper.

AMMOURY. A zoo of two!

MOTHER. Plus your father.

JAWAD. How come you never told us?

MOTHER. Drawing was my secret. A secret that could stretch the walls of the house all the way out to the universe.

AMMOURY. You shouldn't have given it up, Mamma!

JAWAD. You might've become the greatest artist in Iraq since ancient Mesopotamia.

MOTHER. Without a doubt.

JAWAD. (*To* MOTHER.) So I got my talent from you. It's in my blood. Mr. Ismail says—

AMMOURY. Not that hippie teacher again.

JAWAD. —that we had the first art workshops in the world. And the largest. Not only did we invent writing—

AMMOURY. (*A football chant.*) Sumeria! Sumeria!

JAWAD. And build the first cities and temples—

(*The young men surround their mother, harassing each other and vying for her attention.*)

AMMOURY. Goal! Sumeria – 1, the World, – 0.

JAWAD. And the first works of art.

AMMOURY. Goal! Sumeria – 2, World, – 0.

JAWAD. Giant statues—

AMMOURY. Sumeria! 3 – 0.

JAWAD. —so exquisite they were pillaged and taken to museums in London and Paris.

AMMOURY. Uh oh. The World scores in rapid succession on the exhausted Sumerian squad. It's 3-3 folks.

MOTHER. Cut it out!

AMMOURY. Maybe it's just as well they shipped off the art to the West; all we do is fight.

MOTHER. Ammoury! This war with Iran will end.

JAWAD. They've been saying that for years.

AMMOURY. And the trenches get deeper.

MOTHER. (*To* AMMOURY.) You just worry about finishing your service. In one piece. And preparing for your medical exams.

(*To* JAWAD.)

And you. Your father and *his* father washed, and his grandfather, and his/

JAWAD. (*Mocking.*) Great, great grandfather...

MOTHER. It's an honorable lineage.

AMMOURY. Let Jawad apply, Mother. He's got it like a poison in his veins.

JAWAD. Yeah, I do.

(JAWAD *throws a military duffle bag at* AMMOURY. *Time passes. Darkness.*)

SCENE SIX

JAWAD's FATHER *and* MOTHER *are arguing about him.*

FATHER. Ammoury will be a doctor! It's a respected profession.

MOTHER. Ammoury backs him on this.

FATHER. Well Ammoury's not here. He's at the front, doing his duty. Jawad is here and will do his. The answer is *no*.

MOTHER. You know it's one of the best in the Arab world.

FATHER. What is?

MOTHER. The Art Academy. Not just anyone is accepted.

FATHER. (*Matter-of-factly.*) And not just anyone can do what I do, either.

MOTHER. I know that, darling. But just hear him out. It's only for a few years, then he'll come back and work with you.

FATHER. So my wife is against me now, too?

MOTHER. Not against you. Beside you... (*Beat.*) What if it's not his destiny?

FATHER. That's exactly what you said about Ammoury! ...Thank God Hammoudy's around to help me.

(FATHER *exits.* MOTHER *and* JAWAD *stand in silence.*)

JAWAD. Thanks for trying.

(JAWAD *lights a cigarette. His mother grabs the box and takes her own and looks at* JAWAD, *waiting for him to give her a light.*)

MOTHER. Oh don't look at me like that. Just give me a light. And don't tell your father.

(*He does. They smoke in silence for a beat.*)

Why must you make him unhappy? You're selfish. That's what you are.

JAWAD. Yeah. I guess you're right.

MOTHER. Good. I lost that ability. Don't you do the same.

(*JAWAD moves to hug his mother. She holds up her hand to stop him.*)
Save the sentimentality, okay? Until you've accomplished something. Just make sure you are top of the class at the Academy.

(*JAWAD goes to get ready for University, moving to rock music [maybe Mellencamp's "Small Town"], combing his hair back, tucking his shirt in, filled with pride to be going to University. It's the mid- to late-1980s. As* JAWAD *readies himself, he chants:*)

JAWAD. The Challenges of the Avant-Garde!

Art in Renaissance Italy!

The Medieval Islamic Imagination! Bam!

Sculpture of the Ancient World! Ta, ta, ta.

Art history and its methods! Mmmhm.

SCENE SEVEN

JAWAD *is rushing to class on his bike.*

A young man, the campus guard, BASIM, *is reading the papers and smoking. He wears pseudo-official security guard clothes and hat. He blocks the way when* JAWAD *tries to get past him to class.*

BASIM. You're late.

JAWAD. Only two minutes!

BASIM. Two minutes is precisely two minutes too late, man. Sorry.

JAWAD. Come on.

BASIM. Intro to Art History?

JAWAD. Yeah.

BASIM. They call your Professor the "Englishman." 'Cause he's a tight ass, obsessed with time. And you're out of time. Ergo: I can't let you in.

JAWAD. Please, man.

BASIM. No way. He'll blame me. And I don't want him on my ass. Can't lose this gig.

JAWAD. Shit. Shit!

BASIM. You're first year, aren't you?

JAWAD. Yeah. Jawad. You?

BASIM. They call me the gatekeeper of the underworld.

(*JAWAD is suddenly apprehensive.*)

Lighten up. You look like you got bit by a viper. I'm Basim. Been the campus guard here since, well, seems like since Gilgamesh was a grad student. Standing all day ages you prematurely. Anyway, you need to know something, anything, you come to me, okay? Meanwhile, you got an hour to kill courtesy of the Englishman.

(*He hands his newspaper to* JAWAD.)

JAWAD. Thanks.

BASIM. (*Quietly.*) Just military communiques, really. Passing for news.

(*A moment. They suss each other out.*)

JAWAD. I trust we're winning every single battle then, with ease?

BASIM. Like taking candy from a baby!

JAWAD. And triumph is close at hand?

BASIM. Perhaps we'll cross paths at the victory parade where we'll celebrate vanquishing the Persian hordes without losing a *single* Iraqi soldier.

JAWAD. God willing.

(*They laugh.* BASIM *offers* JAWAD *a smoke.* JAWAD *opens his sketchbook and draws.*)

BASIM. Got anyone at the front?

JAWAD. My brother. He's gonna be a doctor.

BASIM. May God keep him.

JAWAD. You?

BASIM. I did. One down.

JAWAD. I'm sorry.

BASIM. One to go. Figure I'll be up next.

(JAWAD *looks intently at* BASIM.)

JAWAD. Your eyes.

BASIM. What about them?

JAWAD. I don't know. The color of…never mind.

BASIM. The color of what?

JAWAD. Coffee. But not what coffee looks like, just how you remember it in your head.

BASIM. Oh. Thanks?

JAWAD. I have a thing about color. When I see something that hooks me—

BASIM. Like coffee eyes?

JAWAD. Yeah. I want to put that color or that line on canvas. Not to recreate it but to…

(*In one breath.*)

And when I can't get it right I can't stop 'cause it keeps driving me, pulling me, spinning me like a.

(JAWAD *suddenly stops.* BASIM *takes this in.*)

Sounds stupid, right?

BASIM. No. It's your calling. Your gift. Shit, I wish I had something big to swallow me up like that. Myself, I dabble in everything. Though I'm a football guy at heart. Al-Zawra lost to Najaf last night by the way.

JAWAD. How'd you know I'm an Al-Zawra fan?

BASIM. I know it all. Plus it was the only game this week.

JAWAD. I can't believe we lost to those shitkickers in Najaf.

BASIM. Skip to the back page. There's a decent article on Borges and Andalucía.

JAWAD. You take classes here too?

BASIM. Nah. Too smart for this place. I studied at the University of Elsewhere. Got a masters in Footballogy, a doctorate in Common Sense, with a minor in No Fuckin' Money.

JAWAD. Listen, I can slip in so quietly the Englishman won't even know I'm late.

BASIM. Afraid not, friend. Next time, get here early.

(JAWAD *pretends he sees someone behind* BASIM.)

JAWAD. Wow. Who the hell is that? What a beauty!

(*When* BASIM *turns to look,* JAWAD *races past.*)

You're not a very good campus guard.

BASIM. I know. And you're right, man. She's a beauty!

(JAWAD *is confused. He looks around. He hears a* VOICE *offstage.*)

VOICE. (*Offstage.*) Just because class is outside today doesn't mean you lose your focus! Now in this exercise, you are on a boat. It's sinking. Act it out. Without words. Who's up?

(BASIM *disappears just as a student steps out.*)

SCENE EIGHT

A young woman, REEM, *appears.* JAWAD*'s eyes are glued to her. She wears flowing black pants and a black T-shirt, her hair very short or tied back in a ponytail. She does the exercise, confident, in control of her body.*

AMMOURY, *in beige fatigues and carrying a duffle bag, now joins* JAWAD, *but doesn't see* REEM. *As they speak,* REEM *continues the exercise.*

JAWAD. (*To* AMMOURY.) I couldn't even move she was so damn fine.

AMMOURY. I been back in Baghdad from the red-hot front line for all of an hour, and the only thing you've done is blab about this Roon/

JAWAD. Reem!

AMMOURY. So me, yeah, I'm fine. Thanks for asking. Dodging Iranian shells like a fucking Gazelle.

JAWAD. She's like a young Zubaida Tharwat, man, I swear.

AMMOURY. I'm a Hind Rostom kind of guy, personally, or Sophia Loren, but/

JAWAD. So I walk up to her after her class...offer her a cigarette.

AMMOURY. A real life Omar Sharif, huh?

JAWAD. Felt like I was walking on a cloud.

AMMOURY. Look, I only got 48 hours leave, so get on with it, playboy.

(REEM *ends her exercise and begins to leave.*)

JAWAD. So I walk up to her and I'm / like:

(AMMOURY *starts to undress out of his Army fatigues and pack them in his duffle bag while they talk. Then he puts on regular clothes as the scene progresses.*)

"I wanted to save you from drowning. But I can't swim."

AMMOURY. Lame opening, man. Did I teach you nothing?

JAWAD. Wait. So she says:

(REEM *speaks to* JAWAD. JAWAD *is in two worlds, talking to both* AMMOURY *and* REEM.)

REEM. Excuse me? What the hell are you talking about?

(AMMOURY *laughs.*)

JAWAD. I know, I know. But. I recover. "The exercise" I say. "This morning. I was sitting in the courtyard and I saw you drowning."

(REEM *lets out a laugh.*)

She laughs like a movie star too, I shit you not. That deep smoky laugh.

REEM. I appreciate your gallantry, but it does me no good if you can't even swim.

JAWAD. (*To* REEM.) Intentions don't count?

REEM. They're crucial, actually. Though not always enough. (*Beat.*) Reem. Theater.

JAWAD. Jawad... Delighted.

AMMOURY. Delighted?

JAWAD. (*Back to* AMMOURY.) Then I see it.

AMMOURY. See what?

JAWAD. Bam!

AMMOURY. She punched you!?

JAWAD. No, dumbass. The ring. The wedding ring!

AMMOURY. Ouch!

JAWAD. Yeah, like a 24-carat smack to the face.

REEM. But tell me, Jamal—

AMMOURY. Jamal?

JAWAD. (*To* REEM.) It's Jawad. Fine arts.

AMMOURY. (*Mockingly.*) Bond. James Bond.

REEM. —how do you know if I'm waving or drowning? Maybe it's you who's drowning?

JAWAD. You think so? Will you save me?

REEM. I'll have to save myself first. But if I can't, well, it was nice meeting you.

(*She disappears.*)

JAWAD. Saw her a couple days later getting into a car. Mercedes. The husband had on gold sunglasses, perfect mustache. Dyed extra black. You know the type.

AMMOURY. What the hell do you want with a married woman anyway? There's plenty of fish in the river.

JAWAD. Not like her.

AMMOURY. Whatever you say. I gotta run, Shrimp. Time's come for this dashing soldier and doctor-to-be to drop in on a certain damsel who waits for her betrothed.

(AMMOURY *takes* JAWAD's *face in his hands.*)

Good to see your face.

(AMMOURY *gives him a loving slap on the cheek. He starts to leave then turns and throws his duffle bag at* JAWAD. *In another space there is a knock at the door.*)

You mind taking that home with you, little brother? See you later for supper, okay?

SCENE NINE

JAWAD *stands with the duffle bag in his arms (c. 1988). He puts it down and opens it. There is a piece of paper, official-looking. He reads it, then he takes out a uniform and unfolds it. It's* AMMOURY's *uniform.*

After some moments FATHER *enters.* JAWAD *composes himself.*

FATHER. Who was that at the door?

(FATHER *sees the uniform. The bag.*)

JAWAD. He's... Ammoury... He's...

(FATHER *whispers prayers.*)

FATHER. *In the name of God, most Merciful, most Compassionate...*

JAWAD. *Here is the body of your... You have taken his...*

FATHER. *taken his soul and separated...separated...*

(FATHER *exits.* MOTHER *enters. She watches* JAWAD, *then she takes the shirt from him and packs it in the bag. She carries the bag away, like the body of her son.*)

SCENE TEN

C. 1990. REEM *and* JAWAD *alone together.* JAWAD, *naked from the waist up, stands with his arms outstretched as* REEM *adjusts and pins a costume on him. The costume looks like half a sheet, made into a big shirt, painted poorly in blue and green.*

JAWAD. Can't this wait 'til later?

REEM. Nope.

JAWAD. Ouch!

REEM. Hold still.

(*The needle pricks* JAWAD *again.*)

JAWAD. Damn it.

REEM. Each time you move I'm going to prick you with the pin!

JAWAD. I'm not moving, I'm just breathing.

REEM. No breathing either.

(*They are silent some moments as* REEM *works.*)

JAWAD. You don't find it belittling to play 'Water'?

REEM. I'm not playing '*Water.*' I'm playing '*Ocean.*'

JAWAD. Well, your Ocean has a terrible costume.

REEM. Well I'm not a designer, I'm an actor. And it's terrible because you won't help me.

(JAWAD *cries out again.*)

JAWAD. But I didn't even move!

REEM. You were thinking about it. That was a preventative prick.

JAWAD. Speaking of pricks/

REEM. Don't. Stand down.

JAWAD. Why? Why the naval blockade... All I want is to send my delegation to negotiate in your territorial waters. Respectfully.

REEM. If I let you, you'll think I'm easy.

JAWAD. You'll never be easy.

REEM. Everyone thinks di-vor-cees are sluts. I'm not.

JAWAD. I know. Kiss me.

REEM. I don't kiss on demand.

> (JAWAD *grunts in disappointment.* REEM *threatens with her pin.*)

JAWAD. I don't think you should play the Ocean. It's a silly part.

REEM. It's the *biggest* part. And this Ocean is smart. She's a bad-ass. At the end of the first act, she roars. Want to hear her roar?

> (REEM *lets out her roar of the Ocean. Long and loud and impressive.*)

JAWAD. Not bad.

REEM. Wanna see my waves?

> (REEM *makes her 'waves' with her body. It's pretty sexy.*)

When are you gonna draw me? That might be the kind of gesture that could help heat up diplomatic relations.

> (*He takes a step towards her, turned on. She holds out the pin with one hand to stop him.*)

JAWAD. I can't. Every time I pick up a pencil I feel sick.

REEM. Why?

JAWAD. I drew Ammoury and he's gone now.

REEM. And if you draw me, then what? I'll disappear, too? Is that what you think?

JAWAD. Maybe.

REEM. Don't be silly.

JAWAD. If you take off your clothes, I *might* be inspired to draw again.

> (REEM *laughs.*)

When I'm with you and I hear you laugh, I don't think about my brother and that feels good.

REEM. So I turn you on *and* I make you forget.

JAWAD. Yes.

REEM. Like a drug?

JAWAD. Is this a trick question?

REEM. I don't want to be your drug, Jawad.

JAWAD. You're not, it's just that since my brother's death… Never mind.

> (*She pricks him again.*)

REEM. If I let you kiss me, you have to remember. And talk to me. Agreed?

> (JAWAD *is silent. She pricks him again.*)

JAWAD. Agreed!

    (REEM *kisses him on the neck. For a moment* JAWAD *is quiet.*)

REEM. Since my brother's death…

JAWAD. Since my brother's death…all my father wants to talk about is Ammoury "the martyr who died liberating al-Faw on April 17th, 1988." He doesn't see me… He hasn't even noticed I stopped drawing. Ammoury…

    (*He stops.* REEM *kisses him again on the neck, waits.*)

REEM. Ammoury…

JAWAD. …Could see who I am, right down to my footnotes. And when I'd leave pieces of myself behind me, he'd pick them up and stuff them back in. Because he knew.

REEM. Knew what?

JAWAD. What I was made of. Even though I didn't.

REEM. You'll never stop missing him, Jawad.

JAWAD. All I want is to tell Ammoury that I was right about you. That you're free now.

REEM. Never felt free. Always seemed as though the earth has a hold of my ankle. I kick at it, try and shake it off, but it won't let go.

    (REEM *kisses* JAWAD *on the mouth and he responds. Then* REEM *steps back and eyes the costume critically.*)

There's something wrong with this costume…

    (*After a moment,* REEM *puts her hand on* JAWAD*'s crotch through the sheet.*)

REEM. What's this?… It seems…a barnacle has appeared in my ocean. Damn it, I haven't rehearsed to include a barnacle in my piece.

JAWAD. Maybe… Maybe you need to…incorporate…the barnacle. Into your…performance?

REEM. You think so? Well, to do that I might have to get into the Ocean… I suppose it doesn't matter. I'm already…wet.

    (REEM *gets into the costume with* JAWAD, *coming up into the 'Ocean' from the bottom. Now they are facing each other, still not touching, standing in the big 'shirt' of the ocean.*)

JAWAD. Reem, I/

REEM. Be quiet. Things will take place. But only on top of the clothes. No exceptions. Agreed?

JAWAD. Absolutely.

REEM. And no more forgetting.

JAWAD. No more forgetting.

REEM. Because the Ocean…always remembers.

> (*They kiss again. As soon as they do, air raid sirens in the distance.* JAWAD *escapes "the Ocean" and hurries into fatigues.*)

SCENE ELEVEN

> JAWAD *stands next to* BASIM (*c. 1990-91*). *They are both in army fatigues, smoking cigarettes.*

BASIM. I'm betting this Kuwait shit won't be a real war. Not like that fucking bloodbath against the Ayatollahs. Who would be stupid enough to get out of one war and end up in another?

JAWAD. Basim, keep your voice down, man.

BASIM. Don't worry. I'm the gatekeeper of the underworld out here, too. I get all the black market shit for the officers in this regiment. Smokes, booze, video tapes. I'm from around these parts, remember? And three times more efficient than the army's useless supply lines.

JAWAD. You really think Saddam has it in him to fight the Americans?

BASIM. Who knows, man. Last I remember, he was their guy.

JAWAD. Their running dog.

BASIM. Who do you think shipped him the poison he used on the Kurds? It was Reagan and his gang.

JAWAD. Damn, it's hot.

> (*The two men take off their shirts.*)

BASIM. Well, this hot-ass plain is my hot-ass plain. Al-Samawa. You know nothing, Baghdad Boy. I'll show you the desert. And Lake Sawa, too. Next time we have a free morning.

> (*They are in the desert now. Shirts off but tied around their heads.* JAWAD *is in awe.*)

JAWAD. There can't be a lake in this desert. No way.

> (*Blue seems to rise up around them.*)

BASIM. See for yourself.

JAWAD. I've never seen anything like it.

BASIM. The only lake in the world fed entirely by ground water.

JAWAD. A blue like this blue.

BASIM. This lake shows up in all the ancient accounts, dates back to pre-Islamic times. Put your hand in it.

> (JAWAD *does.*)

JAWAD. It's cold! And this mud. It's perfect. I'll take some back to the barracks. I'll sculpt a statue of…the King of Lake Sawa! Basim the Great.

BASIM. I don't want to be a king. Just a free man. And a good friend.

(*A fighter jet passes over them, closer now. They both look up.*)

Ignore it. They're not supposed to attack if we're not a threat. They're just:

JAWAD/BASIM. (*Mocking.*) "keeping the no-fly zone clear..."

BASIM. But even from that high up they can hear us breathe. So whatever you do, don't shout at them or point at them or they'll use you for target practice.

(*The men are back in their bunkers.*)

JAWAD. I hate sleeping underground.

BASIM. Like fucking rats, man. But you get used to it.

JAWAD. I hope not.

(*A dull thud in the distance.*)

BASIM. I gotta say, I didn't think that old fart Bush had it in him.

JAWAD. He's pulling out all the stops.

BASIM. The Empire Strikes Back.

JAWAD. The first movie was better.

BASIM. Second.

BASIM/JAWAD. Third was shit.

(*The two men start undressing, down to their underwear. At times we hear explosions in the distance.*)

BASIM. I got guard duty in an hour.

(*They each lay out blankets and lie down with their heads on sand bags.*)

Hey, how's the brooding thespian girl?

JAWAD. Her name is Reem. And she's a woman.

BASIM. Really? So, have you...?

JAWAD. Not yet. Almost, but then I was called up. Her family's rich.

BASIM. Oooh. To a rich girl, poor is sexy, man.

JAWAD. I miss my workshop at the university.

BASIM. I miss keeping late students from class, borrowing books from the lost and found.

JAWAD. Only good thing about being here is I don't have to see my father's disappointed face.

BASIM. Look, friend, tell 'em Basim said you don't have to touch another dead body for the rest of your life!

JAWAD. I bet Caravaggio did. There's no way he could have painted bodies with such anatomical knowledge unless he'd washed them, from the inside out.

BASIM. Is that even possible?

JAWAD. I don't know. But I like it that you listen to me. That you ask questions, that you're interested / in my

BASIM. Now don't go getting soppy on me. (*Beat.*) I am kind of terrific, though, aren't I?

JAWAD. Yeah.

BASIM. You know, when you first told me my eyes were like coffee, I did think it was kinda stupid. But then afterwards every time I looked in the mirror, I saw what you meant. You did that, man. You changed the way I saw myself. I wish I could do that to people.

> (*They are silent for some moments. Then a larger explosion nearby.*)

This is not an even match-up. This ridiculous skirmish is more like a game between Brazil and *Lithuania*.

> (*Another thud.*)

Hey, maybe our officers should propose a match instead of a war. In Basra. Those corn-fed boys wouldn't last one half in this heat!

JAWAD. Thamer Yousif would run circles around them.

BASIM. Oh shit, I can see it!

JAWAD. Falah the Fox!

BASIM. Their bombers would be worthless in a battle against the Lions of Mesopotamia, man. War averted, victory achieved!

JAWAD. Unless they bombed the stadium.

BASIM. Hey, remember Radhi's goal in Mexico City?

JAWAD/BASIM. *O Jogo Bonito!*

> (BASIM *imitates the goal in his underwear, celebrates! He falls down laughing just as there's a huge explosion.* BASIM *gets up.*)

BASIM. Wake up, Jawad. Hurry! They hit the South building. Run! Go!

> (JAWAD *sits up. Then he begins to crawl through the smoke.*)

JAWAD. The smoke's so thick I can't see!

BASIM. The anti-aircraft guns are lit up like a birthday cake! Jawad! Hurry, man! Move! (*Beat.*) What are you looking at!?

JAWAD. Even from 30 meters away, I recognize you.

> (BASIM *now watches his own dead body, which is the sandbag* JAWAD *approaches.*)

You're on your stomach. Your weapon is three or four meters away. Unloaded.

BASIM. Sleeping next to a loaded weapon makes me nervous. You know that.

JAWAD. Not that a rifle would've made much of a difference.

BASIM. Fucking stealth bombers: more like the wind than the wind.

(JAWAD *is now in the present with* BASIM*'s body.*)

JAWAD. Your arm. Fuck, fuck!

BASIM. My left arm is twisted backward, in a weird position. Flip me over, man.

(JAWAD *flips 'the body/sand bag' over.*)

At least my legs are intact. I can still hook one to the top left corner of the net when we play the Americans. Can't say the same for the others that died that day.

(JAWAD *tries to 'wake' BASIM up.*)

JAWAD. No... Hey. Hey! Basim! Can you hear me? Basim! Get up, / man!

BASIM. Okay. That's enough.

(JAWAD *stops shaking* BASIM*'s 'body' and just holds it.*)

My father is gonna ask you, "Did he suffer?" And you'll say "No."

JAWAD. No...

BASIM. But for seven minutes, between the time of the explosion and when you find me, I'm alive. What do you think, Jawad? You think I suffered?

(JAWAD *quietly cradles* BASIM*'s 'body' in his arms.* BASIM *watches his friend grieve.*)

You put your ear to my chest but you can't hear anything. You kiss my forehead. You take me in your arms. Friend, that's not suffering.

(BASIM *steps away, leaving* JAWAD.)

SCENE TWELVE

JAWAD *begins to cough in the smoke. Then he crawls away from the bunker.*

JAWAD. Basim!... Basim?

(*He crawls until he crawls between someone's legs. It's* REEM.)

REEM. Wait! Stop. Only to the knees!

(JAWAD *seems to 'wake.' Now he's with* REEM. *They are in an almost dark.*)

JAWAD. Reem...?

REEM. Keep saying my name... No. Not any higher... No!... Just a tiny bit further...

JAWAD. Yes.

REEM. No...

(JAWAD *now does his best to distract* REEM.)

JAWAD. Let's get out of here. Away from the sanctions.

REEM. No higher! Stop!

JAWAD. I can't stop! My tongue is an avowed anti-Imperialist.

REEM. Jawad! Don't!… Oh, Do, do, do!

JAWAD. It's collective punishment. The Americans want to make us/

REEM. Shut up, keep going!

JAWAD. Now *you* can't forget, even for a minute! Or I'll stop.

REEM. Please, please…

JAWAD. The sanctions…

>		(JAWAD*'s tongue finds* REEM.)

REEM. Ahhhhhh.

>		(REEM *breathlessly recites the embargoes list.* JAWAD *encourages her*
>		*to keep the list going as he keeps going.*)

The sanctions… No toasters allowed in, no… Venetian blinds or Vaseline…

JAWAD. Or voltage regulators.

REEM. Or voltage regulators… No scoreboards… Ohhhhh… No tampons or penicillin, no spark plugs…

JAWAD. No TV sets, no rulers.

REEM. No rulers… Oh, oh, oh, no calculators or candles, no chisels, no clocks… Noooooo

>		(REEM *begins to come.*)

Yes, yes yes… Ohhhhhh.

>		(*Lights come up just when* REEM *is finished. She stands and composes*
>		*herself.*)

So. What did your mother say? About me, the divorced woman?

JAWAD. Not much. My mother's cool. But my father was pretty uncomfortable in your parents' *enormous* house in al-Jadiriyya. He doesn't even own a necktie.

REEM. Well, my father accepts that your father washes dead people, so…?

JAWAD. Let's leave here together.

REEM. What? I can't leave my family.

JAWAD. I'll be your family. We'll go to Europe. London. Italy. Anywhere but here. You can act and I can sculpt and teach at…the University of Elsewhere.

REEM. Can we ride a Vespa through Rome, like Gregory Peck and Audrey Hepburn too?

JAWAD. Not a big Mercedes like Mr. ex-husband? That valiant officer / who

REEM. Is that what you think? That I had it so good?

JAWAD. Well, he was rich and handsome.

REEM. Yes, he was. He used to shower me with kisses, especially on my hands, and especially after—

JAWAD. I don't want to hear this.

REEM. —after hitting me. Yeah. And he'd buy me expensive gifts, promise me that it would never happen again. I thought about telling people, but who was going to believe that an officer awarded three medals by Saddam would beat his wife?

JAWAD. Reem. I didn't know/

REEM. On his second leave, he broke my arm. And when he was killed at the front, I couldn't even cry. Fucker stole years from me. When someone hits you, throws you down the stairs, you get old.

JAWAD. You're not old.

REEM. On the inside I use a cane and wear false teeth. I'm half blind. Is my life already over? Maybe I've no time left at all… You're right. Let's get the fuck out of Iraq while we still can.

JAWAD. I'll start saving up money.

REEM. I want you to draw me, all of me, before it's too late. I'm going to take off my clothes.

(REEM *begins to undress as* JAWAD *fumbles for his pencil and paper; as soon as he's found them, his* FATHER *is suddenly there.*)

SCENE THIRTEEN

FATHER *and* JAWAD *at home (late 1990s).*

FATHER. This was not our agreement! Sure, I know you can paint naked women / and

JAWAD. You've no right to go through my / notebooks!

FATHER. bowls of fruit!

JAWAD. Just hear me out, Father. One of my friends… His father is a contractor. He paints houses.

FATHER. Yes, the houses of corrupt officials getting rich exploiting the embargo!

JAWAD. What does that matter?

FATHER. Ha. Ask your beloved Uncle Sabri if it matters. On this, if nothing else, we agree.

JAWAD. Painting houses is a decent job for the time / being.

FATHER. And our profession isn't decent? You promised you'd come to work with me once you were done with your Academy!

JAWAD. But that was before. Now I need to save up… To marry.

FATHER. And what keeps you from marrying if you are working at the wash house?

JAWAD. Washing does not pay. Not much / anyway

FATHER. You are paid with God's favor! And you and your brother never lacked / for food.

JAWAD. Reem and I are going to leave.

FATHER. Iraq?

JAWAD. Yes.

FATHER. And who will look after your mother and the wash house when I'm gone? That is your duty, Jawad. No. You will stay.

JAWAD. My duty is to make a career. A real living.

FATHER. A real living? How dare / you.

JAWAD. I mean as an artist. There's nothing here. In my field. Not even at the / University.

FATHER. (*Not listening.*) And Reem, she approves of this pursuit?

JAWAD. With all her heart.

FATHER. Ah, what do the young know of heart? I know mine inside out, since my Ammoury was…

JAWAD. I miss him too, Father.

FATHER. I washed a child last week. With green eyes. His father insisted I know his name. Ali.

JAWAD. Please. I don't / want to—

FATHER. You know what took him? Diarrhea. The runs. Nothing more. But the doctors couldn't save him. The sanctions have stopped even the most basic medicines. Tell me, what kind of evil is this?

JAWAD. I'm going to make a name for myself.

(FATHER *looks at his son for a beat, then speaks.*)

FATHER. I never desired such a thing. And yet people know my work, Son. And my name.

SCENE FOURTEEN

Time has passed, we are circa 2002. JAWAD *is working on a sculpture in progress. It looks like some kind of chair, but ominous. He calls to someone who is offstage.*

JAWAD. You were right about the color by the way!… Reem? I think this might be my best sculpture. I'll take some photos of it, for my portfolio. I'm telling you, they're gonna dig my work in Europe! Once we get this wedding business behind us, the great escape will commence. Reem? Did you get a chance to talk to your parents again?

> (*He circles his piece.*
>
> *To himself.*)

Am I a genius. Maybe? Well, no. Of course not... Maybe a little. A little bit of genius? Sure. Why not?

> (*No answer.*)

Honey!?

> (*Again no answer. The lights shift. Time has passed.*)

Reem? Where the hell are you? Hey. Reem!

> (REEM *appears, elsewhere on stage, though* JAWAD *can't see her.*)

REEM. My knees miss you.

JAWAD. Where did you go?

REEM. Far away.

JAWAD. Where?

REEM. Far from you.

JAWAD. No one will tell me anything. Where are you?!

REEM. Far away from myself, too.

JAWAD. What the hell does that mean? Your whole family's up and vanished. It's been over a year! I hear you're in Jordan one day, then Syria, then Sweden, but I can't find an address or a number. It's like you don't exist / anymore.

REEM. And you're ashamed to tell anyone that I left you and you keep saying that we're gonna get married once the sanctions are lifted...

JAWAD. We almost had enough saved / to

REEM. It doesn't matter anymore, Jawad. We missed our chance. Or our chance missed us./

JAWAD. Did I do something wrong? / Did I

REEM. Remember how you loved to draw my hair, the way it fell down my bare back?

Before turning me around and...

JAWAD. Yes. Yes. Baby, I miss / you.

REEM. Well, I'm losing it. My hair. And my chest has a scar. A scar which hasn't healed because I got an infection after surgery.

JAWAD. What are you / saying?

REEM. The breast you used to bite like an insatiable puppy is...gone.

> (JAWAD *takes this in.*)

JAWAD. Then I'll love the other one twice as hard.

REEM. What would that matter? My body isn't mine any more.

JAWAD. Come home. Or I can meet you? We can meet in/

REEM. In Rome?

JAWAD. Sure. Why / not?

REEM. Depleted uranium. That's what the doctor told me. Left behind by the Americans: "My office is filled night and day with Iraqis like you," he said. "If the bombs don't kill instantly, the cancer will take care of the rest."

JAWAD. Should I come to you? Or wait for you to return?

REEM. I used to think that was a beautiful word: return. Now I live in terror of its return. Of this ticking. Like a bomb, attached to my chest.

JAWAD. Reem, we promised to always be beside each / other.

REEM. Don't. Don't try to get in touch with me again, Jawad. It must be like we never met, like you never tried to save me from drowning.

> (REEM *disappears.* JAWAD, *in anger, begins distressing his 'chair' artwork by hitting it with a piece of chain.*)

JAWAD. To hell with this sculpture! What's the fucking point?

> (MOTHER *and* FATHER *appear. They speak to one another.*)

MOTHER. It's daylight but it's pitch black outside.

> (*The distressing of* JAWAD*'s chair continues.*)

MOTHER. Everything is covered in soot. Even the rain is black.

FATHER. Saddam's lit the oil wells to make it harder for their jets.

MOTHER. But the bombs keep falling. This war is not like the other wars. Should we leave Baghdad? We should leave/

FATHER. If God wants to end our lives, he will do so here.

MOTHER. I've taped up the windows.

FATHER. This is not our first bombardment. It's like water running from the same source, a continuous river of war.

MOTHER. This Bush is crazier than his father.

FATHER. (*Calmly.*) Don't forget about the lecherous silver-haired weasel who ground us down for eight years...

MOTHER. How could I? I have nightmares Clinton is sitting on our toilet at night, singing.

FATHER. Same war, same river.

MOTHER. At this point we might as well dig our own graves! Is that what they want?

FATHER. There is no God but God.

MOTHER. And you? Is that what *you* want? To wash and bury everyone until no one's left?

FATHER. No. But if that is what must be done, then yes.

(*JAWAD has finished with his artwork. He examines it.*)

JAWAD. Yeah. Yeah. Okay. Not bad… This just might be something.

(*FATHER looks JAWAD's way, only now he sees the smashed-up artwork.*)

FATHER. (*To JAWAD.*) *This?* This is the art you speak of?

(*FATHER looks carefully at the 'artwork.'*)

Can I touch it?

JAWAD. Yes. Sure.

(*FATHER runs a hand slowly over a part of the sculpture.*)

FATHER. I saw a body like this once. The feet were the only part not broken. When you make this, who are you thinking of? The living or the dead?

JAWAD. Both, I guess. Sometimes they're not so different, right?

FATHER. Well, I will pray for you, Son.

(*We hear the call to prayer, air sirens. FATHER looks up.*)

I will pray for them also. May God forgive them.

(*The sounds of the war as FATHER goes to pray. We hear the whispers of his prayer. An explosion. Closer. Still the prayer continues.*)

SCENE FIFTEEN

Year 2003. Another sudden explosion. Louder than the others, close by. Debris falling. Darkness. Voices in the dark.

MOTHER. (*Offstage.*) Jawad? Jawad! Are you all right?!

JAWAD. Yes. You?

MOTHER. (*O.S.*) And your father?

JAWAD. Praying.

MOTHER. (*O.S.*) Go get him. There might be more strikes!

(*JAWAD goes to find his father. In the dim light we see his father fallen over on his prayer mat.*)

JAWAD. Babba, are you okay?

(*JAWAD gently puts his hand on his father's back.*)

Father?

(*JAWAD realizes his father is dead. He backs away from his father's body.*)

JAWAD. (*Whispering.*) No… No…

(*Then silence. MOTHER appears and the two stand over him for several moments. The ghost of his FATHER sits up.*

Only JAWAD sees his FATHER now.)

FATHER. Well… That's that. (*Beat.*) So who will wash me, then?

MOTHER. You must wash your father's body.

FATHER. Will you wash me, my son?

JAWAD. I can't wash him.

FATHER. Then my soul will not be at peace.

MOTHER. He would have wanted it.

JAWAD. I'm not a washer.

FATHER. If you don't wash me, I will always be alone.

(HAMMOUDY *appears with his camphor.*)

HAMMOUDY. Will you stay?

JAWAD. I've never seen my father naked.

FATHER/HAMMOUDY. *Your forgiveness, Oh Lord. Your forgiveness.*

JAWAD. No.

HAMMOUDY. A son should wash his father.

JAWAD. Well, the son who should've washed him was killed in / the war.

HAMMOUDY. Your father wanted you to do it. He told me.

JAWAD. And once I washed him, he figured the next would be easier, right? And the next and the next.

HAMMOUDY. Jawad.

JAWAD. You do it.

HAMMOUDY. Very well. It will be difficult to take him to Najaf to be buried. I could go with you.

JAWAD. The roads will be dangerous.

HAMMOUDY. We'll take him together.

JAWAD. My father will never forgive me, will he?

HAMMOUDY. Perhaps he'll never know you didn't wash him.

(JAWAD *looks at his* FATHER.)

JAWAD. Oh. He'll know.

(JAWAD *turns to go.*)

HAMMOUDY. Wait.

(HAMMOUDY *digs in his pockets.*)

The keys to the wash house. You should carry them now.

(JAWAD *takes the keys, uncertain.*)

SCENE SIXTEEN

HAMMOUDY *and* JAWAD *on the road to Najaf.* FATHER *sits quietly in the 'back seat.'*

HAMMOUDY. The military spokesman says victory will be ours any minute.

JAWAD. Maybe his watch is broken.

HAMMOUDY. Yeah. We keep racking up victories and keep falling behind.

JAWAD. Everything is upside down.

HAMMOUDY. Not the sun. It'll rise any minute now/

JAWAD. (*Interrupting.*) Americans. Americans! Shit! Pull over. Stop. Stop the car!

HAMMOUDY. God help us.

JAWAD. If we move, they'll shoot.

HAMMOUDY. (*Quickly.*) *Nothing can come to pass and there is no strength without God's will.*

JAWAD. Stay still, do nothing.

HAMMOUDY. They're stopping.

> (*The U.S. soldiers shout orders. Instead of distinct voices we hear brutal, distorted* NOISE, *that only* JAWAD *and* HAMMOUDY *can partly decipher.*)

NOISE. XXXXXXXXXXXXXX

HAMMOUDY. What's he saying, Jawad?

JAWAD. They want us to get out of the car.

NOISE. XXXXXXXXXXXXXXXX! (Put your hands up!)

JAWAD. (*To* HAMMOUDY.) Put your hands up!

NOISE. XXXXX! (Now!)

HAMMOUDY. *May God protect us from all evil.*

JAWAD. Hands up! Up! I think they want us to get away from the car.

> (JAWAD *and* HAMMOUDY *slowly move.*)

NOISE. XXXXXXXXXXXXX! (Down. Down. Get down on the ground!)

> (*They get down on their knees.*)

JAWAD. They're gonna kill us.

NOISE. XXXXX (Shut the fuck up!) XXXXXXXXX (What's on the car?)

JAWAD. My father. It is my father on car!

HAMMOUDY. For Najaf! For Najaf, Holy place!

JAWAD. Dead man. My father! He's dead.

NOISE. XXXXXXXXX (It's a fucking coffin!)

JAWAD. Yes. It is *coffin.*

> (*Noise like nervous laughter.*)

Is this funny? Is this funny, man?

HAMMOUDY. (*Whispers.*) Jawad! Be quiet.

NOISE. XXXXXXXXX (What's he babbling about?)

HAMMOUDY. (*Whispers.*) You'll get us both shot!

JAWAD. You wanna stop me from burying Father in Najaf!

> (JAWAD *gets off his knees. As he does so, we hear the sound of guns being cocked, aimed at* JAWAD.)

Or you want to bury me also? This whole damn country is a fucking coffin.

> (*Silence some moments. After a moment—*)

NOISE. XXXXXXXXXXXX (Let's get the fuck out of here.) XXXX (Clear. Clear.)

> (*The soldiers retreat.*)

HAMMOUDY. Your English is good.

JAWAD. I'm shaking.

HAMMOUDY. Did you see the size of them?

JAWAD. The soldiers or their guns?

HAMMOUDY. Both.

JAWAD. The old man'll be at peace when he lies next to his favorite son. Let's get to Najaf and be done with it.

SCENE SEVENTEEN

> JAWAD *arrives at the wash house, jangling his keys. He "enters" and sees the three spirits of* BASIM, AMMOURY *and his* FATHER *standing there.*
>
> *They all look at each other for a beat.* JAWAD *then begins to sweep, doing his best to ignore them.*

FATHER. It was kind of him to bury me in Najaf.

> (BASIM *spits.*)

BASIM. Najaf? I'll take the shores of Lake Sawa any day.

> (AMMOURY *looks at where* BASIM *has spit.*)

AMMOURY. Don't spit in the wash house.

FATHER. Though he wouldn't wash me.

BASIM. Get over it, old man.

AMMOURY. Jawad, you should've washed him.

JAWAD. Leave me alone.

> (JAWAD *puts in his earphones to block them out, though they continue.*)

FATHER. ...And now there are places on my body without my son's hands / to

BASIM. (*To* AMMOURY.) I think he should forget about this place.

AMMOURY. No.

  (AMMOURY *pulls* JAWAD*'s earphones out and speaks into his ear.*)

JAWAD. Hey!

AMMOURY. He's got to support Mamma.

JAWAD. Stop telling me what to do.

BASIM. Yeah! Stop telling him what to do!

FATHER. *We come from God and to him we return.*

AMMOURY. But aren't you worried about Mamma?

JAWAD. I'm sick of being worried.

BASIM. Good! "You must train yourself to let go of everything you fear. Fear is the path to the dark side." (*Beat.*) Yoda.

AMMOURY. Jawad, where'd you find this windbag?

  (JAWAD *sticks his earbuds back in.*)

BASIM. (*Interrupting, to* AMMOURY.) You calling the wind, Doc?

  (BASIM *farts in* AMMOURY*'s direction.*)

AMMOURY. Wait, how did you do that? We're not supposed to/

BASIM. To be able to fart anymore? Or spit or cry? Simple: I break rules. You, Ammoury? You follow them.

  (*This time* BASIM *takes* JAWAD*'s earphones out and stuffs them in his pants.*)

BASIM. (*To* JAWAD.) Jawad should walk away, and…sculpt a giant Mesopotamian bull!

JAWAD. I'll decide on / my own.

BASIM. Out of radioactive mud.

AMMOURY. This isn't the time for art.

JAWAD/BASIM. It's always the time for art!

FATHER. The pile of bodies is rising.

BASIM. How 'bout a bust of Churchill!? The Brits were the ones who taught the Yanks how to bomb Iraqis, after all.

FATHER. What happens when there is no one left alive to wash the dead?

JAWAD. Not my problem.

AMMOURY. Well you better find some way to take care of Mamma.

  (*To* BASIM.)

Maybe there's a comfy post waiting for him to fill it at the University?

FATHER. Soon the pile of bodies will be higher than the mosques.

AMMOURY. I bet all the old professors are gone now / that—

BASIM. No chance. Those tenured types survive nuclear wars.

FATHER. Higher than the minarets.

BASIM. Hey, I just realized…

FATHER. Who will wash them all?

BASIM. Each of us was taken in a different war.

>(BASIM *points his finger like a gun at each of the spirits, including himself.*)

One. Two. Three. Three wars in a row.

FATHER. Same war, same river.

AMMOURY. Three down.

BASIM. One to go.

>(*The spirits face him.*)

AMMOURY. So?

JAWAD. So?

AMMOURY/BASIM/FATHER. (*Overlapping, to* JAWAD.) What are you going to do?

JAWAD. Don't worry about me. Or Mother./

AMMOURY/BASIM/FATHER. With the wash house!

JAWAD. You mean with these?

>(JAWAD *holds up the keys and jangles them.*)

Let the shadows eat 'em.

>(*Then he throws the keys, hard, into the darkness.*)

I'm closing the wash house down!

>(FATHER *and* AMMOURY *groan.* BASIM *celebrates.*)

Look, I have a plan. I'm an artist, not a washer. And you, old man, you're not alive, so I don't have to listen to you anymore.

>(*To* AMMOURY.)

Or you.

>(*To* BASIM.)

Or you!

>(JAWAD *puts his hand out to* BASIM *who reluctantly passes him his earphones.* JAWAD *puts them in and flips on his music, which roars out across the stage. He dances. And he sure can dance. Angry, wild, blocking out everything else.*)

SCENE EIGHTEEN

>JAWAD *is working on a new sculpture. He works with concentration, studying his sculpture from different angles. He sings as he makes adjustments. For the moment, he's happy.*

A GUARD *appears. The* GUARD*'s face is obscured.* JAWAD *keeps working while they talk.*

GUARD. The building's not safe.

JAWAD. I asked the administration. They said I could be / here.

GUARD. The administration was wiped out in the last bombing, kid.

JAWAD. I know. But I'd like to keep my workshop here. No room at home. This is where I studied.

GUARD. You and half of Baghdad. Sorry. Can't let you squat here.

JAWAD. But I'm in the middle of… Please. I could pay you something.

GUARD. In that case, I'll pretend you're not here.

JAWAD. Thank you. I'm Jawad.

GUARD. I'm the gatekeeper of the underworld.

(JAWAD *stops working. He's apprehensive.*)

JAWAD. Basim?

(*The* GUARD *looks up, lifts her helmet. Now we see that the* GUARD *is a woman.*)

GUARD. Basim?

JAWAD. Oh. Sorry. I thought/

GUARD. Takes me an hour to pin up my hair under this ridiculous hat. Got a headache the size of a fucking watermelon.

JAWAD. I used to know the campus guard. A while back.

GUARD. It's not the best gig, but I'll be damned if I'll translate for the occupiers, get a bullet in my head for the trouble. Not that I can stop the looters if they come. They emptied out the National Library, plucked the National Museum like a chicken, too, all while the Americans looked the other way. I had to buy this flack jacket off a French journalist.

JAWAD. Anyone else still here?

GUARD. Couple of students in and out of the Political Science building. But I'm pretty sure they just use it to shower and sleep. One of the safest places in the city. Until last week. One minute it's a campus, the next—

(*She makes the sound of an explosion.*)

Ripped in two. Science building, vanished. So what're you makin'?

JAWAD. Something for a gig. Bunch of foreigners will be there. This is my ticket to one of their universities. "Iraqi Artists: Out of the Ashes!" That's what the show's called.

GUARD. Nah, too pretty.

JAWAD. I agree, bad title for a show, / cliché

GUARD. (*About the sculpture.*) I mean your sculpture's too pretty. Make something ugly. Really ugly. Then they'll feel guilty. Then they'll like you.

JAWAD. Well, they got to like me for me to get / to

GUARD. The University of Elsewhere.

JAWAD. What did you / say?

GUARD. Anywhere but here. 'Cause there's no shortage of little monsters these days, kid, and they come out at night to play. Militias, gangs, not to mention the Yankees. People are disappearing all over the city. They're throwing corpses in the river. And in Lake Sawa.

JAWAD. Lake Sawa?

GUARD. Never heard of it. Just lock your doors when you get home. And if you can, get to Amman or Damascus. There's a darkness coming.

(*The* GUARD *begins to sing a bright song in Arabic as she leaves.*)

SCENE NINETEEN

JAWAD *and* AL-FARTUSI, *a cleric in a Shi'a robe and turban, stands with* JAWAD *(c. 2006).* AL-FARTUSI *finishes a cup of coffee.*

AL-FARTUSI. But surely your father showed you?

JAWAD. I won't do it.

AL-FARTUSI. Excuse my bluntness, Jawad, but your father, God rest his soul, ran the only Shia wash house—

JAWAD. —in this part of Baghdad. Yes, I know that.

AL-FARTUSI. Look, I've been working for ten years collecting unclaimed bodies.

JAWAD. I know.

AL-FARTUSI. And not for money, God knows. When I started this... calling...I'd no idea the amount of work the future would hold. My two sons shadow me now. Drive with me to the darkest folds and creases of the city, fighting off the dogs and the buzzards who are always the first to... Jawad, people must be cleaned./

JAWAD. Bodies.

AL-FARTUSI. *Bodies* must be cleaned and buried, regardless of who they were or how they died. With the occupation, and with the violence that's been unleashed, people can't even get across the river to have their loved ones washed according to custom.

(JAWAD *is unmoved.*)

If you do not care about pleasing God then think about your mother.

JAWAD. I do. I am. The little jobs I take keep us alive. I even managed to sell a couple of drawings.

And when my mother is re-married and looked after, I'll be free to focus on my art full time, create a body of work in order / to

AL-FARTUSI. Why do they call it that? Why do they call it *a body of work?*

JAWAD. I don't know.

AL-FARTUSI. Well in that case, I've come to the wrong place. I came here for answers.

JAWAD. I gave you an answer. You just didn't like it.

AL-FARTUSI. No. You answered the wrong question. Thank your mother for her hospitality.

JAWAD. What about Hammoudy? He was my father's assistant. He's more… experienced than I am. And he needs the money. Perhaps Hammoudy could reopen the wash house? He'd have to clean and re-stock it.

AL-FARTUSI. I could help with that! And I'll bury the ones that aren't claimed. Of course a percentage would go to you and your mother. Here, take this as an advance. Please.

JAWAD. But I want nothing to do with it. Nothing, do you understand?

AL-FARTUSI. Of course.

JAWAD. I don't even want to talk about it.

AL-FARTUSI. Not another word.

JAWAD. And don't come to me with problems.

AL-FARTUSI. Never.

(JAWAD *finally takes the money.* HAMMOUDY *enters and hands* JAWAD *an envelope.*)

HAMMOUDY. Half again. For this month. I know you said you'd take less but it wouldn't be right.

JAWAD. Thank you, Hammoudy.

HAMMOUDY. Don't you want to stop by and… I've made some changes. In terms of stocking and… To deal with the influx / of—

JAWAD. Would you like some coffee? Or something / to eat

HAMMOUDY. No thank you. I should get back.

Jawad. Do you ever feel when you walk in the streets of this city that you've already disappeared?

(HAMMOUDY *leaves.*)

SCENE TWENTY

MOTHER, *an unlit cigarette hanging from her mouth, turns on the radio. It is war reportage. She changes the channel, finds music. Enjoys it, just as the electricity cuts. There's a loud knock. She hides the money, then the cigarette.* JAWAD *listens just offstage, unseen.*

MOTHER. Who is it?

VOICE. Electrical company.

> (*She picks up a piece of furniture, gives it a swing. That'll do, a makeshift weapon.*
>
> UNCLE SABRI *enters with a suitcase.*)

SABRI. Easy, easy.

MOTHER. Sabri! I almost took your head off. I can't believe you're back!

SABRI. After all this time!

MOTHER. Yes, well, that brother of yours. He left me alone.

SABRI. His loss. Suitors should be lining up outside your door.

MOTHER. Jawad tells me you're thinking of coming back for good, maybe, to settle down? But I don't believe it for a second. Or is it true?

SABRI. I wish! But how could I when the man welcoming me back to my country after all these years is an American!? "Welcome to Iraq!" In English. Imagine! The official, one of *ours*, was wearing slippers! I asked him who decides who's allowed in and he said the Americans. "I just stamp." Then he asked for money. I told him: "At least go to the trouble of wearing shoes before you ask me for a bribe!"

MOTHER. In the old days a bribe felt like a more honorable transaction, it's true.

SABRI. Well, what's clear is that this mayhem has destroyed us, my dear.

MOTHER. We're not destroyed. Look at the two of us?! We're still here, and / we're

SABRI. It's as if Iraq had been wiped off the map.

And this sectarian venom. It's a product of the occupation. I say if we can't all become communists then at least we should become hybrids. Long live the (*Beat.*) Shunnis!

MOTHER. The Shunnis? Always on another planet, my Sabri.

SABRI. Berlin's not quite another planet. But close.

MOTHER. Your hair has grown white.

SABRI. It's not white hair. It's just a bit of snow, from Germany.

MOTHER. So...has the dashing Sabri found a German maiden to take care of him?

SABRI. Ah... Enough about me! How are *you?*

MOTHER. Let me see your hands!

> (*She takes his hands and examines them.*)

Yes... I believe I got them right. Though the thumb is wider here...

> (MOTHER *keeps* SABRI's *hands in hers, and stares into his eyes, boldly.* SABRI *withdraws his hands.*)

SABRI. Hey, I've brought you a book!

(*He gives her a small book, wrapped.*)

MOTHER. Is it a collection of those love poems you're always writing...?

SABRI. Open it.

MOTHER. I remember when your brother and I were first engaged, even then you slipped a poem under my door every night. Right up until the wedding...

SABRI. Oh God. Don't remind me.

(*She takes the book out of its bag.*)

MOTHER. Palm trees.

SABRI. There's nothing more fascinating than palm trees. Now, where's Jawad?

(*Yelling offstage to* JAWAD.)

I need books! Urgently! In Arabic! Germany is a bloody desert. I need my nephew to escort me to Mutannabi Street!

(JAWAD *enters.*)

JAWAD. Uncle Sabri!

SABRI. Look at you. A man!

MOTHER. Which must mean I've grown old!

(SABRI *speaks a line in German.*)

What does that mean?

SABRI. "You're still beautiful enough to make the sand stand upon its own!" And now we must run off, before it's too hot to move.

(SABRI *and* JAWAD *leave.*)

SCENE TWENTY-ONE

JAWAD *and* SABRI *are at the book market, looking at books. At times* SABRI *will speak to booksellers we cannot see.*

JAWAD. What about that one?

SABRI. The author's a pompous hack. Ah, but look. Kanafani. First edition... And there's Mr. Galeano... Ah, and my dear June Jordan... Right next to Neruda! "Yo puedo escribir los versos mas tristes esta noche"... And enough Shakespeare to sink a ship.

JAWAD. Uncle. I've been / thinking

SABRI. Baldwin! Jimmy Baldwin sounds his best read out-loud in Arabic... And this one, Cedric Robinson! You must read it. *Black Marxism.*

JAWAD. There's something I need to/

SABRI. Cedric named the ugly monster: "racial capitalism." I'll take that one and this one. Jawad, this is why the history of secularism in Iraq is a long one. We eat books like termites!

JAWAD. Yes we do. But what I / want to

SABRI. (*To bookseller.*) Qais, how are you, friend?!… Well, as Gramsci said, "Pessimism of the intellect. Optimism of the will!"

(*They move to another stall.*)

JAWAD. You and my mother seemed happy to see each other…

SABRI. (*Ignoring his words.*) It's nice to find a handful of old comrades from the party still around with their heads in place.

JAWAD. I left the two of you alone on purpose. I was thinking / it might be

SABRI. (*To another bookseller.*) You, young buck! I want *masguf.* Where's the best place to eat fish?

JAWAD. No way. The fish are so fat with depleted uranium they glow in the dark.

SABRI. (*To* JAWAD.) Hear that? There's a place where the fish are raised on special farms. Thank God the rich and famous must have their fish uncontaminated. Let's go there. On me.

(JAWAD *and* SABRI *are in the restaurant.*)

SABRI. I can't believe this is Karrada! All barbed wire and tanks. Even the trees look traumatized. This used to be the most beautiful neighborhood / in Baghdad—

JAWAD. Uncle. I have to get out. There's nothing here for me / anymore.

SABRI. (*Not listening.*) I knew what to expect after all these years, but to see it with your own eyes… Believe me, the Americans will make people long for Saddam's days… No easy feat!

JAWAD. So I have a / plan.

SABRI. Where do we go from / here?

JAWAD. (*Shouts.*) Uncle Sabri! I'm leaving. I need to leave Iraq!

SABRI. Yes. Of course. Where?

JAWAD. I've looked into Sweden, France. Even the U.S. But I / think

SABRI. Not the U.S.! They'll never let you in. They're like a restaurant that only delivers. At least to people like us. Won't let us dine in, the bastards.

JAWAD. I've started paperwork for Italy. *The Accademia di Belle Arti,* Florence.

SABRI. And don't rule out Germany, either.

JAWAD. It's just that I can't leave my mother alone. It's the one promise I intend to keep to my father. Which is what I wanted to talk to / you about.

SABRI. Don't worry about your mother. Do. But… I just mean your mother's no flower. She's strong. We'll figure something out.

JAWAD. What if *you* were to come back here? To stay? *You* could take care of Mother.

You've always liked each / other

SABRI. I couldn't.

JAWAD. Yes you could!

SABRI. It's not that simple.

JAWAD. Just hear me out. Iraq needs thinkers like you. Your comrades need you. You and my mother can marry, or…don't. But together, you live off the money from the wash house. It's enough for two if you're careful. And you can do your translating and writing from / here.

SABRI. I can't marry your mother! What's gotten into you / ?

JAWAD. You have my blessing! Everyone knows you've always had a thing for her. Even Father knew it. And you miss / Iraq

SABRI. I'm married.

JAWAD. What? No. No you're not.

SABRI. Yes, I am. To a German woman. Why do you think they allow me to stay in Berlin?

(JAWAD *is dumbfounded.*)

JAWAD. Does Mother know?

(SABRI *shakes his head.*)

You got to be kidding me. Shit, shit… Okay… Okay… Fine. We adjust. We can fix this.

SABRI. We? What's gotten into you?

JAWAD. Divorce the German lady! You can do that in Germany. It was for the passport anyway. And Mother doesn't even need to know you were married. She might not even care.

(SABRI *considers this plan. Then:*)

SABRI. I love her.

JAWAD. I know! Even as a kid I knew you loved my mother.

SABRI. My wife. I love my wife.

JAWAD. No. Don't say that.

SABRI. Helen. Her name is Helen.

JAWAD. Oh, man… How could I be such an idiot?

SABRI. It was…worth a shot, kid. In your shoes I'd/

JAWAD. (*Explodes.*) Then why did you come back here? Just to watch us in this…zoo!

SABRI. Jawad/

JAWAD. Then you'll pick up and leave. Again. Because you can. Back to Berlin so you can write about us and cry for us, pick at the scab of nostalgia from a safe distance. Isn't that fucking convenient?!

(*Beat.* SABRI *is wounded.*)

SABRI. Well, that's a bit unfair, kid.

JAWAD. (*Still angry.*) Is it?

SABRI. But maybe you're right. In a way.

JAWAD. (*Ashamed now.*) I'm sorry I/

SABRI. Send me your portfolio. I'll do what I can. I promise.

(SABRI *touches his hair, checking.*)

I should get back. To Germany. It seems the snow is melting in my hair.

(*A cell phone rings. And then another and another, building and then abruptly cut off.*

SABRI *looks around him, then gets up and leaves just as* MOTHER *enters.*)

SCENE TWENTY-TWO

MOTHER. Hammoudy went to the market to get more camphor.

JAWAD. I told you, I don't want to hear about the wash / house.

MOTHER. Three days ago! He hasn't come back.

JAWAD. What? Are you sure?

MOTHER. His cousins are looking everywhere. The hospitals, the police station,

JAWAD. He's probably just stuck / somewhere.

MOTHER. The morgues.

JAWAD. A curfew or a lockdown on the other side of / the river.

MOTHER. They're searching the corpses, Jawad. Looking for the green ring he used to wear on his left hand.

JAWAD. They wouldn't kidnap Hammoudy.

MOTHER. Oh yes they would.

JAWAD. But he has no money! Why/

MOTHER. Jawad! He's disappeared! Vanished!

(*Beat.*)

JAWAD. Hammoudy will come back!	**MOTHER.** Hammoudy will never come back!

MOTHER. Even the dead aren't safe anymore.

(After a moment:)

JAWAD. Then let's get out, Mother. Let's leave together / now!

MOTHER. We missed that boat a long time ago. Anyway, where would we go? A refugee camp? Unless you have a bag of gold? Or a five-star connection? Do you have either? Well then. They're booby-trapping dead men now, you know that!?

JAWAD. They. *They?* Who do you mean?

MOTHER. The Sunnis! They! Them! Who else?

JAWAD. Mother, you can't—

MOTHER. We can't go out. Hammoudy is gone. Sabri has left us. Again. The wash house is closed. Again. You can't find a job. So I must blame someone, anyone, or I will suffocate.

JAWAD. Then blame the Americans.

MOTHER. The Americans… They are always too far away, even when they are standing at your door. It's too late for me to run. If God wants to end my life he will do so here.

SCENE TWENTY-THREE

AL-FARTUSI *and* JAWAD.

AL-FARTUSI. With all due respect, soon you and your mother will have nothing to eat. You need the income, Jawad.

JAWAD. I won't discuss this again.

AL-FARTUSI. You think I haven't looked for someone else? Hammoudy's gone. There is no one else! Open the wash house!

JAWAD. No.

AL-FARTUSI. No. Again, *No.*

JAWAD. You wouldn't understand.

AL-FARTUSI. You think you're the only person in this country whose life has been derailed? (*Beat.*) I used to write verse. Oh yes. I was a poet. And not a bad one either. I drank and enjoyed women and life. After college I was drafted. Then Saddam invaded Kuwait. Only two survived in my unit, myself and Musa, a young conscript from Ammarah. We were the only ones the Americans didn't blast to bits that day on the highway to Basra. Everyone was running, trying to escape… The jets were hunting humans as if they were insects. People were on fire in the seats of their cars. The smell of burning flesh and hair. Men became lumps of coal. Stray dogs devoured what they could. After I returned to Baghdad, I thought I could put all that behind me. But then the nightmares started: Dogs tearing apart my wife. Or my children, charred, coming apart in my hands… I told a cousin about the nightmares, the insomnia. She said I should go to the mosque and pray. Not turn away from the ills of the world. She was right, because prayer saved me from the madness erupting around me. And this work, it saves me / from

JAWAD. That's your solution? You want me to pray?

AL-FARTUSI. No! I want you to realize what must be done. The dead are everywhere! Stuffed into overflowing fridges! Squeezed into every nook and cranny their grieving families can find. People need to know their dead are at peace.

> (*Suddenly* AL-FARTUSI *grabs* JAWAD *and shakes him violently, almost out of control.*)

You don't fuck with tradition! I won't beg you again! Every time I come I beg. But if God won't knock you down, I swear I will!

> (*The two men stare at one another.* AL-FARTUSI *breaks his grip, realizing he's lost control.*)

I'm sorry… So sorry. I…

JAWAD. I'm all right.

AL-FARTUSI. Forgive me.

JAWAD. Look, I haven't washed in years. I've forgotten the details.

AL-FARTUSI. What matters is *intention.*

JAWAD. What matters is: we'll starve if I don't do it… So. If I agree to wash—

AL-FARTUSI. God keep you!

JAWAD. —it will be a temporary solution. Temporary. Until I find another source of income.

AL-FARTUSI. It'll come back to you, like riding a bike. I'll send Hammoudy's cousin, Mahdi, to help you out. I'll pay his salary to start. He's a fast learner.

> (AL-FARTUSI *turns to leave.*)

JAWAD. The dogs in your nightmares? They leaving you in peace now?

AL-FARTUSI. I suspect the dogs were afraid of what they saw in my other nightmares.

JAWAD. What happens in those?

AL-FARTUSI. You know as well as I do. Just go and look outside.

SCENE TWENTY-FOUR

> *Two years have passed.* JAWAD *and* MAHDI *are "outside" in the courtyard. They are exhausted.*

JAWAD. Mahdi. You can go home now.

MAHDI. Every time we think we're done, Fartusi brings another body.

JAWAD. And another.

MAHDI. Sometimes at the end of the day I'm so tired I just want to lie down on that slab. But lifting all this dead weight, I got the arms and legs of a wrestler. Girls like it.

JAWAD. I bet they do. Hammoudy was good at this. And so are you, Mahdi.

MAHDI. May God rest his soul.

JAWAD. You know, you could work without me now.

MAHDI. I ordered more supplies.

JAWAD. You could take over the wash house, like Hammoudy did. You could run this place alone.

MAHDI. I couldn't—

JAWAD. You could! I'd be / happy to—

MAHDI. I mean, I'm a football player, man, not a corpse washer.

JAWAD. The money's not bad. Think about it, Mahdi. I could / even—

MAHDI. I wanna be Messi. Not Hammoudy. Not you.

JAWAD. You could save up. To marry.

MAHDI. I'm saving up to get the hell out of here. I appreciate the work, respect it, but I've had a plan since I was a kid. They say Barcelona's the most beautiful city in the world. I'll take a boat over there and sneak in for a tryout if I have to.

(MAHDI *moves to go.*)

JAWAD. Take some pomegranates home with you. From the courtyard. They're ripe.

MAHDI. How come you never eat them?

JAWAD. The water from the wash house, it drains to the tree.

MAHDI. Oh. I don't mind. See you tomorrow, boss.

JAWAD. I told you not to call me that.

MAHDI. You're too much alone, boss. It's you who should be saving up for a wife.

(MAHDI *leaves. After a moment* REEM *appears.*)

SCENE TWENTY-FIVE

REEM *stands looking at* JAWAD.

REEM. You should marry.

JAWAD. Who would want to marry me?

REEM. (*Mocking.*) *Who would want to marry me...?*

JAWAD. I'm serious. I used to like walking the streets. Now when I do I look at people's faces and think—

REEM. —who'll end up on the bench next for you to wash?

JAWAD. Let me wash you with my tongue. Tonight, I'll do

REEM. Whatever you want with my body?

JAWAD. Whatever you want with your body.

REEM. I'm not even really here.

JAWAD. Who cares? It's my fantasy.

REEM. Is that why you never kiss the breast that's not there? What's gone is also me.

JAWAD. You're so damn gorgeous you could stop the rain.

(REEM *steps back.*)

REEM. I don't want to stop the rain. You have to let me go.

JAWAD. Never.

REEM. I'm just...your cotton candy.

JAWAD. My tortured muse?

REEM. What if I can't be that anymore?

JAWAD. Kiss me, please.

(REEM *moves away.*)

REEM. Listen to me. With your ears. Not your dick.

JAWAD. I listen all day. To the saddest shit. I just want to be with you. I want to close my eyes and—

REEM. Forget?

JAWAD. Yes.

REEM. No. Jawad, I want to remember. Who I am, what I wanted. I'm going to act again. In movies—

JAWAD. Stop.

REEM. And dance! Which means the next time you conjure me, I'm not coming.

JAWAD. You can't do that.

REEM. Yes. I can.

JAWAD. No!

REEM. In your mind, it's all about you and what you want but I'm real. I need to be able to imagine myself without you and you need to do the same.

JAWAD. Reem, I need / you to

(AMMOURY *appears.*)

AMMOURY. Hey, bro.

JAWAD. Get lost, Ammoury. I'm with Reem.

    (*To* REEM.)

Baby / we could

AMMOURY. You're always with her. What about me?

REEM. I have to go, love. For good.

    (JAWAD *holds onto* REEM*'s arm.*)

JAWAD. (*To* REEM.) No. You can't leave.

AMMOURY. (*Mocks.*) *You can't leave.* Boo hoo.

JAWAD. (*To* AMMOURY.) Shut up!

AMMOURY. You should spend more time with family. She's not family.

    (REEM *breaks free of* JAWAD.)

JAWAD. (*To* REEM.) He's just jealous!

AMMOURY. I came by to let you know that Fartusi's on his way.

JAWAD. I don't care.

    (*To* REEM.)

Let's talk about this.

REEM. Fartusi's bringing you a double harvest this week, Jawad. That's real.

    (AMMOURY *eyes* REEM.)

AMMOURY. I got to admit she's sharp. You've no idea how much I miss Wasan…

    (*Calls.*)

Hey Lake Boy! Get in here.

JAWAD. (*Calling.*) No, don't get in here!

    (BASIM *appears.*)

BASIM. How come you always wanna hang out with her, but not with us, huh?

JAWAD. Don't start.

REEM. Maybe because I'm just *visiting* his mind. I'm not actually *dead*.

BASIM. Sticks and stones, baby.

REEM. Fuck off. Though you are kinda cute.

BASIM. Same to you.

JAWAD. Hey!

REEM. Good-bye, Jawad.

    (REEM *disappears.*)

AMMOURY. Pay attention, bro: Most of the bodies Al-Fartusi's picked up this week have no papers or IDs.

JAWAD. You assholes drove her away.

AMMOURY. No, weirdo, you did.

JAWAD. She left me. Again.

BASIM. She survived and moved on, man. You, not so much.

JAWAD. I'm stuck here!

BASIM. (*To* AMMOURY.) He still doesn't get it.

JAWAD. Oh, I get it. The only way to move on is to leave, once and for all, take my chances at the border. Like everyone else.

AMMOURY. Like I was saying, most of the bodies are unidentified.

BASIM. It's getting worse by the day, friend.

AMMOURY. No names.

JAWAD. And what am I supposed to do about that?

AMMOURY. I'm thinking maybe you could just...

BASIM/AMMOURY. Write down the exact cause of death!

AMMOURY. It's the least you could do. And frankly, you're not doing anything else. Certainly not doing Reem.

BASIM. That was low. Let's just get on with it.

JAWAD. I don't want to get on with it!

(AMMOURY *throws* JAWAD *the notebook.*)

AMMOURY. Bullet in the forehead.

BASIM. Write it down so you can let it go, man.

(JAWAD *gives in and writes.*)

JAWAD. Bullet...

AMMOURY. In the forehead... Strangulation marks around the neck (*Beat.*) Knife stabs in the throat.

JAWAD. Knife stabs in the throat...

AMMOURY. Mutilation by electric drill.

BASIM. You making this shit up, Doc?

JAWAD. Please...

AMMOURY. Med school was like kindergarten compared to this.

BASIM. Keep going. Get it over with.

AMMOURY. Fragmentation caused by suicide bomb.

JAWAD. (*Shouts.*) I don't want to know anymore!

(*The light shifts. It is* MOTHER.)

MOTHER. They've blown up the market at Mutanabbi Street! All those people. All those books. When your Uncle Sabri finds out he'll be... Get up! There's a line outside the wash house.

(*She leaves. Another knock is heard as* JAWAD *dresses for work.*)

SCENE TWENTY-SIX

In the wash house. JAWAD *is still putting on his apron when a* MAN *appears. The* MAN *is reserved and hardly shows his emotions.*

MAN. We have someone…a dead man we want to wash. And shroud.

JAWAD. We?

MAN. My sons and I. They're outside. They don't want to. Watch. (*Beat.*) I'll be honest with you. We aren't Shiite.

(JAWAD *is silent a moment.*)

Please. We have nowhere else to go.

(JAWAD *takes a moment.*)

JAWAD. That's all right. I can do it.

MAN. May God keep you, sir.

JAWAD. Do you have the body?

(*The* MAN *hesitates a moment. Then he holds out a black bag to* JAWAD. *They both regard the bag.*)

MAN. We have only the head.

JAWAD. May God…

(JAWAD *is quietly dumbfounded and doesn't know what else to say. His* FATHER *appears.*)

FATHER. (*To* JAWAD.) Say to him: May God help you and your family, sir. I'm very sorry.

JAWAD. May God help you and your family, sir. I'm very sorry.

(*Then his* FATHER *gently takes the bag from the* MAN *and hands it to* JAWAD.)

FATHER. God be with you, Son. In all my days I never had to/

JAWAD. (*Calls off.*) Mahdi.

(MAHDI *appears. It takes him a moment when he sees the bag, but then he understands.*)

MAHDI. I'll bring the smallest coffin.

FATHER. Of children, you've had your share to wash, but this… *There is no power save in God.*

JAWAD. How are you related?

MAN. He is my son.

FATHER. (*To* JAWAD.) My son—

JAWAD. *May God have mercy on his soul.*

FATHER. —You must brace yourself.

JAWAD. What was his name?

MAN. Habib. His name was Habib. He was studying to be an engineer.

JAWAD. (*To the* MAN.) *May God bless you and have mercy on his soul.*	**FATHER.** (*To* JAWAD.) *May God bless you and have mercy on your soul.*

(JAWAD *holds the bag. Lights shift.*)

SCENE TWENTY-SEVEN

Nightmare: Alone, JAWAD *sits in a chair being interrogated by the dead. They take turns interrogating him, though they never touch him.*

AMMOURY. Your name is Jawad? Jawad Kazim?

JAWAD. Yes.

FATHER. Graduated Academy of Fine Idiots?

REEM. Failed Sculptor?

JAWAD. Yes.

BASIM. Are you a believer, Mr. Jawad?

ALL. Answer the question, motherfucker!

(*At different times during the scene, we hear that* JAWAD *is struck and see him react to the blow.*)

FATHER. You haven't fasted or prayed or gone to a mosque in years, have you?

AMMOURY. And now you desecrate the bodies of martyrs?

REEM. Did you weep for Hammoudy?!

FATHER. Did you weep for your father?

AMMOURY. You ever sculpted anything worth putting up?

BASIM. Or better yet, worth pulling down?

JAWAD. I don't know.

ALL. Shut up!

FATHER. Write down the titles of all the books your uncle ever gave you.

REEM. Hey! Are you Sunni or Shiite?

FATHER. Maybe you're a…so-do-mite?

AMMOURY. You and your friend Basim, huh? Lonely army nights.

REEM. Look at me, did you search for the tit that Reem lost?

BASIM. What can you tell us about the University of Elsewhere?

FATHER. Why didn't you wash your father? Why don't you visit his grave?

AMMOURY. What do you have against the war?

ALL. Same war, same river.

BASIM. By now you should be a fucking fish!

ALL. ANSWER ME!

> (JAWAD's *answer is to let out a tremendous scream, like a roar that becomes the roar of jets.*)

SCENE TWENTY-EIGHT

> JAWAD's *nightmare is interrupted when his* MOTHER *enters pushing a wheelbarrow full of burned books. It's morning. Some of the books are still smoking.*

MOTHER. If you're going, then you need to get an early start. Hurry up. The line for border control will be a mile long by the time you get there! I went to the market this morning and picked up a few things for your journey.

> (MOTHER *hands* JAWAD *a burnt backpack to pack his things.*)

I still can't believe you're leaving. But if you are destined to leave, then you will leave.

JAWAD. Make sure to call Fartusi. We've got an agreement: he'll see that you're taken care of.

MOTHER. Here's the number for your father's cousin in Jordan. / I

JAWAD. Mother. You can come visit me in Amman, or wherever I end up. Soon as I find work I'll send you money. And I'll come back to visit you.

MOTHER. I'll be all right.

> (*She embraces* JAWAD *awkwardly.*)

I want to get enough of you. I can't.

> (JAWAD *is about to leave.*)

Did you know that there are as many palm trees in Iraq as Iraqis? Millions.

JAWAD. No. I didn't.

> (*His* MOTHER *tries to keep* JAWAD *with her a little longer.*)

MOTHER. Some have had their fronds burned. Some have had their backs broken by time. Some of the palms have been mutilated, or uprooted and exiled from their orchards. Some have allowed the invaders to lean on their trunks.

JAWAD. I've got to go.

MOTHER. But some remain, keep growing, despite everything. Do you think I'm stretching the palm tree metaphor too far?

JAWAD. I'll call you when I get there.

(JAWAD *leaves.*)

MOTHER. Which kind of tree will each of us be in the end?

SCENE TWENTY-NINE

JAWAD *is standing in line for border control.*

AMMOURY *and* BASIM *appear.*

AMMOURY. There's the little shit!

BASIM. Trying to give us the slip, huh?

(JAWAD *puts on earphones while he stands in line, blocking them out.*)

AMMOURY. (*To* JAWAD.) Hey! You can't go, Shrimp!

BASIM. Not without us!

(JAWAD *moves forward in line again.* AMMOURY *and* BASIM *follow.*)

AMMOURY. (*To* BASIM.) Can he do this? Go without us?!

BASIM. Calm down, Doc.

AMMOURY. I always thought it was just a bluff. But he's really leaving this time!

BASIM. (*To* JAWAD.) Not with those black bags under your eyes, you aren't. You're like a walking mugshot, man. Close the castle gates! The filthy Moor approaches!

AMMOURY. He's ignoring us.

(AMMOURY *lifts one of* JAWAD's *earphones. We hear a flash of loud, energetic music.*)

Jawad?! What the hell are you doin'?!

(BASIM *lifts the other earphone.*)

BASIM. Hey raghead!

AMMOURY. (*To* JAWAD.) Don't go, you stupid—

BASIM/AMMOURY. Camel jockey!

(JAWAD *doesn't respond. They drop the earphones back in place.*

JAWAD *moves forward in line.*)

BASIM. Should we go with him?

AMMOURY. Can we cross borders?

BASIM. Why not? They're just imaginary lines. Drawn randomly through the map by the French and the Brits! Me, I'm sick of this furnace. I'm getting out. And once we get into Jordan, I'm crossing the river into Palestine, man.

AMMOURY. But there's no lake in Jerusalem.

BASIM. Then we'll move Lake Sawa to Jerusalem.

(*They both turn back to* JAWAD *and lift his earphones and shout at him.*)

AMMOURY/BASIM. Jawad?!

AMMOURY. We're coming with you!

(AMMOURY *and* BASIM *both get in line behind* JAWAD.)

BASIM. So if you want to get through the border check, look alive. Smile!

AMMOURY. Coulda used a shave but that's okay.

BASIM. You're almost at the front of the line.

AMMOURY. Look them straight in the eye, Brother.

BASIM. Drop a Jedi mind trick on 'em. "This is *not* the lonely single Arab man you are looking to turn away. You *will* let him pass."

AMMOURY. You're up next. Get out your passport!

BASIM. Stop sweating.

AMMOURY. He's dripping like a popsicle!

BASIM. We're almost out, man.

AMMOURY/BASIM. Almost out!

(JAWAD *takes out his passport.*)

BASIM. No more dismembered corpses!

AMMOURY. No more camphor and lotus!

BASIM. No more radioactive dust!

AMMOURY. No more death!

BASIM. *'O jogo bonito'!*

BASIM/AMMOURY. The Beautiful game awaits!

(BASIM *and* AMMOURY *let out celebratory whoops as* JAWAD *holds out his passport to the authorities. Then* FATHER *appears behind him.*)

FATHER. (*Calmly.*) You would leave without saying goodbye?

(JAWAD *turns to his* FATHER, *stares at him, then:*)

JAWAD. Father.

FATHER. I'm not here to stop you, Son. I came to watch you go. So go! And may God help you find what you are looking for.

(*They look at one another a moment.*)

JAWAD. (*Steady.*) I didn't wash you, old man. I was afraid... There was a way you touched the bodies, a tenderness in your hands I tried to recreate but couldn't find, not even in my brush, or with clay. I should have told you that.

THE CORPSE WASHER

FATHER. Jawad. What matters is intention. What we do, it has meaning when it is a choice. The living die or depart, but the dead always come. Life and Death are not two separate worlds with clearly marked boundaries.

> (JAWAD *now looks at his* FATHER, *listening*.)

They are conjoined, *sculpting* each other.

JAWAD. How can you be sure?

FATHER. Because this (*Beat.*) This is what you taught me.

> (JAWAD *takes this in. His* FATHER *disappears. After a moment,* JAWAD *steps out of line*.)

AMMOURY. Oh shit.

BASIM. Shit.

AMMOURY. What's he doing?

BASIM. What are you doing?!

> (JAWAD *walks away*.)

AMMOURY. Jawad!

BASIM. What the hell!

AMMOURY. He's getting out of line!   **BASIM.** Don't get out of line!

> (BASIM *starts to follow.* AMMOURY *holds him back*.)

BASIM. Where's he going?

AMMOURY. To Najaf. To visit Father's grave.

> (JAWAD *arrives elsewhere, and drops to his knees*.)

SCENE THIRTY

> JAWAD *is kneeling at his father's grave.*
>
> *Now we hear the sound of jets approaching. They fly directly over* JAWAD.

JAWAD. Hey! Hey! Over here, you fuckers!

> (JAWAD *gets up, challenging the jets*.)

Hey! That's right, that's right! (*Beat.*) Listen to me: We're not going anywhere. Do you hear me? *I'm* not going anywhere! Every single one of us you kill: I. Will. Wash!

> (*As if in answer, and with a sudden burst of noise, the jets disappear in to the distance.*
>
> JAWAD *watches them go, then he turns and steps into the wash house.* JAWAD *has a new energy and focus*.)

SCENE THIRTY-ONE

A man appears at the wash house, naked but for a towel around his waist. (The actor playing FATHER *is the corpse that* JAWAD *will wash.) Neither show any recognition.*

THE CORPSE. How much is the fee?

JAWAD. Whatever you can manage. Plus the cost of the shroud. Who are you?

THE CORPSE. I don't know. I forgot my name. I...

JAWAD. It's all right. Come.

(MAHDI *appears with a bucket of water.*)

How did you die, friend?

THE CORPSE. I can't remember.

MAHDI. *May God have mercy on your loved ones.*

THE CORPSE. Am I alone?

JAWAD. Please, lie down on the bench. I will wash you. You are not alone.

(*The* CORPSE *approaches the bench and lies down on it. For the first time we will see a part of the ritual of washing the body with water. It is a careful, confident, and beautiful performance by* JAWAD *and* MAHDI.

MAHDI *and* JAWAD *speak the proper supplications, which may be repeated:*)

JAWAD. *In the name of God, most Merciful,*

MAHDI. *most Compassionate.*

JAWAD/MAHDI. *Your forgiveness, O Lord, your forgiveness.*

MAHDI. *Here is the body of your servant who believed in you.*

JAWAD. *You have taken his soul and separated the two.*

JAWAD/MAHDI. *Your forgiveness, O Lord*

JAWAD. ... *Your forgiveness.*

And the shroud...

(MAHDI *holds out the shroud. A faint knocking in the distance.*)

EPILOGUE

The Present. As in the beginning. JAWAD *is on break. From the shadows, the spirits are watching him.* JAWAD *begins to light a cigarette but is interrupted when there is a KNOCK on the door.* MAHDI *enters.*

MAHDI. Jawad. They're here with another one. We need to get started.

JAWAD. All right. Give me a minute. I'll be right there.

> (JAWAD *takes a deep breath. Then he leaves the stage, with purpose, to continue his work, just as lights black out.*)

End of Play

POSSIBLE EXTRA PRAYER LINES FOR END:

—*This is your servant and the son of your servants coming to you.*

—*We know nothing of him but goodness.*

—*Replace him among his household. With your mercy.*

—*Oh God, grant forgiveness…to all men and women…the living among them and the dead.*

SUGGESTED READING/VIEWING

Books

Abdullah, Thabit A.J. *A Short History of Iraq*. London: Routledge, 2016.

Al-Ali, Nadje Sadig. *Iraqi Women: Untold Stories from 1948 to the Present*. London: Zed Books, 2007.

Antoon, Sinan. *The Book of Collateral Damage*. New Haven: Yale University Press, 2019.

Catherwood, Christopher. *Churchill's Folly: How Winston Churchill Created Modern Iraq*. New York: Carroll & Graf, 2004.

Cockburn, Patrick. *The Occupation: War and Resistance in Iraq*. New York: Verso, 2007.

Ditmars, Hadani. *Dancing in the No-Fly Zone: A Woman's Journey Through Iraq*. Northampton, MA: Olive Branch Press, 2005.

Drumsta, Emily, editor and translator. *Revolt Against the Sun: The Selected Poetry of Nazik al-Mala'ika*. London: Saqi Books, 2020.

Jamail, Dahr. *Beyond the Green Zone: Dispatches from an Unembedded Journalist in Occupied Iraq*. Chicago: Haymarket, 2007.

Kukis, Mark. *Voices from Iraq: A People's History, 2003-2009*. New York: Columbia University Press, 2011.

Otterman, Michael and Richard Hil with Paul Wilson. *Erasing Iraq: The Human Costs of Carnage*. London: Pluto Press, 2010.

Parenti, Christian. *The Freedom: Shadows and Hallucinations in Occupied Iraq*. New York: The New Press, 2004.

Scahill, Jeremy. *Dirty Wars: The World is a Battlefield*. New York: Nation Books, 2013.

Sluglett, Peter. *Britain in Iraq: Contriving King and Country*. New York: Columbia University Press, 2007.

Reports

International Physicians for the Prevention of Nuclear War, Physicians for Social Responsibility (U.S.), & Physicians for Global Survival. *Body Count: Casualty Figures After 10 Years of the "War on Terror": Iraq, Afghanistan, Pakistan*. Washington, D.C.: Physicians for Social Responsibility; Berlin: Internationale Ärzte für die Verhütung des Atomkrieges/Ärzte in socialer Verantwortung; Ottawa: Physicians for Global Survival, March 2015. https://www.psr.org/blog/resource/body-count/

Films

About Baghdad. Directed by Sinan Antoon, Bassam Haddad, Maya Mikdashi, Suzy Salamy, and Adam Shapiro. 2004.

HOW TO DEFEND YOURSELF
by Liliana Padilla

ABOUT *HOW TO DEFEND YOURSELF*

This article first ran in the Limelight Guide *to the 43rd Humana Festival of New American Plays, published by Actors Theatre of Louisville, and is based on conversations with the playwright before rehearsals for the Humana Festival production began.*

In your daily life, how often do you think about your personal safety? Maybe it's not something you've ever been that concerned about, compared to other people you know. Or it is, and so you've developed a set of habits that are supposed to keep you from being mugged, or followed, or sexually assaulted. Don't carry cash. Take a different route home from work every day. Never leave a drink unattended. Maybe you used to worry sometimes, and now you don't. You're not going to live in fear, you've decided. Or you simply feel too exhausted, even powerless. In the back of your mind, though, do you ever think about fighting back? What if you could learn how? A group of female college students attempts to do just that in Liliana Padilla's daring, visceral play *How to Defend Yourself.* In an empty campus gym, they gather for a series of self-defense workshops only a few days after two fraternity brothers rape a classmate named Susannah. But as they memorize attackers' weak spots, practice wrist escapes, and throw punches, they wonder: will any of it keep them safe?

Self-defense, according to workshop co-organizer Brandi, is about more than physical training. A senior with a black belt in karate, Brandi tries to instill in her peers a shift in mindset as well—they should think like fighters, not victims-in-waiting. First-year student Diana is all in, amped to discover how to neutralize threats. But for her, and for the rest of the class, self-defense techniques don't instantly lead to empowerment. Fellow first-year Mojdeh freezes up during the first exercise, and wallflower Nikki balks at one of the class's core tenets: Your body is a weapon. "Maybe your body," she jokingly tells Brandi. Meanwhile, the workshop's other facilitator, Kara, is struggling to process what happened; Susannah is Kara's best friend and one of her and Brandi's sorority sisters. With grit and surprising humor, Padilla traces how these five women all contend with the same question: "What does it mean to carry around a lifetime of feeling like you need to defend yourself?"

During the second workshop session, two upperclassmen in the same fraternity as Susannah's attackers show up. Asked by Brandi to participate, Eggo and Andy are eager to stand against rape and be good male allies, but they aren't always sure what that means. They're not alone in their confusion: in the midst of the class's exercises and training drills, women and men alike are wrestling with gender roles, consent, and the fundamental messiness of sex and desire. And although Eggo and Andy's presence initially sparks conflict, guys aren't the enemy here; for Padilla, vilifying individuals or certain groups is beside the point. "So much of my own journey," they reflect, "is not about pointing to capital-V villains, but working through internalized oppression, which is systemic." Throughout *How to Defend Yourself*, Padilla explores how everyone is both complicit in and hurt by rape culture—a social environment that normalizes sexual assault and is rooted in, in their words, "the belief that you have to dominate another person in order to have power."

In a refreshingly frank way, *How to Defend Yourself* depicts coming of age in a world where violence against women is so common that there are classes they can take to deal with it. To Padilla, the play also serves as a gift for their younger self, isolated in the aftermath of being sexually assaulted. "It's just to keep company," they say. "That's it." But the writing process has illuminated something else about how survival and art might connect. Padilla shares insight gleaned from Kim Rubinstein, a mentor and early influence on *How to Defend Yourself*: "As artists, we're often channeling painful feelings in order to learn that we can stand them. And when people come to the theatre, they see that they can stand them too." Similarly, for the play's richly imagined ensemble, a self-defense workshop becomes more than a chance for them to practice punches and kicks; it's also about bearing witness to each other's lives and metabolizing their own complex experiences, turning them into fuel to meet whatever might come next.

"How hard it is to be open with someone else—that was something I thought about a lot as I was working on *How to Defend Yourself*," Padilla recalls. Despite its challenges, they firmly believe that vulnerability is an essential strength, not a weakness. But another word for vulnerable is defenseless, and Padilla pairs their conviction with a clear-eyed understanding of why closing ourselves off is often a safer choice. The result is a play that they aptly call "fierce, chaotic, and sweaty," in which being taught how to fight back leads to a broader reckoning with the necessity—and the limitations—of self-defense. Shouldn't the responsibility of rape prevention fall on all of us, not just on potential victims? In the meantime, self-defense students in classes all over the country are trying to get stronger and hit harder. They're carrying their keys between their fingers. They're learning to use their bodies as weapons. It's about muscle memory, as Brandi says. You have to practice every day.

—Jessica Reese

BIOGRAPHY

Liliana Padilla makes plays about sex, intersectional communities, and what it means to heal in a violent world. Their play *How to Defend Yourself* won the 2019 Yale Drama Prize and was a 2018–2019 Susan Smith Blackburn Prize Finalist. It was produced in the 2019 Humana Festival of New American Plays and at Victory Gardens Theater in 2020. Padilla's work has been developed with Oregon Shakespeare Festival, Ojai Playwrights Conference, Victory Gardens Theater, INTAR Theatre, Hedgebrook, Seattle Rep, the Playwrights' Center, and San Diego Repertory Theatre. They received their MFA from the University of California, San Diego, and their BFA from New York University's Tisch School of the Arts. Padilla is currently commissioned to make new plays with the National New Play Network, Colt Coeur, and South Coast Repertory. They are also a director, actor, and community builder who looks at theatre as a laboratory for how we might be together. For more information, please visit lilypadilla.com.

ACKNOWLEDGMENTS

How to Defend Yourself premiered at the Humana Festival of New American Plays in March 2019, in association with Victory Gardens Theater. It was directed by Marti Lyons with the following cast:

DIANA	Gabriela Ortega
MOJDEH	Ariana Mahallati
BRANDI	Anna Crivelli
KARA	Abby Leigh Huffstetler
NIKKI	Molly Adea
ANDY	David Ball
EGGO	Jonathan Moises Olivares
SUSANNAH	Phoenix Gilmore

and the following production staff:

Scenic Designer	Kimie Nishikawa
Costume Designer	Dina Abd El-Aziz
Lighting Designer	Heather Gilbert
Sound Designer	Luqman Brown
Movement Director	Stephanie Paul
Fight Director	Drew Fracher
Stage Manager	Jan Hubert
Dramaturg	Jessica Reese
Casting	Emily Tarquin
Dialect Coach	Rachel Hillmer
Associate Scenic Designer	Kelvin Pater
Properties Master	Heather Lindert
Production Assistant	Margaret Rial
Assistant to the Director	Lex Turner
Assistant Dramaturg	Alonna Ray
Directing Assistant	Emily Moler
Stage Management Apprentice	Em Hornbeck

This play was developed by the University of California, San Diego's Wagner New Play Festival in collaboration with Kim Rubinstein; Victory Gardens Theater's IGNITION Festival of New Plays 2018; the Ojai Playwrights Conference; and was supported by residencies at the Blue Mountain Center and the Anderson Center at Tower View.

CHARACTERS

MOJDEH, 18, she/her/hers, Iranian-American. Desperate to lose her virginity.

DIANA, 18, she/her/hers, Mexican-American. Loves guns.

NIKKI, 20, she/her/hers, person of color. Pulls in all her tentacles to disappear.

BRANDI, 21, she/her/hers, white. Sorority VP and a black belt in Karate.

KARA, 21, she/her/hers, person of any race/ethnicity. Into rough sex and not afraid to say it.

EGGO, 20, he/him/his, person of color. Wants to be loved, by anyone really.

ANDY, 21, he/him/his, white (but also, maybe not necessarily). He's trying to be an ally, he's really trying.

SUSANNAH, 6, she/her/hers. A young child of color who makes a wish.

AUTHOR'S NOTES

/ indicates an interruption, the next character speaks

In choral scenes, featured text is in **bold**

[ ] indicates gestural language

( ) is whispered

In my experience, community agreements and daily physical practice as a company have been helpful in creating a room that supports what this work requires.

You may also find it deepens the work and extends the community to collaborate with a local rape crisis center and self-defense teachers. Access to mental health resources and supportive body work may also support the process and is also a great idea.

Sending you much love with this journey,
Liliana

A LENGTHY ACKNOWLEDGEMENT SECTION, BECAUSE LET'S BE REAL, THIS HAS BEEN HELD BY A VILLAGE

How to Defend Yourself has been held by many hands, hearts, souls and communities. I am eternally grateful for those who have given themselves— brave, raw, vulnerable, human, curious—to this journey. The following acknowledgements come close, but this play (and I) have been held by infinitely more beings. Thank you.

Thank you to the wisdom-keepers and truth-tellers who have come before, alongside and after me. Thank you to the collective energies of transformation. I am honored to be alive in this moment of seeing and healing.

To Kim Rubinstein, thank you for teaching us to stand on the bones of our feet. Thank you for encouraging me to finish this play and for shepherding the journey that made it possible. I am more awake because of you.

To my beloved Dylan, the first reader on everything I write. You are a gift in this world and a true seer.

To Marti Lyons, thank you for crossing this threshold with me and encouraging me to dream bigger.

To Steph Paul, you bring love, presence and possibility everywhere you are!

To my therapist Karen, who created a space for me to feel safe and grounded enough to go into the cracks and try to piece it together.

To my parents Ben and Maria Padilla, who taught me to always ask questions and try to see things from many angles.

To my Grandmother Anita, with whom I told my first stories.

To my cohort at UCSD—Ali Viterbi, Mara Nelson-Greenberg, Ava Geyer, Steph del Rosso, Anna Moench and Dave Harris. Your genius and love are in this play.

To Naomi Iizuka, thank you for growing what you saw in me, thank you for creating space for me to follow my instincts and say what I mean.

To Deborah Stein, thank you for helping me see more of myself and encouraging me to go to the edges.

To Allan Havis, thank you for always encouraging me to explore the subconscious, the raw.

To my dear friends Orion Johnstone, Ruth Moir, Mojdeh Rezaeipour, Mary Glen Fredrick, Riley Teahan, Jana Fredricks, Tegan Ritz McDuffie, Desiree Mitton, Clayton Fox and Korde Tuttle, for being all of who you are.

To Community Centered Solutions, the rape crisis center in San Diego, and specifically the many gifts of Phoebe Morris and Allison Johnson.

To the many actors who have given life to this play: Ariana Mahallati, who I met under a tree and have been blessed to grow with since, the limitless Molly Adea is brave everyday, Mary Rose Branick who asked the big questions that helped make Kara who she is, Garrett Schulte who is honest where it hurts, Trevor Rinzler who makes me laugh till I cry and then actually just cry, Andrea van den Boogard who can do anything in the universe, Fedra Ramirez, the voice and spirit of an angel. Anna Crivelli is a true goddess whose capacity to work and glow is limitless, Abby Leigh Huffstetler taught me about how voice is the courage to connect, Gabriela Ortega, whose love and creativity is pure energy, David Ball who lived into bravery, Jonathan Moisés Olivares helps me remember I am cosmic, Phoenix Gilmore knew what she was up to and graced us from the future. Netta Walker, you queen, I am so grateful to know you on this journey. Jayson Lee, you surprise and inspire me everyday. Isa Arciniegas, you are a tender heart with undeniable truth, Andrea San Miguel, you helped me learn about seeing and being seen (and blue hair dye), Ryan McBride, you are a generous soulful artist. Thank you to Layla Khoshnoudi, Mary Glen Fredrick, Calum Bedborough, Andrea Abello, Amara Granderson, and Esaú Mora for helping us find and feel into childhood in a December 2018 workshop of the end of the play. Thank you to Yonatan Gebeyehu, Ali Viterbi, Hannah Finn, Jennifer Kim, Sam Ressler, Camille Umoff, Xavier Clark, Krystal Ortiz, Arti Ishak, Sasha Smith, Ryan McBride, Tommy Rivera-Vega, Kiah Stern, Maggie Scrantom for workshopping this play in various cities and times. All of you have helped this piece become what it is.

Thank you beautiful dramaturgs: the generous, brilliant and infectious Sasha Emerson, the wise and loving Jess Reese, the multitalented, smart as hell Ali Viterbi, the loving, precise Gabe Greene and the wondrous question asker Kat Zukaitis who all helped me believe in and know this piece.

Thank you powerful, loving creative producers: Naomi Iizuka, Emily Tarquin, Zach Meicher-Buzzi, Amy Wegener, Jenni Page-White, Robert Egan, Chay Yew, Erica Daniels, Kanomé Jones, Erica Sandvig.

Thank you Kanomé Jones, for embodying love and leadership.

Thank you dear designers: Minjoo Kim, Yi-Chien Lee, Steven Leffue, Annie Le, Heather Gilbert, Kimie Nishikawa, Kelvin Pater, Luqman Brown, Dina Abd El-Aziz, Paul Toben, Christine Pascual, Thomas Dixon, Yu Shibagaki and Bren Coombs.

Thank you Stage Managers, Amber Dettmers, Jan Hubert and Alison MacLeod.

Thank you to my representatives, Michael Finkle and Scott Halle, for believing in what I have to say and who I am becoming.

Thank you apprentices, crew and staff of Actors Theatre, all the folks at UC San Diego and Victory Gardens. Thank you New York Theatre Workshop and Rachel Chavkin for taking this journey with me in the future.

Thank you reader.

Thank you, brave child.

Thank you, ancient one.

This play exists because of your love and presence.

Thank you.

Ariana Mahallati and Abby Leigh Huffstetler
in *How to Defend Yourself*

43rd Humana Festival of New American Plays
Actors Theatre of Louisville, 2019
Photo by Crystal Ludwick

How to Defend Yourself

SCENE ONE

MOJDEH *and* DIANA *enter the gym. It's empty.* DIANA *is mid-story*—

DIANA. A gun

MOJDEH. A gun?

DIANA. Like an m16 m14 / m-something

MOJDEH. Machine gun?

DIANA. looked like one

I've never seen one in real life but it looked like one

she disarms him and I mean /

he had a fucking gun

MOJDEH. This class?

DIANA. This *technique*

MOJDEH. Whoa.

DIANA. tiny white girl

tiny hands, tiny

BAM. disarmed him.

BAM. her hand at his throat.

BAM. probably could have killed him.

BAM. she makes him her bitch.

MOJDEH. sounds like propaganda

DIANA. NO!

It's totally real

I think I'm more powerful than I think I am. you know?

MOJDEH. This video was on the news? The actual news?

DIANA. Linked on that Facebook invite from Zeta Chi you sent me.

So Good

To have hard skills.

Mexican women have like hella hard skills

Americans have none.

In Juarez, we had to work on like

like not getting kidnapped

and like

speaking in code

249

because

MOJDEH. You were four

DIANA. I remember it completely

MOJDEH. Uh huh

DIANA. In my bones

My mom—total warrior

Warrior spy

Totally focused on like

protecting our family

our community and and we get here and here she's like

buying shit on Amazon and reading op-eds

and sitting on her ass

Complacent as fuck!

I mean, I mean your mom was a LITERAL REBEL

MOJDEH. Well—

DIANA. That shit is *crazy*

Total whiplash to be here

In this in this fiction of safety

But still—still

You gotta be prepared Cuz you DO NOT KNOW

If someone's gonna mug you or like gun you down or like...

　　　　(*She inhales. She thinks: rape you.*)

Yeah

　　　　(*She swallows.*)

Is that girl still in the hospital?

MOJDEH. Susannah?

DIANA. Yeah, Susannah

MOJDEH. I don't know

DIANA. Every time I'm in a parking lot I'm like

check the corner check the corner check the corner

I went to a Billie Eilish[1] concert and the security bitch confiscated my mace

and I was like really? really that's safer?

GLOBALLY?

that's safer?

you're afraid I'm gonna hurt someone?

---

1. Or change to mainstream pop star of the moment that a college freshman might love.

I weigh like 117 pounds,
>   (MOJDEH *smirks*.)
like 120, like, sometimes one twenty three, four
but I was on my period
like
I am tiny
you should not take my mace
you take my mace
you vulnerabilize me even more
so basically if something happens to me
that's blood on your hands
literally

…

literally.
>   (*Beat.*)

MOJDEH. People are just posting on Susannah's wall like "get well soon" and "praying for you."

DIANA. It's so weird how you stalk all the Zeta Chi girls.

MOJDEH. It's research. It's how I found out about this class.
>   (MOJDEH *gets lost in her phone.*)

DIANA. And thank you very much.
I wanna get abs by my 19th. You think that's possible?

MOJDEH. Not if we keep eating cupcakes.

DIANA. (*Beat. Then, re:* MOJDEH's *phone.*) You're addicted, dude.
>   (*Beat.*)

Anyone on there?

MOJDEH. Lots of options, lots of options.

DIANA. Anyone good?
>   (DIANA *walks over to look at* MOJDEH *swiping on her phone.*)

Which one is he?

MOJDEH. Polo.

DIANA. There's like 10 guys in polos.

MOJDEH. Tall one?

DIANA. Weird teeth.
>   (*Swipes next.*)

MOJDEH. Aw, baby goat!

DIANA. I bet he's met like one goat. For THIS PHOTO.

MOJDEH. He's cute!

DIANA. He looks like a cannibal.

    (*Swipes.*)

Golf? Automatic no. Next.

    (*Swipes.*)

Oh this guy wants you to know he loves his mom!

MOJDEH. I think that's his girlfriend.

DIANA. That's his mom.

    ...

WOW.

MOJDEH. What?

DIANA. Looking for a nice girl to play with? Seriously?

MOJDEH. / I am a nice girl to play with

DIANA. Ew

    (DIANA *throws* MOJDEH*'s phone away.*)

MOJDEH. Hey!

DIANA. It's fine!

    (DIANA *gets up, starts throwing warm-up punches.* MOJDEH *stands.*)

MOJDEH. You got anyone better?

DIANA. You're going out with that guy, right? from—?

    (MOJDEH *joins* DIANA, *they shadowbox throughout the following.*)

MOJDEH. Bio. James Preston.

DIANA. (*As a cartoony James.*) Ooo shit "I'll show you biology."

    (MOJDEH *laughs.*)

When?

MOJDEH. Wednesday—tomorrow!

DIANA. Hump day

MOJDEH. Aaaaaa!

DIANA. Aaaaaaa!

MOJDEH. AaaaaaI'm so nervous.

DIANA. It's just a date.

MOJDEH. Yeah well—

DIANA. Ooo

MOJDEH. Maybe

DIANA. (*Playing the hype woman.*) My girl's gonna get her cherry POPPED!

MOJDEH. D! Sh!

DIANA. See, inside you there's a little cherry.

A maraschino

And your partner puts in his dick and it just pp

  (*She gestures popping.* MOJDEH *falls to the ground.*)

MOJDEH. You are such an asshole.

  (DIANA *approaches her, a playful straddle.*)

DIANA. You're gonna geeeet it—

MOJDEH. I don't / know

DIANA. (*Sex noises.*) Uh uh uh uh uh uh James uh uh Jaaaaames

MOJDEH. He is—

  (*So fine.*)

An Adonis.

DIANA. Aaaaaaa!

MOJDEH. Yeah!

DIANA. Aaaaaa!

MOJDEH. Yeah!!!

  (DIANA *spots a zit on* MOJDEH'*s chin.*)

DIANA. Yo, stay still.

You've got a massive zit.

  (*She picks at the zit.* MOJDEH *shadowboxes out the pain.*)

MOJDEH. If we get in

DIANA. *When*

MOJDEH. (*Pain.*) Oh fuck

DIANA. Stay still

MOJDEH. (*Fine.*) And live in Zeta Chi

  (*Pain.*)

I promise—

Oh Sweet Lord

DIANA. Got it.

  (DIANA *shows her yield.*)

MOJDEH. Oh fuck that's a good one.

DIANA. I know.

MOJDEH. I promise to help you become, like…the best version of yourself.

DIANA. (*Touched and a little embarrassed.*) Oh, Mojz. Same.

  (DIANA *licks her finger, dabs saliva on* MOJDEH'*s wound.*)

MOJDEH. My cousin Sanaz was a Zeta Chi. Do you remember Sanaz?

DIANA. The bitch who taught us drinking water made you full?

MOJDEH. That was a long time ago. She's an architect now, who is married to a lawyer. Who is HOT. Anyway. One Halloween she said she and her sister—not bio sister—sorority sister

DIANA. I gotchu

MOJDEH. Went to Taco Bell and ordered a Chalupa and a Soft Taco Supreme each / and like

DIANA. I thought she was anorexic

MOJDEH. It's complicated. Anyway through the magic of the Taco Bell Gods, they received two dozen of each. Suddenly they've got all this friggin' Taco Bell and they go home and they ring the all call—

DIANA. What's an all call?

MOJDEH. Like a system

Like a bell?

I don't know

They can all talk to each other

And they say that they've got a fuckton of Taco Bell

And they spread it in their room like a picnic

And drunk girls pour in and sit on the floor and chow down

Sanaz said some girl started crying because she was lactose intolerant

Sanaz said it was her best Halloween ever.

DIANA. That's gonna be US!!!!

MOJDEH. I dunno. One in ten girls get in.

DIANA. Girl, we're at least 90th percentile. At least.

Gimme them cinnamon twisty things

MOJDEH. What?

DIANA. From Taco Bell, those, those cinnamon—

> (BRANDI *and* KARA *enter in lululemon.* BRANDI *looks around. It is so much emptier than she'd thought it would be.* DIANA *and* MOJDEH *act casual.*)

BRANDI. Oh. Is this the right room?

KARA. North Gym Room 2. This is North Gym Room…2.

BRANDI. (*Just to* KARA.) What time is it?

KARA. 4:59.

BRANDI. Yeah, ok, huh.

> (*To* MOJDEH *and* DIANA.)

Hi!

> (*To* KARA.)

Facebook said 30?

KARA. 22 yeses and 8 maybes. It was last-minute—

BRANDI. Uh huh

KARA. And most of the girls are busy with Polish Week, so…

BRANDI. People really don't give a fuck, do they?

…I'm glad we're doing this.

KARA. Hm. Me too.

BRANDI. Hi warrior princesses!

DIANA. Uh hi

MOJDEH. I'm so glad you're doing this

So important

I've always wanted to take self-defense

> (DIANA *clocks this: what?*)

BRANDI. Hell yes

MOJDEH. I can't believe you have a black belt

I YouTubed you

Ha

BRANDI. I've just been training for a while—anyone can do it

Everyone should, honestly

MOJDEH. True. So true.

> (*Beat.*)

BRANDI. (*Referencing a small notepad.*) Intros are first! Hello hello, I'm Brandi Jones. I'm here because I know Susannah very well and I have a black belt.

MOJDEH. Mojdeh. Mojdeh Ebrahimi. I am so thrilled to learn from you and also rush Zeta Chi!

Diana's rushing too.

> (DIANA *does a little wave.*)

BRANDI. Cool.

KARA. This isn't a Zeta event.

MOJDEH. No no totally—that was a sidebar. Cuz I know you're both on exec and—

KARA. They're doing Polish Week.

MOJDEH. What's Polish Week?

KARA. It's where we prep to recruit PNMs.

MOJDEH. What's a PNM?

KARA. You're a PNM.

BRANDI. Potential new member.

MOJDEH. That's amazing.

KARA. It's whatever.

This is an us thing.

MOJDEH. I'm sorry.

BRANDI. 100 percent fine. Can you tell me your name one more time, beautiful?

MOJDEH. Mojz-day

BRANDI. I love it. And you?

DIANA. (*Pronouncing DeeAHna.*) Diana Rodriguez. Question: will we be working with guns?

KARA. What?

DIANA. In the krav video

BRANDI. It's a self-defense class, so we're mostly learning defense?

DIANA. I realize that: in the video on Facebook there were people working with guns?

BRANDI. Oh! Yeah that—

KARA. I just linked a video as sort of a / teaser

BRANDI. I'm trained in hand to hand.

DIANA. Cool.

BRANDI. Cool

DIANA. Yeah, that's cool!

> (*Beat.*)

KARA. Kara. Hello. I'm co-host of this workshop. I don't have fighter skills but I have…promotional skills. So.

BRANDI. And you will get fighter skills! You all will.

I'm a fighter

> (*Making it into an exercise.*)

I am a fighter

Repeat

I am—

> (*They join in.*)

ALL. (*In varying rhythms.*) A fighter

I am a fighter

I am a fighter

I am a fighter

KARA/MOJDEH. I—

BRANDI. How'd that feel?

> (*Beat. They each respond non-verbally.*)

Good, right?

> (KARA *stifles a laugh.*)

You ARE fighters.

KARA. (*Getting a candle, addressing the group.*) And um, I brought this candle for Susannah.

Who is at Scripps Hospital right now. Fighting in her own way.

> (*Lighting the candle.*)

Um. I just thought it would be good to remember why we're here. Why we're really here.

So maybe we can hold her in prayer? Send her love—light or something.

> (*A moment of silence.* MOJDEH *tries to grab* BRANDI *and* KARA*'s hands. Oh, that's not happening.* BRANDI *nods solemnly.*)

KARA. Thank you.

BRANDI. Thank you.

> (*Beat.*)

FIND YOUR WEAPONS!

FIND YOUR WEAPONS!

FIND YOUR WEAPONS!

DIANA. What? I'm sorry what?

BRANDI. FIND A WEAPON!

DIANA. Ok.

> (MOJDEH *freezes.* DIANA *springs into action, emptying her backpack. The following overlaps quickly.*)

MOJDEH. Didn't bring

/ Didn't bring any weapons…what?

KARA. Brandi I didn't FB that

DIANA. C'mon Mojz

MOJDEH. I didn't know this was a requirement

KARA. You didn't tell me to FB that

MOJDEH. Was this emailed, was this?

KARA. I could have FBed that

MOJDEH. I don't have any weapons

BRANDI. Anything can be a weapon

Use your fucking imaginations

Anything in this room

YOU NEED ONE WEAPON

What can you use to protect yourselves?

GO!

Ten...Nine...You're wasting time...Eight...What can you use...Seven...One weapon...Don't think too hard...Six...outside of the box

> (*As* BRANDI *counts,* MOJDEH *and* KARA *run to their belongings. They empty their backpacks. Notebooks. Pens. Tape. Books. Condoms spill out of* KARA*'s backpack—"embarrassing!"* MOJDEH *sees, totally jealous. While she stares at* KARA, *a spoiled apple rolls out of* MOJDEH*'s backpack and across the room toward* BRANDI. BRANDI *watches* MOJDEH *pick it up.*)

BRANDI. Five...ok...four...three...two...one!!!! Line up.

> (*They return to make a small line with objects.* DIANA *has a pen, a shard of bleacher, an X-ACTO knife, a weight.* MOJDEH *has an apple.* KARA *holds her keys between her fingers.*)

Explain. Diana.

DIANA. Ok, so! I've got four.

BRANDI. I asked for one.

Go ahead.

DIANA. One, pen to the temple or the larynx.

BRANDI. Good

DIANA. Thank you, and I think this is a shard of bleacher. Rusty. Nice edge. Could give a decent slice. And this is an X-ACTO knife—I take studio art, and this is obviously a weight.

BRANDI. Yeah, well. Do you see the problem here?

DIANA. ...

BRANDI. Your hands are full.

DIANA. Oh! Yeah! Well, I would pick one if—

BRANDI. I *asked* you to pick one

DIANA. Yeah, I would if—

BRANDI. If what?

DIANA. If this was a real crisis.

BRANDI. Ah, the distinction between real and simulated crises. Don't do that.

DIANA. This is a class.

BRANDI. Of course! Just play pretend in here! Does that make you feel safe? Treating something like a warm-up? A throw-away?

(*Beat.*)

I asked for one, so, next time—

DIANA. Yeah.

BRANDI. Practice makes perfect, excuses make mistakes! But good job! Mojdeh.

MOJDEH. I'm sorry

BRANDI. Sorry not accepted.

MOJDEH. I'm not sure I understood the exercise.

This is disgusting—

BRANDI. How would you use that…apple? Core? To defend yourself?

(NIKKI *enters. No one notices her.*)

MOJDEH. I was looking for the trash can

I guess I could throw it at someone? Like a diversion? I don't know.

And if that didn't work, I could stab them with my pen.

BRANDI. OK!

MOJDEH. In their temple. That's a pressure point, right?

DIANA. That's what I—

BRANDI. Side of the neck is better.

Do you mind if I?

MOJDEH. Go for it

(*She demos on* MOJDEH. MOJDEH *giggles.*)

BRANDI. Right there, see?

MOJDEH. Oh

DIANA. / So she says to some rapist,

BRANDI. (*To* MOJDEH.) Do you feel that?

DIANA. "Hey! please stay still so I can jam this in your neck?"

BRANDI. (*Pronouncing Die-ana.*) No, Diana

DIANA. (*Pronouncing Dee-AH-na.*) Diana

BRANDI. If someone is attacking you, it's your life or theirs and you fight with every piece of rage and skill you have. Muscle memory, which is why we practice.

(*Beat.*)

You try on me.

DIANA. That's ok

BRANDI. Do it.

DIANA. No, that's ok

BRANDI. Seriously. I'm trying to train you.

DIANA. Ok.

I would stab you…

Here

BRANDI. Higher. Back. Higher. Yes. Do you feel the difference?

DIANA. Yes.

BRANDI. Good.

      (BRANDI *gestures to* KARA.

      DIANA *loudly dumps her objects on her backpack.*)

KARA. They say to hold your keys between your fingers

When you're walking to your car or whatever

NIKKI. (*Soft.*) Wolverine.

KARA. Excuse me?

BRANDI. Oh hi, come on in. One more.

      (BRANDI *grabs the sign-in sheet.*)

MOJDEH. (*Just to* DIANA.) You ok?

DIANA. Yeah.

NIKKI. (*Louder.*) X-Men?

KARA. Yeah, I don't watch "comics," but

DIANA. Totally like Wolverine.

BRANDI. Ooo, yeah.

KARA. YEAH! I go Wolverine on them.

BRANDI. (*To* KARA.) Actually, that's not effective. You'll only hurt yourself.

      (*To* NIKKI.)

What's your name sweetie?

NIKKI. (*Soft again.*) Nicollette? Um, but I go by Nikki. It's a new thing.

BRANDI. I'm sorry, love, I can't hear you. Do you want to come join us?

      (NIKKI *laughs uncomfortably.*)

NIKKI. (*Only slightly louder.*) It's Nikki. Nikki.

      (BRANDI *hands* NIKKI *the sign-in sheet.*)

BRANDI. Nikki, Hi, Welcome

I bet you have a weapon on you.

NIKKI. What?

BRANDI. We're doing an exercise on impromptu weapons.

      (*Beat.*)

NIKKI. Um yeah

To be honest,

I don't think I have anything which would count as a weapon.

BRANDI. Nothing?

NIKKI. No.

BRANDI. I don't believe you.

NIKKI. Uh! Believe it.

(*Beat.*)

BRANDI. You've got arms,

NIKKI. Yeah

BRANDI. And teeth, and feet, and fingers, and hips.

So I'd say your body is a weapon.

(NIKKI *self-consciously covers her body. She shrugs.*)

NIKKI. Yeah, ok.

BRANDI. It is

NIKKI. Doesn't feel like it.

BRANDI. If you learn to use it

It's a very serious weapon.

NIKKI. (*Like it's a joke.*) Maybe your body.

BRANDI. Your body

NIKKI. Your body

BRANDI. Your body

NIKKI. Your—My body

BRANDI. Yes

NIKKI. Aaaaaahaahahaha

(NIKKI *shrugs and laughs, deeply uncomfortable that everyone is looking at her body.*)

BRANDI. You're uncomfortable.

NIKKI. Yes

BRANDI. Why

NIKKI. Oh I don't know

BRANDI. Why

NIKKI. Cuz people are

People are looking at my body...

KARA. Did you all sign the waivers?

BRANDI. This is your dojo. And these situations will be triggering but we're gonna stick with it.

(KARA *distributes a clipboard.* MOJDEH, DIANA *sign waivers.*)

When I think of Susannah being—when I think of—when I think of—when I think of—any woman, person, being brutalized, it makes me want to kill someone. And I know I could, you know? With my bare hands. I could. I could tear them apart. I could choke them until they stopped breathing. I could open their ribcage, rip their heart out of their chest, and hold it in my palms as it took its very last beat.

    (*A shift.*)

Done, everyone?

    (*They hand over their waivers.*)

With self-defense, the most important thing is to get away.

And get to safety.

Your most powerful weapon is your—

…

…Voice.

I want you to practice using your voices. Line up across from each other. And say no.

NO.

    (KARA *and* NIKKI *pair.*

    MOJDEH *and* DIANA *pair.*)

MOJDEH. No	**DIANA.** No	**KARA.** No	**NIKKI.** …no	**BRANDI.**
No	No	No	no	
	NO	NO	no	Say get away
Get away				
GET AWAY	Get away	(KARA	Get—get—	
	GET THE	*walks to*	get away	
GET!	FUCK	NIKKI:)	from me	
	AWAY			
(MOJDEH	GET AWAY			
giggles.)	FROM ME			
				And stay
D, this is	Get away	GET	Stay back	back
really freaking	Stay back!	LOOOST	Go back	
me out…	STAY AWAY	STAY		
	I WILL	BACK		
	FUCK YOU	NOT A		
	UP	CHANCE		
		IN HELL	Aaaaaaaaa	
		GET AWAY-	Sorry.	
		YYYYYY		

BRANDI. That was great. YES. Just using your voice is an excellent defense. But, in cases where that doesn't work, you've gotta play offense and target your attacker's weak spots. Where are they?

KARA. Balls

BRANDI. Excellent. Yes. Groin or inner thigh.

MOJDEH. Eyes

BRANDI. Eyes

DIANA. Kidneys

BRANDI. Very painful. Good—

No matter how much an attacker bulks up, the head and neck and the *groin* will always be vulnerable.

Kara will you demo with me?

> (KARA *joins her.*)

Side of neck—you know this one—

> (*She slow-mo karate chops the side of* KARA's *neck.*)

Please be careful, you can make someone pass out like that,

> (KARA *laughs.*)

And here

> (*She slow-mo bumps the heel of her palm in* KARA's *nose.* KARA *acts like OW!*)

(You don't need to do that)

And here

> (*She knees* KARA's *groin with an exhale.*)

Step into your attacker.

Now in new pairs.

Who's the attacker?

> (DIANA *and* KARA *raise their hands.*)

Who's the victim?

> (MOJDEH *and* NIKKI *sort of shrug.*)

Go!

NIKKI.
This is my first karate class?

MOJDEH. (*So thrilled.*)
Hey

DIANA.
Is that a question?

KARA.
Yeah, so you want to go first?

NIKKI.
Oh my god, no.
**This is my first
karate class.**

DIANA.
Cool.

DIANA.
Wanna go first?

NIKKI.
Sure.

    (NIKKI *hammer
    strikes weakly.*)

    (NIKKI *hammer
    strikes with more
    force.*)

NIKKI.
Arggghhh.
Sorry.

DIANA.
Why? She just—

NIKKI.
I don't—
sorry—
yeah, go.
  (DIANA *does a
  hammer strike to*
  NIKKI*'s neck.*)

  (NIKKI *flinches.*)

BRANDI.
**And give yourself
an argghh as you
release.**

BRANDI. (*To
MOJDEH.*)
**We'll get to that in a
minute**

MOJDEH.
**Sure! Unless you
want to!**

KARA.
I don't care.

    (MOJDEH *delicately
    goes for the nose.*)

MOJDEH.
How was that?

KARA.
I mean, fine? You're not
touching me

MOJDEH.
I'm gonna go for your
kidneys now

KARA.
Ok.

    (MOJDEH *tries to
    find the kidneys.*)

MOJDEH.
**I don't really know
how to punch**

KARA.
**I used to roll my
pants up like that,**

MOJDEH.
Yeah?

DIANA.
You ok?

NIKKI.
Oh yeah. T-totally.
You can do more.

(DIANA *does a few
more.
They switch.* NIKKI
palm heels.)

NIKKI.
Sorry I'm sweaty.

(NIKKI *wipes her
hand on her shorts.*)

DIANA.
**That's okay. You have
a body. Can I—?**

(NIKKI *nods.*)

(DIANA *palm heels.*)

DIANA.
**This one shoots your
nose bones into your
brain.**

NIKKI. Really?

DIANA. I think so.

KARA.
**In like middle
school.**

MOJDEH.
Oh

KARA.
**You're taking me
baaaaack**

MOJDEH.
**I just—I don't have
like, cool—these are
what I had—**

KARA.
**No, no, no, no I love
it. Honestly. It's very
80s.**

MOJDEH.
Yeah!

KARA.
Scrunchie.

MOJDEH.
Thanks.

KARA.
**Are you going to the
Alpha Ep party on
Thursday?**

(KARA *slo-mo palm
heels* MOJDEH *in the
nose.*)

BRANDI.
It's mostly cartilage.
Sadly.
But you stun the
attacker and have
time to get away.

BRANDI.
(*To the group.*)
And groin strikes.

KARA.
I'm wearing teal
for Susannah—like,
consciousness
raising—

NIKKI. Cool

DIANA. Oh.

NIKKI. Oh.　　　　Knee up. And step
　　　　　　　　　thru.

MOJDEH.
Cool.

(DIANA *mimes*
the groin strike on
NIKKI.)

KARA.
That's the color of
rape. Awareness.
Are you going?

(NIKKI *is sort of*
frozen.)　　　　Good, good, again?

MOJDEH.
I'm not Greek

(DIANA *does it again*
with vocals.)

　　　　　　　　Nice up.

KARA.
Oh right, sorry.

MOJDEH.
But I'll watch all the
(NIKKI *tries to*　　Good! Nikki?　　**stories! Yeah, I—I**
balance and knee　　　　　　　　**hope you have fun!**
DIANA's *groin.*
It makes her　　　　　　　　**KARA.**
uncomfortable.)　　　　　　　　**It's more of a**
　　　　　　　　　　　　　statement. Are you
　　　　　　　　That's good!　　**gonna rush Zeta Chi?**
　　　　　　　　Grab her shoulders
　　　　　　　　and say no.　　**MOJDEH.**
NIKKI. No.　　　　　　　　**I mean, maybe? Yes.**
　　　　　　　　Louder.　　　**Yes that's the plan.**
NO.
　　　　　　　　　　　　　KARA.
　　　　　　　　　　　　　You should.
DIANA. That was　　　　　You really should.
good.　　　　　　　　　　We're doing values on
　　　　　　　　　　　　　Friday.

NIKKI. **I don't want to actually hurt her.**

Yes—hesitation is natural, but

MOJDEH.
Values.

KARA.
Like sisterhood, honesty, academic integrity.

MOJDEH.
Those are literally all my values

KARA.
Maybe I'll even be your big. Big sis.

MOJDEH.
Whoa. I've always wanted a sister.

DIANA.
We gonna have one of those dudes come in?

Like covered in padding and you beat the shit out of him?

You ever do that?

BRANDI.
Ha.
Unfortunately, no

KARA.
But shhh don't tell anyone.

That's dirty rushing. Not. Allowed. I would get in big trouble.

Just like go ham?

NIKKI.
Cool.

BRANDI.
Yeah, it's amazing.

MOJDEH.
I do not want you to get in trouble.

DIANA.
That is amazing.

BRANDI. Thank you. Ok, great! Great. Line up. Kara? Music?

(KARA *makes a sorority gesture to* BRANDI *like: I gotchu.*
BRANDI *makes it back: thanks.*
KARA *plays athletic, sexy music you'd wanna punch to—something like "Jump" by Rihanna. It plays throughout the following.*)

MOJDEH. (*To* KARA.) I'm like the least athletic person.

KARA. Me too.

MOJDEH. Like zero percent athletic.

I have core issues.

KARA. Does anyone *not* have core issues?

BRANDI. Who's thrown a punch before?

(DIANA *raises her hand.*)

Uh huh.

DIANA. I have brothers, so.

BRANDI. Anyone else?

(*No one else has thrown a punch.*)

Wow. GENDER, amirite? If we were a bunch a boys, I bet the numbers would be different—but if we were a bunch a boys, we wouldn't be here!

DIANA. I wish girls fought more. Like beat the shit out of each other for fun. I wish that was like a, socially acceptable thing to do. Fight club, you know?

NIKKI. (*Kind of into it.*) Uh huh uh huh

MOJDEH. I'm glad it's not.

KARA. If it was me and you, I think I'd win. No offense, but I think I'd win.

BRANDI. Let's get in fighting stance.

(BRANDI *gets in fighting stance. The others line up with her.*)

Eyes up. See your opponent. You want to stare down your attacker. And take a half step back. See, if someone's gonna come at me, I can back up

(*She does.*)

Or come forward.

(*She comes forward, throws some punches.*

She shuffles back and forth, retreating and attacking.

The girls are impressed.)

And you wanna protect your—what?

KARA/DIANA. Face.

MOJDEH. / Heart.

BRANDI. Aw.

But yeah, protect your face.

(BRANDI *demos her hands at her face.*

She throws punches, exhaling on the throw.)

BRANDI. (*Exhaling.*) Huh. Huh. Huh. Huh.

(*The following text can be drowned out by the blaring music.*

It's more what we see than what we hear.

As they learn, we enter a world of full-on music video.

The team assembles, gathering their power,

punching and moving together.)

Shoulders relaxed.

When I throw a cross, I use my hips as power.

(BRANDI *demos three right crosses.*)

Imagine you're going through your target.

(*They do.*)

See my hips?

(NIKKI *spontaneously laughs.*)

NIKKI. [I'm sorry, it's not you.]

BRANDI. Bend your knees. Yup. There you go.

(BRANDI *walks around, checking form.* DIANA *and* MOJDEH
practice next to each other.

MOJDEH *throws punches weakly.*

BRANDI *holds up a foam arm shield.*)

Line up, and one by one, come in and punch right here. Don't worry, you
won't hurt me.

(BRANDI *gestures to the center of an X on the arm shield.*

They line up. NIKKI *is suddenly the front of the line, on accident.*)

NIKKI. Oh I'm—

(*She goes to the back of the line.*

DIANA *throws a punch at the shield. Hard.*)

DIANA. Do you want one punch exactly or?

BRANDI. If you've got more in there…

(DIANA *punches three times—hard.*

The third knocks BRANDI *back a bit.*

The rest are impressed.)

Good job

DIANA. Thank you.

(MOJDEH *goes up to the shield. She exhales, nervous, then throws a
weak punch.*)

BRANDI. You can actually hit the bag.

(*She does, weakly.*)

MOJDEH. I'm literally 0% athletic.

DIANA. Come on Mojz—you can—

BRANDI. This is a wonderful starting point.

MOJDEH. Right.

BRANDI. It is, just bend your knees, uh huh. Perfect.

And activate your hips. Like your hips are actually propelling your fist forward, ok?

(MOJDEH *tries it. Her fist thwacks on the arm shield.*)

MOJDEH. Whoa.

BRANDI. How do you feel?

MOJDEH. Whoa.

BRANDI. Yeah.

It's addictive.

(MOJDEH *goes to the back of the line.*)

Kaykay?

(KARA *approaches the bag. She throttles on it.*)

KARA. (*Loud, the only thing we hear above the music.*) **Fuck you Spencer fuck you Tom fuck you Spencer fuck you Tom fuck you Spencer fuck you Spencer fuck you Spencer FUCK YOU FUCK YOU.**

BRANDI. Ok good. Good. Nikki?

(NIKKI *takes a deep breath. Stands by the bag.*

Throws a punch, her eyes closed.)

That was great. Literally perfect form, wouldn't change a thing

NIKKI. Thanks

BRANDI. Just a little hesitation on the execution.

So let's try it again.

(NIKKI *punches the bag again.*)

Better? How about this?

Imagine this X is someone you hate.

(NIKKI *closes her eyes to imagine. She swallows. Nods. She starts to throw a punch. Stops herself. She can't finish it. She feels dizzy. She waves her hands.*)

Ok, How about we go on a water break?

(*They do.* BRANDI *turns down the music.*)

What were you thinking about hun?

NIKKI. Just some guy

BRANDI. Huh, some guy.

NIKKI. Yeah, some guy I blew in a gas station.

KARA. Heh—been there.

NIKKI. Heh.

BRANDI. What happened?

NIKKI. I gave him a blowjob in the bathroom. The toilet was leaking. It was gross. He was sad.

BRANDI. Did you want to?

KARA. Brandi, c'mon.

(BRANDI *puts her hand up like:* KARA, *let me work.*)

NIKKI. Yeah. I mean. Yes.

BRANDI. But you're angry? At him?

NIKKI. I have a tendency to be dramatic. He gave me a free Heath Bar on my way out.

(*Beat.*)

KARA. Literally everyone has given a shitty blowjob amirite?

DIANA. Haha.

MOJDEH. Haha!

KARA. It's like you look up blowjob in the dictionary, there's a girl shrugging going "eh!"

(NIKKI *laughs.*)

Each time, I'm like, did I want that?

I figure it's sort of like community service, or like I don't know,

Throat yoga.

(NIKKI *laughs.*)

I try not to shame myself

NIKKI. Mmmm

KARA. Cuz it's all like, life experience!

NIKKI. Mmmm

KARA. One day, we'll be old and look back on photos of RIGHT NOW

And we'll be like:

That was crazy

I gave a blowjob in a gas station! I was so crazy

NIKKI. I was so crazy

(*They laugh.*)

Totally

BRANDI. Are you okay?

NIKKI. I'm fine!

BRANDI. But—

NIKKI. I have a tendency to be dramatic.

SCENE TWO

The women stretch at a ballet bar in unison.

NIKKI *is a ballerina. They are all ballerinas.*

For a moment the space transforms—they are girls and women at the same time.

Lights up and two men are by the door. NIKKI *sees them:*

NIKKI. So. There are two dudes in the doorway?

BRANDI. Oh! They're here!

(BRANDI *leaps to let the men in.*)

DIANA. Who?

BRANDI. Thank you so much for coming!!

ANDY. Hey B

(BRANDI *and* ANDY *hug.*)

DIANA. I thought this was a women's self-defense class.

KARA. It's an assault prevention workshop.

DIANA. So we need some assaulters?

EGGO. Sup

(BRANDI *and* EGGO *side-hug.*)

DIANA. (*To* MOJDEH.) You said it was for—

BRANDI. Ladies…this is Andy and Eggo.

MOJDEH. D, can you stop?

ANDY. Sorry we're late.

KARA. How is Susannah?

ANDY. We didn't see her.

KARA. What?

ANDY. We asked but the hospital chick was like: Family only.

KARA. She is family.

ANDY. I know.

BRANDI. Aw

KARA. Fuck that.

ANDY. Yeah, totally. So, Eggo and I just waited it out in the trauma wing with this bigass cardstock card.

BRANDI. What's the card?

ANDY. A little something from Alpha Ep. All the guys signed it for Susannah. We do not get down with that rape shit. Full stop. Every woman I'm with, every woman I've ever been with, consents *affirmatively*, ok? Like lemme tell you. *A-ffirm-a-tive-ly.*

(MOJDEH *giggles.*)

BRANDI. Hell yes.

ANDY. It's important. Shit! It's so important. It's not just a woman's body, it's her soul.

(BRANDI *nods appreciatively.*)

I mean, I have two sisters. And they're pretty. Like, gorgeous, okay?

EGGO. Good Genes.

ANDY. Anyone touches 'em, I'd kill 'em, bare hands, go to jail, don't care. Susannah's dad was in the waiting room. Destroyed. Totally destroyed. I said to him, I said, Sir, I just want you to know that we do not condone the violence that befell your daughter.

KARA. Befell?

ANDY. We do not support that culture. We do not support those men.

EGGO. Fucking Tom.

KARA. Spencer can go to hell.

ANDY. Did you watch the video?

EGGO. I put it on Insta.

BRANDI. What?!

ANDY. NO! Not *that* video.

The boomerang, with the card—

MOJDEH. I saw it.

ANDY. Kinda cute, right? Handing it to her dad.

Like—

(*He mimes handing the card to Susannah's dad.*)

Just important to put a message out there that we're in solidarity, you know?

(EGGO *nods.*)

Cuz we are. I was telling the boys that this has been a women's issue for too long. But I'm putting it in the Man Box, ok? I'm putting it in my Man Box.

MOJDEH. What's a Man Box?

ANDY. It's all the roles we're supposed to play as men. Provider, aggressor, decider, non-crier,

DIANA. Dominator.

ANDY. Heh. Yeah. Etcetera. Etcetera.

KARA. It's not all bad.

ANDY. No, I mean, gender can be fun too, right?

(MOJDEH *shrug/laughs.*)

But the point. The point is—The work we've been doing with Man Boxes for the past year is to burst out of the conventional bullshit, you know? It's time to listen. To show up for you, however you need to be shown up for.

BRANDI. Thank you, Andy. I'm so glad you're here.

ANDY. When you asked the guys to come participate, I was like FUCK YES. And Eggo was down too.

(EGGO *nods.*)

So just thank you, for sharing your space with us. I know that's—I know that's a special, very trusting thing. Assault prevention, it's big, important stuff.

BRANDI. It is. Yesterday the girls and I learned basic self-defense.

ANDY. Ka-Ra-Te!

BRANDI. Kind of

ANDY. No shit!

BRANDI. Yeah!

MOJDEH. Brandi's a black belt

ANDY. Fuck yeah, little lady.

BRANDI. Not so little.

ANDY. Sorry.

BRANDI. And today we're gonna explore another, possibly *yummier* facet of prevention.

DIANA. Guns.

BRANDI. Ha. No. Has anyone taken a consent workshop before?

ANDY. Nope.

MOJDEH. First time.

DIANA. Virgin Voyage

(MOJDEH *looks at* DIANA *like: shut up.*)

EGGO. Nah.

NIKKI. Maybe?

BRANDI. What did you do?

NIKKI. In cotillion, we talked about how to say no to boys without hurting their feelings.

KARA. Brandi and I are trained peer counselors here on campus. And so is Andy.

(ANDY *waves.*)

BRANDI. If an issue comes up in the workshop that you want to explore, just tell us and we can unpack it.

ANDY. I am also available.

BRANDI. This workshop requires your consent to participate. Do we have your consent?

DIANA. What are we going to do?

BRANDI. GREAT POINT.

Kara, can you?

KARA. Oh!

(KARA *wheels in an old-school chalkboard. She scribes.*)

BRANDI. One aspect of consent is CLEAR ASKS AND EXPECTATIONS

First, locate yourself. Where am I?

DIANA. Right here.

MOJDEH. North gym room two

ANDY. The floor.

BRANDI. What do I desire?

EGGO. Tacos

MOJDEH. What don't I desire?

DIANA. Uhhh

NIKKI. Chocolate chip

ANDY. Well

(KARA *draws stick figures with genitals, and hearts for eyes.*)

BRANDI. What am I asking of my partner?

KARA. Or, partners?

BRANDI. That's fun.

(KARA *draws a third stick figure. She draws speech bubbles.*)

BRANDI. Am I being **clear** and **honest**?

(KARA *doesn't know how to draw this.*

She writes: CLEAR! HONEST!)

So for today, the exercise is around 20 minutes long

DIANA. Kay

BRANDI. With sex—with *everything* I think it's important to consider: what are your boundaries of time?

DIANA. Yesssss. It's the worst when you're thinking—how long is this gonna go on? You're like [hand job] come on. Okay. Come on.

KARA. Totally.

ANDY. Unless you're in trance state.

MOJDEH. What's that?

ANDY. Well, in trance, time gets fluid, gets revealed for the construct that it is. Sometimes when I make love,

DIANA. Ha.

...

[go on]

ANDY. I start to get downloads that aren't from me, they're from beyond me. It's—well, it's dissolution of self, actually. You don't exist.

MOJDEH. Whoa.

BRANDI. Not everyone wants to dissolve. Right? I would like to exist. Thank you. Soooo. Boundaries of time! And *body*. How would you like your body to be touched and engaged with? It's YOUR body after all.

We're taught that it's not—

like, you know when you're a kid and they make you hug all your relatives?

MOJDEH. Oh yeah.

DIANA. Fuck that.

BRANDI. Yeah. But um. Um...The fact is, the fact is: You do NOT have to touch anyone you don't want to! It's your body! It's yours.

(*Beat,* BRANDI *gets a little lost.*)

And...Heart. Yes. What are you letting into your heart? Kara.

(*She gestures: draw that. A triangle.*)

Kara, the triangle. Do you remember the triangle?

(KARA *draws a triangle diagram with body, time and heart at the points.*)

No, heart goes on top. Yeah, there ya go. Clear boundaries of time, body and heart.

This exercise asks you to work in pairs exploring touch from the elbows down. Raise your hands like this if you consent.

(BRANDI *indicates: hands up.* ANDY *mouths the word "elbows" to* MOJDEH *who laughs.*)

DIANA. Elbows down as in *genitals* or elbows down as in fingertips?

BRANDI. Important clarifying question from my favorite student...

DIANA. I'm your student?

BRANDI. Peer. Peer. Thank you.

Elbows to fingertip.

Raise your hands if you want to play.

(KARA *raises her hand.* ANDY *raises his hand.* MOJDEH *raises her hand.* EGGO *raises his hand.* NIKKI *raises her hand.* DIANA *raises her hand.*)

ANDY.
You wanna?

MOJDEH.
(*Gestures to
herself "me?"
Nods.*)
Mmmhmm!

ANDY.
I'm Andy.

MOJDEH.
Mojdeh.

ANDY.
Oh shit.
Slower?

MOJDEH.
Mo-j-deh.

ANDY.
Can I call you
Mo?

MOJDEH.
…Sure.

KARA.
Me and you?

EGGO.
I consent

KARA.
Haaa

EGGO.
Eggo.

KARA.
**Eggo is short
for?**

EGGO.
Eggo.

KARA.
**Cool. I'm
Kara.**

EGGO.
I know who
you are.

KARA.
Yeah?

EGGO.
I noticed you.

DIANA. (*To
herself.*)
Uhhh.

NIKKI.
Partners again?

DIANA.
Yeah, sure.
Diana.

NIKKI.
I know your
name.

DIANA.
**Do you mind
that I'm a
girl?**

NIKKI.
**Why would
that matter?**

DIANA.
No, right, right,
totally

NIKKI.
The principles
will apply
either way—

KARA.
Of course.

DIANA.
Duh, yup.

NIKKI.
And girls can
be—

DIANA.
Yeah

NIKKI.
Too

BRANDI.
So you start
kneeling and
looking at each
other.

(*They kneel
and look at
each other.*)

(*They kneel
and look at
each other.*)

(*They kneel
and look at
each other.*)

And just
breathe
together.

ANDY.
You a yogi?

MOJDEH.
I'm bad.

ANDY.
Believe that.
(*Wink.*)

This is sitting
warrior in yoga

MOJDEH.
Mmm cool.

(ANDY *leans
in to begin.*
MOJDEH *is
like: OK! They
do feeding
breaths.*)

You can try
feeding breaths,
so what that
looks like is
you inhale and
exhale as your
partner inhales
and then they
exhale as you
inhale. Get as
close as you are

(*They do
feeding
breaths.*)

(DIANA
notices
MOJDEH *and*
ANDY *going
for it.*)

**comfortable.
Make sense?**

DIANA.
You wanna?

NIKKI.
Yeah

**EGGO.
Sorry, I just
ate garlic
shrimp. Do
you mind if
we?**

(*They do
feeding
breaths.*)

**ANDY.
Your breath
smells like
cinnamon,
or jasmine.
Like some, like
exotic tea.**

(*He moves
slightly further
away.*)

**MOJDEH.
Thank you. I
think it's Crest
mouthwash?**
The purple
bottle.

KARA.
Oh sure, uh—
it's fine but—

(*They keep
doing feeding
breaths.*)

NIKKI.
I'm getting
dizzy.

ANDY.
Must just be you
then.

(*Then maybe
they just
look at each
other.*)

DIANA.
Yeah, stop.

**KARA.
Are you in
pain?**

EGGO.
I'm trying not
to blink.

KARA.
You can blink.

EGGO.
As a personal
challenge

BRANDI.
And when you're
ready, describe
the kind of
experience you'd
like to have with
your partner.

KARA.
Ok, I'll do it
too.

Today. **How do
you want to
feel after this
exercise?**

ANDY.
I'd like to feel
connected—
yeah to a new
friend.

MOJDEH.
I'd like to feel
brave

NIKKI.
I'd like to feel
strong?

DIANA.
I'd like to
feel like
I've—learned
something
new.

KARA.
Uh. Relaxed.

EGGO.
Ooh I like
that. Relaxed
too.

(ANDY
chuckles to
MOJDEH.)

BRANDI.
Plant that
intention of
what you can
give your
partner deep
inside you.

And now, ask
your partner
to touch you,
exactly as
you'd like to be
touched. But
from the elbow
down, ok? Elbow
to fingertip.
Let's respect that
boundary. We're
strangers here,
for the most part.

(NIKKI *and*
DIANA
wonder who
wants to go
first. They
laugh at
this.)

ANDY.
Tell me how
you want me to
touch you.

MOJDEH.
Oh

ANDY.
From the elbow
down, don't get
any ideas.

MOJDEH.
Uh um.

NIKKI.
Maybe you can
just rub my
palms?

ANDY.
How do you
want me to
touch you?

MOJDEH.
I really don't
know.

ANDY.
Hey, all answers
are the right
answer.

MOJDEH.
Ha, ok

ANDY.
Any way you
want.

MOJDEH.
Yeah, so—

ANDY.
Brave, right?

MOJDEH.
Yeah, thanks for
remembering

ANDY.
Say what you
want

MOJDEH.
I'll take a graze?

EGGO.
Ladies first.

KARA.
You go first.

EGGO.
Oh. Ok. Can
you breathe?
on my palms?

KARA.
Huh?

EGGO.
Just like
breathe on my
palms. Like
(*He breathes as*
if fogging up a
mirror:) **Ah.**
Ah.
Ah.

KARA.
That's really
fucking weird
bro.

DIANA.
Sure

NIKKI.
Is that ok? Do
you want to
do that?

DIANA.
If you want to,
sure.

NIKKI.
If you want to.

DIANA.
It's fine. Good.

(DIANA
rubs NIKKI*'s*
palms.)

NIKKI.
That feels nice.
And can you
thread your
fingers?

DIANA.
Just like—

(DIANA *tries*
it.)

NIKKI.
And rotate
my—
Yup

From inner
elbow to
fingertip?

ANDY.
Nice. And?

MOJDEH.
That's nice. Just
keep doing that

(ANDY *does.*)

MOJDEH.
That's not a
graze

ANDY.
Sorry.

MOJDEH.
And a massage?
I'd like you to
massage my
hand

ANDY.
How's that for
pressure?

MOJDEH.
I can take harder

ANDY.
Ok, that?

MOJDEH.
Yeah

EGGO.
Nevermind

KARA.
I'm in.

(*She breathes
on his
palms.*)

EGGO.
That's good

....

Warm

...

**Can you lick
my forearm?**

KARA.
...

EGGO.
Nevermind.

KARA.
No it's ok, I'm
just thinking

(DIANA
rotates
NIKKI*'s
wrists.*)

DIANA.
**Your hands
are real soft—**

(NIKKI *closes
her eyes.*)

NIKKI.
**Do you mind
if I close my
eyes?**

DIANA.
No sweat.
(DIANA *rolls
out* NIKKI*'s
wrists.*)

NIKKI.
We—we switch?

DIANA.
Can you scratch
my inner arm?
Actually, tickle
my elbow?
Actually just
hold my elbow?

NIKKI.
Like that?

DIANA.
Yeah.

BRANDI. (*To
MOJDEH.*)
Be specific

ANDY.
Harder?

MOJDEH.
Right. Oh.
Right there.

(*She licks his
forearm. She
cough/spits.*)

ANDY.
Knot. You work
too hard.

MOJDEH.
Maybe!

NIKKI.
Sorry—I need
to pee.

(NIKKI
*goes to the
bathroom.*)

KARA.
Garlic.

EGGO.
**That makes
sense.**

KARA.
Anything else?

EGGO.
No, that was
good. Thanks.
**Do you
wanna go? I
can—I follow
directions
very well.**

KARA.
**No—no
thanks.**

BRANDI. What's the issue here?
KARA. We did it
BRANDI. You both went?
EGGO. / No
KARA. Yes
BRANDI. You both need to—need to go
KARA. Yeah, it's not really my thing?
BRANDI. What's not your thing?

KARA. I'm not trying to offend, B.

But this exercise is kinda—not my style.

BRANDI. It's about communicating desire. That's a growth edge for you, Kara.

KARA. Why?

BRANDI. I think you can—

KARA. Brandi, when I'm in bed I don't have to fucking talk.

BRANDI. Using your voice can be scary

KARA. If Todd was like, "How do you want to feel?"

I'd be like: 1) gross. 2) Are you a woman? 3) I don't know

BRANDI. You don't know, huh

KARA. Huh

BRANDI. Maybe that's because you're not in touch with your desire

KARA. I am so in touch with my desire

BRANDI. Are you

KARA. Are you?

BRANDI. I'm—I'm getting there

KARA. Maybe I desire to be told what to do

Maybe I desire to be useful

Maybe I desire to be used

Maybe I desire to be the object of HIS desire

Maybe that is what I desire

BRANDI. Honey, that's the conditioning of the patriarchy

KARA. It's what I like

/ It's what gets me off

BRANDI. Here's an opportunity for you to feel your own cells, your own—

KARA. I want a man who just takes me

Uses me

Tosses me on a bed

Makes me a little animal

I don't want to think

I don't want to talk

        (NIKKI *comes back from the bathroom.*)

I just wanna get totally fucked

Like totally fucked

Till I have no idea what's going on

Till I'm just holes

I'm just holes

Getting fucked

When I'm fucking I wanna get fucked, sorry!

BRANDI. I need to apologize for Kara

KARA. No you don't

BRANDI. I think it's important

I think it's important to understand the context of Kara's sort of—

KARA. The context? I'm not saying anything new

BRANDI. Kara is it ok if I—?

KARA. I'm saying what I honestly like

Isn't that your point

BRANDI. It sounds like abuse

It sounds like violence, not sex

KARA. Because those things are sooooo different

BRANDI. It sounds like what happened to Susannah.

    (*Beat.*)

KARA. It's nothing like what happened to Susannah.

BRANDI. Well...

KARA. You asked how I like it, that's how I like it

BRANDI. Maybe you can interrogate why you like that

KARA. Maybe you can interrogate why it scares you

    (DIANA *laughs.*

    KARA *exits, clearing the chalkboard out of the room.*)

BRANDI. (*To* DIANA.) You wanna add something?

DIANA. Um. I think Kara has a point.

MOJDEH. D. Sh.

BRANDI. Do you?

DIANA. Sometimes I don't know what I want, you know?

So answering is like: ??

Like I'm not sure if I want to but I kind of could want to?

EGGO. This is where I get confused.

DIANA. I'm at a 40% yes but if he's at an 80 then I convert to 60 plus.

Or I start at 30, get to a 50 and I'm like, yeah, that was fine.

EGGO. This is why it's better to not fuck anyone.

You can't fuck anyone anymore.

ANDY. Eggo's an incel.

EGGO. I'm not an incel, asshole.

MOJDEH. What's an incel

ANDY. Involuntary Celibate.

He doesn't have sex

EGGO. I totally have sex.

And half the women are like: hit me, baby, please hit me

And I'm like, oooh are you sure? Can I get you asking on tape? On a contract?

They're like: shutup—just do it—stop thinking

Well, I gotta think, ok? Cuz my bros who don't—well—

I'm not trying to be a douchebag here

I am only speaking for myself. I want that to be clear.

I can go to the gym and like bite off your thong or whatever it is you want me to do. But I'm not gonna read your fucking mind. I can't read your fucking mind. Girls want you to read their fucking minds and then be everything to them. If you're flirting with me, if you come up to me at a bar and press your tits on me, I'm assuming you want to fuck, sorry!

BRANDI. Well, you shouldn't

EGGO. Is that problematic? Is that the wrong thing to say? To think?

Cuz from my vantage point, pressing tits equals desire to do *something*. And then girls are like "ha ha ha didn't mean it"; Well, what did you mean?

BRANDI. They're just flirting

EGGO. Don't flirt like that! My last kind of girlfriend, fuck if I know, she was like: "I'm a virgin" which was NOT TRUE and she asked me to fuck her gently which I did like a gentleman, then she broke up with me cuz I couldn't satisfy her and it's like BITCH if you want me to SATISFY you then tell me what you want.

BRANDI. Tell me what you want, see?

EGGO. And she says, you look like the kind of man who can't satisfy me.

I was like, how, how do I look like that?

And she goes, you know what I mean

Bitch, I don't know what you mean, if I knew what you meant I wouldn't ask

—"Don't make me say it"

—I'm making you say it

—Don't make me say it

—I'm making you say it

—You're so soft and sweet and cuddly. I can't imagine you fucking me the way I want to be fucked.

Turns out she'd been fucking Justin

KARA. Ugh Justin

EGGO. Said the sex always felt like a surprise

Loved how it was a surprise

Now riddle me this: what's the difference between sex that is a SURPRISE and assault?

Cuz I don't want to be a surprise that winds up in jail.

BRANDI. First of all Eggo, I'm so sorry for your loss.

EGGO. She's a bitch

BRANDI. Can you use a different word?

EGGO. No.

BRANDI. That experience sounds really painful

ANDY. (*Just to* BRANDI.) Don't bother—

BRANDI. What?

ANDY. He's always [going on and on and on] about Tasha.

Just let him go

EGGO. You wanna say something?

ANDY. Nah

EGGO. Legit, it seems you wanna say something, you can say something.

ANDY. Nah.

EGGO. Do it

ANDY. Nah

EGGO. Do it

ANDY. Fine. If you fuck a woman well enough, she won't complain. She won't leave you. I don't think you should whine, that's all.

EGGO. WOW—

BRANDI. Can you break that down for us, Andy?

ANDY. Sure. Ok. So, here's my theory: sex is the shadow world, ok? All the stuff we can't put or be in the world gets to come out and play—fuckin Gladiator shit. You can be anything. You are limitless. You are beyond thought. If sex is too clean, too polite, too planned—it kinda defeats the purpose.

KARA. I know what you mean

ANDY. Yeah?

KARA. Sometimes you can't really explain the things you want.

DIANA. That's true.

ANDY. Yeah?

KARA. When I was little I used to spray Mr. Clean into my vagina

EGGO. The bald guy?

KARA. I'd sneak into the bathroom and talk to him and just like, hold him and spray him inside me

MOJDEH. Didn't that hurt?

KARA. YEAH.

ANDY. Yeah

KARA. Haha—yeah

BRANDI. How old were you?

KARA. Four, five years old?

BRANDI. Did someone tell you to do that?

KARA. No. I liked it, ok?

BRANDI. / That's not the right developmental stage for—

ANDY. I'd make my sister's Barbies scissor

DIANA. Everyone does that

MOJDEH. I decapitated them

DIANA. I'd sneak into my brother's room and grab his G.I. Joes

ANDY. Ay-o!

DIANA. And lay on the floor.

ANDY. Uh huh!

DIANA. And put them on his bed, sort of towering over me like watchmen and imagine they were spitting all over me.

MOJDEH. Spitting?

ANDY. Like [spitting]?

KARA. Drenched.

DIANA. YEAH.

BRANDI. This is a little much, Kara

KARA. Is it?

BRANDI. This feels like it's coming from a trauma space, / which is—

KARA. Sorry, wanna go back to elbow to fingertip?

BRANDI. Actually yes, we can learn a lot from subtlety.

KARA. And we can pretend that means anything? That that's applicable at fucking all?

BRANDI. It's just an exercise to get you listening to each other's bodies. / It really works!

KARA. Might as well just do a crossword puzzle. Sudoku.

BRANDI. Honey, you ok?

KARA. Pretty amazing, actually

ANDY. I am so into consensual whatever

And I mean *whatever*

KARA. Yeah?

ANDY. Real pleasure can be terrifying

KARA. That's what makes it good.

EGGO. See, he can pull off that George of the Jungle shit. I try that? Tasha's like "thanks for trying."

ANDY. You gotta make sure you're with a girl who's down for that.

DIANA. I bet you could pull that off?

BRANDI. Down for that—so you mean consent!

EGGO. Yeah?

DIANA. Totally

ANDY. Exactly.

BRANDI. / You mean consent.

ANDY. Then it's aces.

BRANDI. I think we're saying the same thing.

KARA. Sex makes Brandi nervous.

BRANDI. Sex makes everyone nervous.

> (DIANA *shrugs*. ANDY *catches this, smiles at her.*)

Anyway.

Did this feel helpful?

ANDY. Absolutely, I'm having a great time

KARA. (*Just to* ANDY.) Me too

> (EGGO *gestures "time."*)

BRANDI. / Obviously there's lots more to learn

EGGO. Yo, Andy, we gots to go PREP

ANDY. Oh shit / yeah.

BRANDI. This is just the tip of the…iceberg.

ANDY. Yeah. Sorry to be rude, ladies, but gonna jet—we're having a party tomorrow—

BRANDI. A party?

ANDY. I'm on cleanup crew and Eggo's

EGGO. I'm the DJ

DIANA. Cool

MOJDEH. What's the theme?

ANDY. Decidedly retrograde, brace yourself.

"Workout Bros and Yoga Hos."

I lobbied to get it changed, or at least the language changed, but I'm not on events.

Bright side: outfits should be easy, amirite?

BRANDI. I can't believe you're hosting already.

ANDY. The assault didn't happen on our grounds, so.

Tom and Spencer banned, obviously…

DIANA. Aren't they in jail?

BRANDI. Detained.

KARA. For now.

ANDY. I mean, it's awful. It's really staggering. I'm so glad you're doing this. I'm sad we need to. But so glad we're here.

> (*Beat.*)

Great workshop, Brandi.

Same time tomorrow?

BRANDI. Yep.

ANDY. Dope. You should come by, if you want.

> (BRANDI *smiles weakly.*
>
> *He and* EGGO *exit.*
>
> BRANDI *approaches* KARA.)

BRANDI. So this is a class, not a bar

KARA. Sorry I didn't play your game right.

DIANA. It's hump day! Where you meeting James Preston?

MOJDEH. I'm freaking out

Can I show you my dress?

DIANA. Fuck yeah.

MOJDEH. Right now?

DIANA. Yeah.

> (MOJDEH *exits.* NIKKI *packs up.*)

BRANDI. Are you aware one of our sisters is in the hospital right now?

KARA. Well aware. /

Did I take her or did you?

BRANDI. Are you taking any of this seriously?

KARA. Yeah, I think so.

> (*She performatively checks in with herself.*)

I *feel* serious, but I don't feel guilty. Do you?

BRANDI. Why would I?

KARA. I dunno. Do you?

BRANDI. About what?

KARA. If she was my little, I don't know…

I'd just—I never let my little out of my sight.

BRANDI. She asked me to leave her.

KARA. Let her go with them…

BRANDI. She *asked* me to leave her.

KARA. Strength in—

BRANDI. SHE ASKED ME TO LEAVE HER ALONE.

KARA. And you listened. Ooof.

BRANDI. You were still there.

KARA. I didn't know she was on my watch.

You coulda told me.

At some point, I got this gut feeling, thank God. Who knows how long she woulda lain there.

BRANDI. (*As in: if you're gonna blame me, just say it.*) What? *What?*

KARA. Yeah, I don't know. Nothing.

Nevermind B.

(*Beat.*)

Don't blame yourself.

BRANDI. I don't blame myself.

KARA. Good.

BRANDI. I don't

KARA. I think it's healthy.

It's healthier your way.

BRANDI. Ok.

KARA. Honest.

BRANDI. Yeah.

KARA. You could drive yourself insane.

(KARA *unplugs her phone from the sound system.*)

BRANDI. Will I see you later?

KARA. Maybe. Text me.

(*A very long silence.* BRANDI *tries to recover.* NIKKI *looks for her phone.* BRANDI *checks her phone on the PA system. For a moment,* BRANDI *starts to tear up.*)

NIKKI. Are you crying?

BRANDI. No

NIKKI. What are you doing?

BRANDI. No

NIKKI. Are you ok?

BRANDI. Yeah, I'm just.

I'm just—

I'm just being silly

Please, don't look at me. Just for a second—

NIKKI. Ok

BRANDI. Thank you.

      (NIKKI *exits.*)

DIANA. Are you crying?

BRANDI. DON'T LOOK AT ME

DIANA. I'm not looking at you!

      (*Beat.*

      MOJDEH *emerges in a skin-tight dress.*)

MOJDEH. So this is what I was gonna—

DIANA. Mojz! You look—

BRANDI. You look incredible.

MOJDEH. I have a date.

BRANDI. / Oooh laaa.

DIANA. When did you get that dress?

BRANDI. I'm liking how much body you're giving in this outfit

MOJDEH. When I went to the mall

BRANDI. Clavicles AND cleavage.

MOJDEH. Thank you

DIANA. When did you go to the mall?

MOJDEH. Brazilian Tuesday

DIANA. You got a wax?

MOJDEH. Yeah

DIANA. Oh

      (MOJDEH *holds up a bra, pulls her dress down to reveal another.*)

MOJDEH. Which one do you think?

DIANA. They're both—

MOJDEH. What?

DIANA. Kind of—

MOJDEH. What?

DIANA. Nothing.

MOJDEH. Great. Great.

BRANDI. White one. White one is hot.

MOJDEH. Thanks.

DIANA. Can you share your location with me?

MOJDEH. You're so fucking paranoid.

DIANA. That chick is literally in the hospital

I'm not paranoid

MOJDEH. One girl gets raped and suddenly all men are rapists?

DIANA. That's not what I'm saying

MOJDEH. Should I just stay home?

Wait till I'm like, betrothed?

/ Shit I'm gonna be late

(*They pick up their pace. As they're leaving:*)

DIANA. That's not what I'm saying

MOJDEH. It's what you're saying

/ Bye Brandi

BRANDI. Bye

DIANA. Just share your location with me.

MOJDEH. He tries anything I'll Wolverine!

DIANA. I know. I know. Please?

(*And they're gone.* BRANDI *takes a breath, alone.*

She leaves a voicemail for Susannah.)

BRANDI. Hey Susannah. Whenever you get to listen to this. Maybe someone can put it to your ear, or. Maybe we're in the future. Our room feels really empty. There's this—you space. I put Mister Froggerson in there, he's keeping it warm. What am I like six years old? Ok. I'm six years old. Ha. Everyone's thinking about you. Sending you love and light [or…] I'm. Yeah. I'll see you soon. I want to say: there's a part of you no one can touch. That sounds all—I don't know if you need to hear that or maybe I need to hear that?—I'm sorry. I'm bad at voicemails. But I—ha—I leave you my voice. Right. Here.

SCENE THREE

NIKKI, MOJDEH, DIANA, *and* BRANDI *before class.*

MOJDEH. I was like, do you always take showers with girls? He's like: I'm following my intuition.

DIANA. Uh huh

MOJDEH. We're in the shower. Perfect temp. And he looks like an angel. Steam angel. I'm thinking: this is surreal. Is this happening? In the shower? James Freaking Preston.

DIANA. He have a boner?

BRANDI. I hate that word

NIKKI. (*Quietly.*) Boner.

MOJDEH. We weren't doing stuff, we were just talking like, soaping each other. I am staring into his crystal blue eyes.

BRANDI. So sweet.

MOJDEH. (*To* BRANDI.) I kept, you know, checking in with myself like you said. Do I like this? Do I feel comfortable? Do I trust him? Do I want this?

NIKKI. How can you trust someone after six hours?

MOJDEH. I did. Can't explain it. My body just knew his body.

BRANDI. James Preston has a great body.

MOJDEH. I. KNOW. And I was the one touching him and soaping him.

DIANA. And then?

MOJDEH. Then we go to his room.

And he picks me up to put me on the bed

BRANDI. (*Sing-songy.*) Vv bride across the threshold!

MOJDEH. He's strong.

His sheets are this deep purple.

BRANDI. Hot

MOJDEH. And then he checks in with me,

He did the whole nine, like,

…

He did this move with my bra that I can't even explain

Amazing

Then he—

He puts a condom on,

DIANA. Good

MOJDEH. And then um—

NIKKI. What did he do?

MOJDEH. It's more a me thing than a him thing

DIANA. WHAT. HAPPENED.

MOJDEH. Then it doesn't

It doesn't

It doesn't quite

DIANA. WHAT DID HE DO

BRANDI. Fit. It doesn't fit.

MOJDEH. Yeah.

DIANA. Aaaa

NIKKI. Hm

MOJDEH. It doesn't.

He's trying and I'm trying and I want to

I make that clear. With my words.

But it's—is it supposed to be that painful?

DIANA. YES. My first time, my boyfriend literally forgot hymens existed. Just "p"—straight in!

NIKKI. I think I broke mine riding horses?

>   (*They look to* BRANDI.)

BRANDI. Oh.

DIANA. When did you "break your hymen"?

BRANDI. Oh, I don't remember.

DIANA. What?

BRANDI. Yeah, I don't remember.

DIANA. Come on.

BRANDI. It was a while ago

DIANA. How old are you?

BRANDI. 21.

DIANA. So…when did you?

BRANDI. …I don't.

Yeah!

So, it doesn't fit…

MOJDEH. He's being SO NICE about it

BRANDI. (*Aw.*) James.

MOJDEH. But like, it will not go in.

>   (*Faux silly but also totally serious.*)

How do I get it in?!

NIKKI. Practice?

DIANA. Jimmy P could go downtown.

Did he eat you out?

MOJDEH. (*Not answering.*) Uh.

I googled about it and there's actually a medical term. Vagin—vagin—

NIKKI. You have the rest of your life to be a...post-virgin.

MOJDEH. Ha yeah. I gave him a blowjob which was—it was fun.

DIANA. Did he cum?

MOJDEH. Yeah. I swallowed! Woo!

DIANA. Really?

MOJDEH. Yeah.

BRANDI. And you spent the night

MOJDEH. Yeah, I woke up and he had eggs and bacon going which—which I don't, but then he made me toast with cinnamon sugar.

BRANDI. Nice!

MOJDEH. I haven't texted him, cuz I know, three days, right?

BRANDI. Did you friend him?

MOJDEH. Yeah. I mean, I don't want to crowd him, maybe he's with another girl, you know, that's fine—but I would like him to know, I'd like him to know that I had a good time, just so he doesn't have to worry about that.

(BRANDI *is on her phone.*)

DIANA. I'm sure he's fine.

BRANDI. Hey, can someone help me grab the mats today? Kara normally— but it seems she's not coming today—the guy with the key wasn't there when—

NIKKI. Yeah, ok.

BRANDI. Thank you! Be back in a bit.

(BRANDI *and* NIKKI *exit.*)

DIANA. Dude, I think it's good you took your time.

Plenty of time with plenty of James Prestons or whatever.

MOJDEH. He's nice.

DIANA. Nice. Good!

MOJDEH. ...thanks

DIANA. Yeah.

MOJDEH. He felt sorry for me?

And I think he wanted me to go...or do it. Or go. Which makes sense. And in my head I'm like: "I want to do it, I just can't. I literally can't. Fuck you body."

DIANA. Don't worry, it'll happen

MOJDEH. Yeah?

DIANA. In its own time, or whatever. Take your time.

MOJDEH. Fuck you take your time.

You fucked DJ when you were 14

DIANA. Yeah and I'm not sure I really / wanted—

MOJDEH. Do you enjoy it?

DIANA. What?

MOJDEH. Do you get off on telling me your "crazy stories"?

Does that make you feel like, extra [...]?

Like I'm your little sister, your little / baby

DIANA. You ASK to hear them

Mojz, you literally BEG me / to describe every fucking detail to you

MOJDEH. I'm so sick of pretending I know what the hell you're talking about.

DIANA. You watch porn. You know what I'm talking about.

MOJDEH. Not in me. I have no IDEA what anyone is talking about. / I thought it would happen ninth grade, nope, tenth grade, nope, eleven, twelve, nope!

DIANA. You're not missing much.

MOJDEH. Maybe I'm supposed to be a virgin forever. I'm like an incel.

DIANA. No you're not.

MOJDEH. Yeah, I'm—no one really wants to fuck me.

DIANA. Wamp wamp. James Preston wanted to fuck you. The shower? Come on. He wanted to fuck you.

MOJDEH. I showered alone.

He said he likes a girl to be clean

Before he—

DIANA. Oh, Mojz.

MOJDEH. Yeah, so—

DIANA. Wow. I'm sorry.

MOJDEH. It's fine.

DIANA. Why would you lie about that?

MOJDEH. What?

DIANA. Why would you make up some Prince Charming—why would you lie about that?

MOJDEH. Um. I don't know.

DIANA. And the cinnamon sugar...?

      (*Beat. No. No toast.*)

MOJDEH. I was on the spot, I was—I was just—

DIANA. ...

MOJDEH. I froze, whatever.

Are you judging me?

DIANA. It's a little weird.

MOJDEH. What was I supposed to do?

DIANA. I dunno—tell the truth?

MOJDEH. People know him. He's a senior—people know him.

DIANA. So what? James Preston can treat you like garbage cuz he's popular?

MOJDEH. It wasn't a big deal—

I know he didn't mean / anything by it.

DIANA. It's ok to tell the truth, Mojdeh.

You don't need to like, protect /

MOJDEH. I know Zeta Chi doesn't matter to you

DIANA. What?

MOJDEH. I know you think the handshakes and rituals are dumb

But I don't.

DIANA. I mean, they're kinda—

MOJDEH. I know you don't give a fuck whether we get in or not

DIANA. We'll get in.

MOJDEH. Not if you don't try. YOU'RE NOT TRYING.

DIANA. I'm being myself.

MOJDEH. Be the nice version of yourself!

DIANA. What does that mean?

MOJDEH. I know you're like WHATEVER about EVERYTHING

Except like guns

DIANA. Hm.

You're tripping over yourself to impress that white girl.

MOJDEH. I'm not.

DIANA. You gonna start straightening your hair again?

MOJDEH. D—

DIANA. Did you bring your calorie journal?

MOJDEH. I don't do that anymore.

DIANA. You know you can't buy your way into being white, right?

MOJDEH. Just because I want a social group and traditions and lots of friends,

I'm suddenly

I'm suddenly

I'm suddenly some kind of racist?

Some kind of brown traitor?

DIANA. Maybe.

> (*Beat.*)

MOJDEH. I just—

I just want to become the best version of myself.

Of *myself.* And I—

I—

I—

I I just want to be the kind of person people want!

DIANA. You are the kind of person people want.

MOJDEH. I just want

to feel what it's like for someone to really

really

really

want to touch me.

> (*Mini beat.*)

and uh uh not because I'm um I'm um um um some girl?

Or like exotic

Or uh like

there,

but because I'm—me.

Specifically me.

Really just—me…[?]

> (DIANA *kisses* MOJDEH. *After a second,* MOJDEH *recoils.*)

MOJDEH. Whoa

DIANA. I'm—

MOJDEH. Whoa—

> (MOJDEH *steps back.* DIANA *starts laughing a little.*)

DIANA. Hey

I'm sorry—

I thought you were

[nevermind]

Dude, read that wrong, sorry.

MOJDEH. Mmm

DIANA. You were like—leaning

And—

Rewind, please, haha

MOJDEH. Cool.

>   (MOJDEH *fumbles with her water.*)

DIANA. What are you thinking?

>   (*Beat.*)

MOJDEH. I don't need you to like, pity kiss me, or—

DIANA. Oh, Mojz I—

MOJDEH. That's not gonna make me feel better

DIANA. No that's not—

MOJDEH. And I'm not fucking gay. I'm not.

What?

"I'm Diana, I kiss everyone, might as well just throw a bone to my loser / friend—"

DIANA. That's not what I was thinking

MOJDEH. What were you thinking?

DIANA. That you—that you—wanted to?

MOJDEH. I DON'T WANT TO.

DIANA. Ok!

I think you're making this a big deal.

MOJDEH. Do you have to fuck everything you see?

DIANA. I I—don't

MOJDEH. Oh my god thank you so much for showering me in your sexual attention, Diana.

DIANA. Come on Mojz.

MOJDEH. I I'm not even into girls.

And if I was, I wouldn't be into you.

>   (*Beat.*)

DIANA. Ok.

MOJDEH. No offense.

DIANA. That's fine.

>   (*Beat.*)

MOJDEH. Anyway, it's really not a big deal.

DIANA. We cool?

MOJDEH. Yup.

>   (DIANA *picks on her skin, silently. She goes to show* MOJDEH, *changes her mind.*

A long moment of sharing the space before:

BRANDI *and* NIKKI *enter carrying gymnastic mats.*)

BRANDI. Did it! Strong women! What?!

(BRANDI *high-fives* NIKKI. *They lay down the mats.* MOJDEH *goes to get a drink of water.* DIANA *goes in the opposite direction to stretch. A painful silence.* NIKKI *notices.*)

NIKKI. Huh.

SCENE FOUR

ANDY *and* EGGO *at the gym before the workshop, getting a pump.*

ANDY. My dad said it's important to show remorse but not guilt. Like "I'm sorry I made you feel that way" is different than "I'm sorry for x." Legally.

EGGO. Hm.

(*Beat.*)

ANDY. Did you see the video?

EGGO. Am I an evil fucker if I say yes?

ANDY. Yes

EGGO. Then no.

ANDY. It was online for like an hour.

EGGO. I was up.

ANDY. Doing what?

EGGO. Doing me.

ANDY. Ok. And what's on it?

EGGO. You watched it.

ANDY. Nah

EGGO. You watched it.

ANDY. I didn't.

EGGO. Really?

ANDY. What's on it?

EGGO. It's barely lit and like 15 seconds long.

ANDY. Uh huh and what can you see?

EGGO. Honestly? Hardly anything.

ANDY. Any bodies?

EGGO. It's barely lit. You can see like their legs. Like you can tell people are fucking, but nothing graphic.

ANDY. Ok

EGGO. Spencer and Tom are fucking sociopaths. I heard her jaw's broken.

ANDY. Bruised, not broken—

EGGO. Ah, ok. Good. Who told you?

ANDY. Kara, the girl with the—

EGGO. Yeah. She licked my arm.

ANDY. Cool.

(*Beat.*)

EGGO. Are you ok man?

ANDY. How does the video end?

EGGO. Oh, it just cuts out. It gets bright for a second then it cuts out.

ANDY. Cool.

EGGO. I had a mad thing for Susannah last year. Before me and Tasha—god, she's one of those girls you wanna be with cuz they're nice. You know? Like she is so actually nice. Karma, man. I don't know.

ANDY. If I tell you something, do you think you can just like—

EGGO. What?

ANDY. Nevermind. I'm sorta trippin' balls about all of this.

EGGO. You care man. You care. That's a good thing. That can go in the Man Box.

ANDY. I think I—I was dancing with Vanessa Lee

EGGO. Oh shit Vanessa Lee!

ANDY. I know. And I went upstairs to just like, take a piss and brush my teeth.

EGGO. With their toothbrushes? That's

ANDY. Nah, man. Like finger in my mouth.

EGGO. Respect.

ANDY. And I open the door, and I see people fucking. So I close the door. I'm not sure, but I'm pretty sure it was—

EGGO. Tom and Spencer and

ANDY. Susannah

EGGO. What—what did you see?

ANDY. It was like five seconds.

EGGO. Five seconds is a long time, what did you see?

ANDY. Nothing. I mean, I was pretty fucked up

EGGO. Uh huh

ANDY. I was just like: this is not the bathroom.

EGGO. Uh huh

ANDY. And then I found the bathroom.

EGGO. Ok

ANDY. They weren't hitting her or anything—

EGGO. What were they doing?

ANDY. I don't remember

EGGO. Like what position?

ANDY. Doggie.

EGGO. Ok

ANDY. And Spencer is jacking off near her face. Which is Totally a thing girls have asked me to do.

EGGO. Uh huh

ANDY. Yeah

EGGO. No, that's cool, I'm sure that was hard to see.

ANDY. No, it wasn't hard to see, that's the point. I didn't like, know, what I was looking at. I got a little hard.

EGGO. Really?

ANDY. I dunno man.

EGGO. Damn.

ANDY. Yeah but now, I'm like, fuck, like, do I, do I tell someone? Do I? Did she see me? Her eyes were closed but

EGGO. Her eyes were closed?

ANDY. People close their eyes all the time during sex, ok? Ok? That's not like an emergency, ok?

EGGO. So then what?

ANDY. I went to the bathroom and brushed my teeth and found Vanessa Lee and went to her place.

EGGO. You gonna tell someone?

ANDY. I'm telling you. You gonna tell someone?

(*Beat.*)

EGGO. Nah man, what's the point?

ANDY. Thanks, bro. I guess.

(*Long beat.*)

EGGO. How long do you think they'll get? In jail.

ANDY. Shit, I don't know.

EGGO. How long do rapists normally get?

ANDY. I think it depends.

EGGO. Yeah, it depends.

>(*Beat.*)

I was talking to my sister and she said rapists should get the same as someone who beats someone up enough to give them a permanent disability.

>(*Beat.*)

Susannah was like the first girl to say hi to me. When I got here.

ANDY. Ok

EGGO. It's not relevant but—yeah.

>(KARA *walks in in sunglasses, hungover.*)

KARA. Whattup bitches.

ANDY. Yo

EGGO. Hey

>(KARA *drops her bag. She pulls out a water bottle and drinks. She laughs at the boys. Beat.*)

You're good at moving.

KARA. Excuse me?

EGGO. I saw you um dancing at um the party last night?

And you're good at...it.

KARA. Haha. Yeah, ok, yeah thanks.

EGGO. I wasn't like staring at you, I just noticed you.

KARA. That music was lit. I was like aaaaa/aaaaa

EGGO. (*About to take credit for the music.*) Oh. Yeah. That. Um. I—

KARA. And that Faderade?

ANDY. INSANE.

KARA. INSANE! When I woke up I thought I was actually dead.

ANDY. Dead dead dying dead.

KARA. Thank God for / coconut water

ANDY. Oh my god I love coconut water

KARA. But you gotta get the pure shit

ANDY. Duh

KARA. Like seven dollars a bottle but—

ANDY. Totally worth it

EGGO. My dad used to be a big partier—back in his day.

He turned me on to Alka-Seltzer.

KARA. Hm.

EGGO. He was like "Eggo, the seltz
can bring you back to life"

KARA. Cool.

I'm like that's bullshit Dad. That's
bullshit.
Then freshman year I'm at this rager
People getting CRAZY

ANDY. Kara, heads up.

**It was the night I did my first
kegstand
Which I'm pretty good at,
actually.**

(ANDY *tosses* KARA *a coconut
water.*)

I wake up the next morning
Destroyed.
And coconut water won't do shit
And I'm like OK Dad, let's try it.

ANDY. I had a good time.

I drag my ass to Rite Aid

And buy some Alka-Seltzer

KARA. Oh yeah, cool. Cool. Me
too.

And yeah. Yeah. It is amazing.
Settles your stomach. And makes
this cool sound.
      (EGGO *makes a fizzing noise.*)

ANDY. Eggo's right about one thing,
you are good at dancing.
KARA. Heh. Thanks.

You can get a hundred for like five
bucks.
That's a lot of—wild nights.
Anyway, it's an option.

I ran home.
Literally, I ran all the way home
And then ate tortilla chips
till I passed out.

      (BRANDI *enters with a bouquet of
      flowers.*)
BRANDI. Kara.
Kara!

      (KARA *looks at* BRANDI.)

BRANDI. Thanks for joining us.

KARA. You bring me flowers?

BRANDI. They're for Susannah. Let's jump right in.
Starting with wrist escapes.

>(NIKKI *enters*. DIANA *enters*.)

So pair up.

>(DIANA *pairs with* ANDY. NIKKI *pairs with* EGGO. KARA *is like "I'll watch."*)

BRANDI.
Really, Kara?

ANDY. Hello!

EGGO. Hey—

KARA. I'm
watching.

DIANA. What?

NIKKI. Hi

ANDY. Pair?

EGGO. How
are you?

DIANA. Sure

NIKKI.
Chillin. You?

BRANDI. So!
Someone is
grabbing your
wrist.

EGGO. I'm
fine.

DIANA. Ladies
first.
>(DIANA
grabs ANDY's
wrist.)

EGGO. You
wanna?
>(NIKKI *grabs*
EGGO's
wrist.)

ANDY. Heh
heh okay.
>(*He escapes.*)

BRANDI. Find
their weakest
point of
contact. Where
is it?

NIKKI. Um

DIANA. Nah,
let's go again.
>(*He escapes.*)

Again.

>(EGGO *taps*
the space
between
thumb and
forefinger

on NIKKI's hand.)

EGGO. Here?

NIKKI. Yup. So you'd—

EGGO. Sorta rotate.

NIKKI. Your hands are big.

EGGO. Sorry.

NIKKI. No, mine are just. (*They compare hands.*)

NIKKI. You wanna go?

EGGO. You can go tighter.

(*He flips! He's out. NIKKI's turn.*)

EGGO. Is that good?

NIKKI. I could take more pressure. Ok, roll toward... and—
(*She gets out.*)

(*She really holds on. He escapes.*)

DIANA. Yeah, whatever, (*To* MOJDEH.) **Hey!**

(*To* ANDY.) Ok your turn.

(*She offers her wrist.* ANDY *holds* DIANA's *hand. She escapes, effortlessly.*)

DIANA. Don't take it easy on me

ANDY. Alright. (ANDY *holds* DIANA's *wrist. She can't get out. It's really pissing her off. She pulls her arm toward her.* BRANDI *joins them.*)

DIANA. Yup.

Ok.

(*She gets out.*)

(MOJDEH *enters.*)

(*She head bumps* DIANA *in response.*)

(*She goes to* KARA.)

MOJDEH. What are we doing?

KARA. I wasn't really listening Something about the thumb

MOJDEH. Do you want to practice— (*Maybe they try one and* KARA *is like, oh no, that'll make me vomit.*)

KARA. Yeah, uh, I'm uh [I'm observing.]

BRANDI. YES! Thumb, right? Twist your wrist—**Mojdeh! work with Kara!**—toward the weak spot and flip your way out of it. Good! Good.

Slow at first. Switch.

BRANDI. (*To* DIANA *and* ANDY.) **Gut instinct says to pull away from your attacker but NO. Muscle memory**. You *roll* toward your target. You take the path of least resistance.

(*Re:* DIANA *getting out.*)
YES.

NIKKI. Nice! Another time?

EGGO. Cool.

(*She gets out again.*)

NIKKI. You're honestly not taking it easy on me?

EGGO. Honestly.

NIKKI. Please don't—

EGGO. I'm not.

DIANA. Okay technique!! Again!

(*She escapes again.*
They repeat.
They switch.)

DIANA. I think we nailed it. Wanna try a choke hold?

ANDY. We haven't learned that yet.

DIANA. I know how to choke you.

ANDY. Oh do you?

(DIANA *shrugs like: yes.*)

(MOJDEH *practices alone.*)

BRANDI. Great! Great, we got that? YES.

BRANDI. OK who would like to learn about getting trapped?

(*Beat.*)

And getting out of being trapped when someone is on top of you?

(NIKKI *raises her hand.* DIANA *raises her hand.* KARA *is like, yeah I guess I'll raise my hand.* MOJDEH *checks in with* ANDY. *Raises her hand. Smiles.*)

Awesome. Can I get a hand?

EGGO. Oh! Yes!

NIKKI. Yup

(*They grab a mat together.*)

EGGO. I don't really need help but—

(DIANA *and* MOJDEH *go to the same mat. They look at each other.*)

DIANA. (Hey)

(ANDY *waits for his mat.*)

MOJDEH. Hi…   **ANDY.** I

NIKKI. Uh—   *(They set*   gotchu.
yeah. Me neither.   *up the mat.*   *(ANDY grabs*
                        DIANA *walks*   *his mat, sets*   **BRANDI.**
(They smile,   *to* MOJDEH.   *it up alone.)*   Thanks, thanks
they set up   MOJDEH   team!
their mat.)   *walks away.)*

BRANDI. Ok first I'll demo alone.

You're lying down. Mmmhmmm. And someone is on top of you and
Number one, you buck your hips. You destabilize their center.

(She does. The others mimic her from standing and sitting.)

And then you capture their torso. Right away.

And then you break their hold. Schwoop.

And you roll toward their arm.

(She's now on her hands and knees.)

Now they're the victim.

Make sense? It'll make sense.

Ok. Try that alone.

(They do. KARA sits it out.)

Good. Good.

Buck. Capture. Break. Roll.

Ok, good. Yeah, you have to use your hips. Kaykay, are you?

KARA. I'm sick

BRANDI. Alright.

Who wants to demo with me? Andy, do you want to? If you're cool with—

ANDY. Sure B

BRANDI. Ok great, so I'm gonna lie down again.

(She does.)

Maybe I'm asleep or—

Yeah.

And Andy, you can come over here and just straddle, over my over my hips
like you're—

(He does.)

Yeah that's it.

Yeah.

Um.

(BRANDI*'s breath catches.)*

Actually you know what?

>   (BRANDI *taps* ANDY*'s thighs twice.*)

I can explain this better if someone else is doing it.

Up?

Thanks. Thank you, Andy.

Does anyone—can I have a volunteer to be in the subm—the bottom position?

>   (BRANDI *looks around.* NIKKI*'s hand shoots up.* NIKKI *looks at her hand, surprised by herself.*)

NIKKI. I'll do it.

BRANDI. Oh! Nikki! Okay!

>   (NIKKI *lies down.*)

ANDY. Is it ok if I—?

NIKKI. Yeah. Yeah.

>   (ANDY *straddles* NIKKI.)

BRANDI. So let's review the form

Buck, Capture—

>   (*Before* BRANDI *can finish,* NIKKI *bucks* ANDY. *He flies forward. The others are impressed. She captures his arms. She bucks him again. She rolls. It all happens in a split second. The others applaud.*)

Wow.

MOJDEH. Whoa

EGGO. Whoa

NIKKI. Wow

ANDY. Wow

NIKKI. That was.

Fuck yeah!

ANDY. You're strong

NIKKI. Aaaaa

BRANDI. That was wonderful!!!

>   (*Beat.*)

Eggo, Diana, you can practice together, Mojdeh, Andy. Get in position. And start slowly. Really feel the mechanics. Buck, Capture, Break, Roll.

EGGO. Can I?	**MOJDEH.** I can be
DIANA. Yeah	the attacker this time.
	If you want to like
DIANA. And Buck	**ANDY.** Sure.
EGGO. Cool	I'm gonna buck.

DIANA. And big hug

EGGO. Ha

DIANA. And then
break your arm

EGGO. Yeah, please
don't

DIANA. Ooh! Pa-pow.
Now I'm the aggressor

EGGO. Ok, I'm gonna
buck you now

DIANA. Yo, I know
what you're gonna—

EGGO. Yeah, but
Just like—
overcommunication is
better than—

DIANA. Sure

EGGO. Buck, Capture,
Break

(DIANA *starts
laughing.*)

EGGO. What?

DIANA. Nothing,
you're great.

EGGO. And I'm gonna
roll toward you

DIANA. Bam!

(*They high five.*)

MOJDEH. Ha—no,
go on.

ANDY. In, arm grab,
and roll.

MOJDEH.
My turn!
So I—like, buck

Thanks
And then I

Like a hug!

ANDY. Go for it

MOJDEH. Ka-pow

Roll!

Can I try one more
time?

ANDY. I am here for
you.

MOJDEH. Why thank
you. Hips.
Hug.
Ka-pow.
Roll!

BRANDI. Hips

Yes capture

And then the arm grip

And roll

That was great.

EGGO. How was that?   **ANDY.** That was
                                        good!

DIANA. Perfecto.

BRANDI. That's it for today. Really great, everyone.

(*The rest of the class starts to pack up. Except* KARA *who's lying on her back.* MOJDEH *is on top of* ANDY.)

MOJDEH. Wait, hold up.

ANDY. You ok? Did I hurt you?

MOJDEH. Yeah, just be still

ANDY. Ok...

(MOJDEH *swipes an eyelash from* ANDY's *face. She holds it in front of him.*)

MOJDEH. Make a wish.

(ANDY *concentrates, blows.*)

What'd you wish for?

ANDY. World peace.

MOJDEH. World peace. What'd you really wish for?

ANDY. Um. I can't tell you.

MOJDEH. Ok.

(*Jokey.*)

How was that for you?

ANDY. Kinda weird

MOJDEH. Oh, I'm sorry—

ANDY. Not you—the whole, the whole class feels kinda—nevermind!

MOJDEH. What?

ANDY. Like, you're learning to protect yourself from—from guys who look like me.

MOJDEH. (*Flirty.*) I'm not protecting myself from guys who look like you.

ANDY. Ha. Yeah. Sorry, it's basically nothing, compared to what you women ...go through.

MOJDEH. Right.

(*Beat.*)

ANDY. I have no idea what it's like to be inside your body.

MOJDEH. I mean—same.

(*Beat.*)

I'd want a blowjob.

ANDY. What?

MOJDEH. If I was in your body, I'd want a blowjob.

> (*She makes her body into his body.*)

ANDY. Ha. I'd want someone to pick me up. And like hold me, hold me against a wall and like—take me. Ravish me?

MOJDEH. Same.

ANDY. Or like dance, I wanna know what it feels like to dance in a body like yours.

> (MOJDEH *smiles.*)

Do you want to be friends on some form of?

MOJDEH. I'm on all the platforms.

ANDY. Cool.

MOJDEH. Ebrahimi like Abraham with an E and then two Is.

> (ANDY *whips out his cell phone.*)

DIANA. Hey Mojz—

MOJDEH. Hi

DIANA. Can we talk?

MOJDEH. Sure!

DIANA. Like…[alone]

> (MOJDEH *doesn't move.*)

Ok

MOJDEH. What's up?

DIANA. Do you want a ride home?

I'm thinking of going to Sprinkles for a—

ANDY. (*Re: his phone.*) I think I found you.

DIANA. Cupcake.

MOJDEH. (*Glancing at his phone.*) That's me!

No, I'm good D.

> (*Beat.*)

DIANA. Ya sure?

> (MOJDEH *nods.*)

Are you gonna walk—or?

BRANDI. Oh wait! Before we leave, can we all gather for a photo please? For Susannah? Like on the mat would be good. Maybe punching? Yeah, yeah, all of you if you're willing? Okay, looking good.

> (*They pose for a photo.* DIANA *is off to the side.* MOJDEH *and* ANDY *are together.*)

And now a positive one like "get well soon!"

(They try to show that.)

And we're fierce.

> *(DIANA drifts off. She goes to get boxing gloves.)*

Great.

And one with me.

> *(They take a selfie.)*

Thank you, that's gonna be really great. Thank you.

ANDY. Do you want a ride?

MOJDEH. I live on Laurel is that on your way?

ANDY. It can be on my way.

MOJDEH. Ok—ok!

DIANA. *(Half heard.)* Bye—

> *(MOJDEH and ANDY exit together. DIANA waves at her. She doesn't know what to do with her body. She punches the wall throughout the following:)*

BRANDI. Honey, can we check in?

KARA. Check it in

BRANDI. Are you alright?

KARA. Is anyone alright?

BRANDI. Ok. Philosopher over here.

KARA. I'm not a philosoph—I'm not a

> *(BRANDI smells KARA's breath. She grabs KARA's bottle.)*

BRANDI. Are you serious?

KARA. Orange juice. *(Sing-song.)* Tropicana.

BRANDI. Go home

KARA. Hospital. I'm ready for the hospital.

I brought a card for Susannah

BRANDI. I'll tell her you say hello

KARA. What the fuck Brandi?

BRANDI. You're a mess

KARA. Brandi I'm fine. / See? I'm fine. Hello my name is Kara I can walk in a straight line

BRANDI. She needs stability right now

I think you would do more harm than good.

KARA. Susannah you look good I love you see I'm fine.

BRANDI. Next time.

KARA. This is our window. This is, This is.

This is our window.

> (KARA *grabs onto* BRANDI*'s wrist.* BRANDI *deflects her, violently.*)

KARA. B!

BRANDI. Muscle memory.

I'll say hi

Fuck I really need to go

What were you thinking? You're such a *mess.*

I'll check on you tonight or something.

> (BRANDI *exits.*)

KARA. You're a mess.

You're the fuckin' mess!

I'm not a mess

She's like—

Afraid of the entire fuckin' world

Scared little bitch

DIANA. Hey she's your friend

KARA. You don't know me

Who the fuck are you—

DIANA. / I don't.

KARA. Susannah! Susannah is my friend!

Brandi's a Barbie

Got a plastic vagina

Nothing's going in there

> (KARA *puts on boxing gloves.*)

I bet in bed she's like

Be gentle be gentle be gentle

I'm like break me break me break me

Would you fuck Spencer?

DIANA. Spencer who raped Susannah?

KARA. (*Banging her fists together, rhythmically.*) 1 2 3

DIANA. No. / What?

KARA. (*Banging her fists together, rhythmically.*) 1 2 3

DIANA. Why?

KARA. Fight me bitch

DIANA. No thanks.

KARA. Fight me

DIANA. No

KARA. You don't even need to use gloves

> (*She flings off the gloves.*)

We can go skin to skin.

DIANA. Crazy bitch

KARA. You wanna go fight club? GO FIGHT CLUB. DO IT. DO IT. HIT ME. HIT ME!

Or do you only like it when your little girlfriend hits you?

> (DIANA *socks* KARA.
>
> KARA *stumbles back.* DIANA *goes to get her stuff to leave.* KARA *drags her onto the mats.* KARA *goes to strike her. They wrestle. They roll.* DIANA *bucks* KARA *off of her.* DIANA *gets up. She yells at* KARA. KARA *pushes* DIANA. DIANA *pushes* KARA. *They lock horns. They yell. They yell. They yell.* DIANA *pushes* KARA.)

KARA. Hit me.

> (DIANA *pushes* KARA.)

KARA. I wanna feel it. Hit me.

> (DIANA *pushes* KARA.)

KARA. Hit me.

> (DIANA *pushes* KARA *with both hands.*)

KARA. I wanna feel it.

> (DIANA *punches* KARA *in the face.*
>
> *She goes down.*
>
> DIANA *sits down, exhausted.*)

KARA. I asked Spencer to fuck me till I bled
And then he actually did.
I told Susannah that Spencer was good in bed
I said, He's crazy. I don't mind sharing
I don't mind sharing
And then he—

DIANA. Yeah.

KARA. Maybe I knew

DIANA. No

KARA. Somewhere—
Maybe I—
Did I?

DIANA. No / girl no.

KARA. Did I give him some sorta like, pass?

DIANA. It's not that hard to like, *not* rape someone.

It's not like, actually, that challenging.

KARA. …

DIANA. Right?

KARA. I am so disgusting. I am so disgusting.

(*Beat.*)

DIANA. When I read the article about Spencer and Tom and Susannah…I thought that is deeply fucked up, is she okay and then I—I got the urge to—masturbate.

KARA. Did you?

DIANA. …yeah.

(*Beat. Silence.* KARA *extends her leg to tap* DIANA'*s foot. Beat.*)

KARA. I got a frog card. Susannah's really into frogs. I got this—it said, I know you'll hop out of it.

DIANA. That's fucked up.

KARA. I know

DIANA. That's really fucked up

KARA. I know.

DIANA. Damn.

(*They laugh.*)

SCENE FIVE

A day later. EGGO *is in the gym, dancing by himself. He's childlike, he's in his body. He's really enjoying himself.* DIANA *and* KARA *enter together talking—they watch* EGGO. *He realizes, goes to shut the music off.*

KARA.	**DIANA.**
Hey!	Hey Eggo!

EGGO. 'Sup.

KARA. What is this music?

EGGO. Just a little—

mix.

DIANA. You made this?

(EGGO *shrugs like, yes—the answer is yes, and he's kind of sweating under these compliments.* DIANA *and* KARA *run towards him to give him some love.*)

KARA. Amazing!

EGGO. Thanks.

KARA. D shot a gun this morning.

DIANA. Who cares.

KARA. No, you got yourself to a shooting range and you fuckin' did it.

DIANA. Yeah, I did.

EGGO. What was it like?

DIANA. SO loud.

And it goes up your whole arm.

Like,

> (*She shows it.*)

I'm imagining this guy right?

Like—a specific man

And I

I—

Dead center

And and all this energy rushes through me

Obliterating him

And I liked it

I really fucking liked it

> (*She breathes into this complex feeling of obliteration, joy, power as they watch.*)

DIANA. I'm not gonna like join the NRA

KARA. I'm in the NRA

DIANA. Really?

KARA. No! Come on. I've never shot a gun.

DIANA. You wanna go with me? I think I'm gonna go again next week.

> (EGGO *thinks about it. They all begin to stretch.*)

KARA. I've got all this Rush stuff.

DIANA. Ditch

KARA. If I ditch, I'll get dissociated.

DIANA. What?

KARA. Like—literally that's what it's called when you quit—dissociation.

EGGO. Yup.

DIANA. Kay. You'll be polishing or whatever and I'll

Bam, bam, bam.

Practice for the end of the world.

(BRANDI *enters. She beams—they're there! And they're warming up!*
Class is going well. KARA *notices* BRANDI:)

KARA. How is she?

BRANDI. Susannah?

KARA. Yeah.

BRANDI. She's—she can't quite talk yet / but she wanted

EGGO. Fuck

BRANDI. Me to give you this

(BRANDI *makes a sorority gesture to* KARA.

KARA *repeats it back instinctively.*)

KARA. Really?

BRANDI. Yeah

KARA. To specifically me?

She really [gesture]?

BRANDI. Yeah

KARA. Suz. She could do that?

(BRANDI *nods.*)

BRANDI. And she loved your card.

Her eyes got sparkly.

KARA. Did she laugh?

BRANDI. Kinda.

KARA. Right.

DIANA. (*Touching her jaw.*) Yeah. Ow.

BRANDI. She's stable.

I think she heard all those prayers

EGGO. Cool.

BRANDI. Do you guys wanna—start?

DIANA. Let's do it.

(*They do a physical warm-up. They count ten jump squats. As they
do,* BRANDI *coaches their form.*)

BRANDI. Hips back

Shoulders dropped

And try it without your arms

DIANA. That is harder

KARA. Oh shit

BRANDI. And punches

(*They get in formation to punch.*)

4 right crosses – 4 left crosses – 4 – 4 – 2 – 2 – 2 – 2 – 1 – 1 – 1

And we're just gonna keep switching.

Keep it crisp!

(*As they're doing the punching warm-up,* NIKKI *runs in breathless.*)

Whoa. Hey. You ok?

(*She stops at the door, catches her breath.*)

NIKKI. Uh uh uh uh uh uh

BRANDI. Honey—

KARA. Do you need some water?

NIKKI. I walked just like you said

Head up, eyes alert. Wolverine in my hands.

DIANA. You okay?

NIKKI. And this guy starts following me, and normally I I I do this thing where I hold my breath and try to disappear from the planet and honestly it usually works, I just pull in all my t-tentacles and usually mostly people don't know I'm there, I'm gone, but I decide not to. I decide to like, stay where I am. I've just been to the pool, I swam when I was a kid and I thought— maybe I'll swim again—and I do and I feel I feel I feel so alive alive!

(MOJDEH *and* ANDY *enter, laughing and playing with each other.*)

And I'm like yeah make my day—

BRANDI. Oh

NIKKI. And he starts walking behind me, "Hey Mermaid, hey Mermaid."

I say "I'm late to this class, sorry."

Keep walking.

He says "I can smell your pussy and it smells delicious"

DIANA. Gross

NIKKI. I keep walking, but then I'm like NO, hell no, I'm not afraid of you, I turn around and I say "what you smell is chlorine, ok, fucker?" and he grabs my wrist I do the—I do the wrist escape. I did it. I did it like perfect.

BRANDI. YES!

NIKKI. But his fingers are easily twice the size of mine and he just starts laughing. He's laughing his ass off. I take my free hand and I go to punch him in the face but he catches my hand before I can reach him

and holds that one too and he's dangling me, he's dangling me. And he says

It's funny how scared you are

It's funny how scared you are

It's funny how scared you are

It's funny how scared you are

BRANDI. Oh honey

NIKKI. Shut up

BRANDI. Ok

NIKKI. Don't teach us things that don't work

BRANDI. It works

NIKKI. It doesn't work

BRANDI. If you get the angle just—

NIKKI. It doesn't FUCKING WORK

BRANDI. You did so well last class, with the straddle escape—

NIKKI. And it doesn't FUCKING WORK

BRANDI. Have a water

(BRANDI *hands* NIKKI *a water bottle.* NIKKI *tosses the water on* BRANDI.)

NIKKI. The poster. The poster said: HOW TO DEFEND YOURSELF. I didn't learn how to defend myself. I didn't learn shit.

KARA. Oh my god your wrists.

(NIKKI*'s wrists are bruised.*)

BRANDI. Do you want me to call counseling services?

NIKKI. What? So I can talk about my feelings? Same fucking feelings I have everyday. Not special feelings. Not a special feeling. Not any different from YOUR feelings. I feel like. I feel like. I feel like a body that can be attacked any time. And you know what? I am. I can be attacked at any time.

BRANDI. The grabs can work. They can. If you get the right angle. I didn't teach you clearly enough. Do you guys want to—want to try some more? Do you want to ?

KARA. Do you need an ice pack?

NIKKI. Yeah ok—so I'm gonna go.

I don't really know why I—

I'm gonna

I'm gonna go now.

BRANDI. No, honey

KARA. Do you want someone to walk you?

ANDY. Yeah I can—

EGGO. Or I can

DIANA. We could—

NIKKI. No, no that's ok.

KARA. Where are you going?

NIKKI. Home

KARA. What are you gonna do at home?

NIKKI. Um. Yeah. I'm gonna

I'm probably gonna bake one cookie, I get the pack and I bake one at a time...And I'll probably watch a TV show

KARA. What do you watch?

NIKKI. Like *America's Next Top Model* or *Arrow* or *Shark Tank*. Mostly *Shark Tank*. I watch in bed and balance the cookies on my stomach and think about how I should really be doing homework, or maybe I'll think about you guys.

KARA. That sounds nice

NIKKI. Yeah

BRANDI. You should stay, we're doing choke holds this afternoon.

NIKKI. That's really ok

BRANDI. It's an important hold, if someone's coming up from behind you

NIKKI. Yeah good luck

BRANDI. I really want to teach you.

NIKKI. You can send me a video.

BRANDI. I'm really sorry.

NIKKI. I think what you're doing is—well, I think you're really trying.

BRANDI. I would have shot him.

The man who—

NIKKI. That's ok.

> (NIKKI *arranges her keys in her hand like Wolverine. She grimaces in an almost-smile.* NIKKI *exits. A long long silence.*)

BRANDI. It works

It does

> (MOJDEH *nods politely.* EGGO *exits to follow* NIKKI.)

Yes it does

I've done the form with

With so many men? Of all sizes?

It works.

> (*Beat.*)

That's why you train

You train everyday

You train everyday

Everyday everyday

And your reflexes—yeah?

They get honed

So you don't need to think

You think? you get stuck

You get stuck you get—

       (Maybe a silent scream.)

And

YEAH

It's not one-size-fits all

It's not guaranteed, because

it's it's oooo it's an approximation

It's it's better than nothing?

It's

That's why you get strong

As you can

So

A chance?

A

I don't

I have a tendency to be dramatic

I don't

Your cells actually

And your body actually

Cuz when you repeat the

When you shrink enough

Quiet enough

Quiet enough

Yes enough

Fine enough

Sh enough

When you do it do it do it do it

enough times

enough times

When you do it enough times

You a learn a new

I'm learning a new language

A new normal

You learn a new

A new

A new becomes an old

A new

Anewanewanewanewanewanewanewanewewerahekk[ ]

> *(She begins speaking in gibberish, the gibberish echoes and expands.*

> *A pop song of the moment bursts in, VERY LOUD.*
> NIKKI *and* EGGO *stumble in with Solo cups.*
> *Suddenly,*
> *We're in a HUGE WILD party.*
> BRANDI *keeps speaking in gibberish but we can't hear her anymore under the music. Her mouth keeps moving.*
> *Someone approaches with a red Solo cup and pours a drink down her throat.*
> *She spills all over herself.*
> *Someone throws up.*
> *People grind, play beer pong.*

> *Music shifts—something that was popular four years ago.*
> *We're in a high school party.*
> *Someone's playing spin the bottle.*
> *Someone's getting fingered in the corner.*
> *Someone is telling an amazing story.*
> *The bottle lands,* KARA *and* NIKKI *share a kiss.*
> NIKKI *enjoys herself, joyful.* KARA *is kind of awkward. The bystanders cheer.* KARA *smiles performatively.*

> *A pop song from four years before that.*
> *A middle school party.*
> *Maybe a dance.*
> *They separate by gender.*
> *They are learning their bodies.*
> *They are trying to grow up fast.*

> *A child's song from six years before that.*
> *An elementary party.*
> *There are balloons.*

They play tag.

It's a blast.

A boy lifts up a girl's skirt.

BRANDI *enters holding a cake.*

Beside her is SUSANNAH, *a young child of color.*

We are in the past.

We are at SUSANNAH*'s sixth birthday party.*

We are also in the present.

We are present in the theatre with this young child.

The actor playing BRANDI *hands the actor playing* SUSANNAH *the cake.*)

ALL. *Happy Birthday to you.*

Happy Birthday to you.

Happy Birthday Susannah,

Happy Birthday to you.

(*Beat.*)

DIANA. Susannah!

NIKKI. Susannah!

KARA. Make a wish!

(*The actor playing* SUSANNAH *inhales.*

She closes her eyes.

She is illuminated by candlelight.

She exhales.

Lights go out.)

End of Play

WE'VE COME TO BELIEVE
by Kara Lee Corthron, Emily Feldman, and Matthew Paul Olmos

All inquiries concerning rights, including amateur rights, should be addressed to:

For Kara Lee Corthron: APA, 135 West 50th Street, 17th Floor, New York, NY 10020. ATTN: Beth Blickers, bblickers@apa-agency.com.

For Emily Feldman: William Morris Endeavor Entertainment, 11 Madison Avenue, 18th Floor, New York, NY 10010. ATTN: Derek Zasky, dsz@wmeagency.com.

For Matthew Paul Olmos: bluedog86@hotmail.com.

ABOUT *WE'VE COME TO BELIEVE*

This article first ran in the Limelight Guide to the 43rd Humana Festival of New American Plays*, published by Actors Theatre of Louisville, and is based on conversations with the creative team before rehearsals for the Humana Festival production began.*

Human history is brimming with bizarre tales of sudden, collective hysteria and mass delusions. From the notorious 1692 witch trials in Salem, Massachusetts, to mysterious "dancing plagues" that swept across Europe between the 11th and 16th centuries, stories about communities gripped by irrational convictions can be found in virtually every century and on every continent. A brief survey of the last 100 years in America offers a plethora of colorful examples. Think of cult members willing to meet their untimely ends for a confounding ideology—remember the Branch Davidians, Heaven's Gate, Jonestown? Or think of UFO enthusiasts who journey to Roswell, New Mexico, for a glimpse of a real flying saucer. Or even sports fans who think their absurd superstitions will help their teams win.

The phenomenon of mass delusion—in equal parts hilarious and disturbing—provides the inspiration for *We've Come to Believe*, this season's Humana Festival show written for the Professional Training Company (PTC). The PTC is an immersive program designed to provide hands-on training for early-career theatre practitioners of every stripe. Members of the company work with Actors Theatre staff and guest artists throughout their time in Louisville, while producing their own full season focused on new work. Every year, Actors Theatre of Louisville commissions a group of playwrights to collaborate on a piece for the Festival—it's performed by the PTC's twenty acting apprentices, and supported in myriad ways by its production, administrative, and artistic apprentices. For the Professional Training Company, *We've Come to Believe* is a celebration of months of hard work and growth, and an opportunity to share their talent with a wider audience.

The process of building the show from the ground up is a massive undertaking that unfolds over the course of nine months. The project kicked off in the summer of 2018, when three intrepid writers—Kara Lee Corthron, Emily Feldman and Matthew Paul Olmos—teamed up with director Will Davis and dramaturg Jenni Page-White to investigate why folks sometimes lose their ever-loving minds in unison. The creative team traded research via phone and email, and began to zero in on the ideas that would fuel the writing process: for example, how easy it is to be swept away by the seductive power of groupthink, or what it feels like to be the only person shouting "The emperor has no clothes!" After a handful of vigorous discussions, the playwrights went off on their own to each craft a series of short scenes riffing on the theme. From a piece that pokes fun at the ongoing saga of "witch hunts" in America, to one that depicts a fringe group preparing for the (nonexistent) genocide of the white race, to one that takes place aboard a boat that may or may not have transported its occupants to another dimension—the material these imaginative writers have generated offers a kaleidoscopic view of mass delusion, by turns meditative, eerie, and ridiculously funny.

With drafts in tow, the playwrights then travelled to Louisville in December 2018 to continue developing their pieces during a weeklong workshop with the director, dramaturg and members of the PTC. Bolstered by some ingenious ideas from the design team, the workshop provided the opportunity to begin weaving these short pieces into a singular theatrical experience—one that highlights both the distinctive voices of the writers and the cleverness of this season's acting apprentices. All in all, it's a highly collaborative process that harnesses the creative energies of a huge number of artists.

In fact, the sheer size of its cast is one of the most unique aspects of this annual project. Director Will Davis relished the rare chance to work with an ensemble of twenty performers, especially in a play that raises provocative questions about herd mentality. Known for physically adventurous work, Davis comes from a background in dance. So in keeping with that sensibility, *We've Come to Believe* uses the spectacle of bodies onstage to explore pattern and uniformity, and to illuminate how an individual's internal compass can stop working in the midst of an impassioned crowd.

What moves people to join a group that espouses a baffling or dangerous philosophy? How do otherwise sensible people wind up holding utterly ludicrous beliefs, despite superior evidence to the contrary? There's no question that it happens; history has shown us that charismatic leaders are able to dupe hundreds of followers, and entire communities can become seized by irrational panic that ends almost as soon as it starts. The question, then, is how? How can something objectively false capture the imagination— nay, the unshakeable conviction—of so many? Depending on your outlook, that question can inspire bewildered laughter, or it could be deeply unsettling. But either way, at the core of this line of thinking is an epistemological concern: if we were the ones who were deluded, how would we know? *We've Come to Believe* invites you to wrestle with these questions, in a mind-bending journey through the world of collective delusion.

—Jenni Page-White

BIOGRAPHIES

Kara Lee Corthron is a playwright, author, and TV-writer based in Los Angeles. Her plays include *AliceGraceAnon* (New Georges), *Holly Down in Heaven* (Forum Theatre, Washington, D.C.), *Listen for the Light* (Know Theatre of Cincinnati), *Welcome to Fear City* (Contemporary American Theater Festival and Kansas City Repertory Theatre), and *What Are You Worth?* She's the author of the young adult novels *The Truth of Right Now* (Simon & Schuster/Simon Pulse) and *Daughters of Jubilation,* coming in 2020. Corthron currently writes for the Netflix drama/thriller *You* and the upcoming thriller *The Flight Attendant* (HBO Max). Her awards include the 2019 Otis Guernsey New Voices in the American Theatre Award, the Parents' Choice Gold Award, Vineyard Theatre's Paula Vogel Playwriting Award, the Princess Grace and Helen Merrill Playwriting Awards, and residencies at MacDowell (four-time fellow), Camargo (France), Bogliasco Foundation (Italy), Skriðuklaustur (Iceland), and Hawthornden (Scotland). She's a proud member of New Dramatists. Her work has been developed at Ars Nova, Atlantic Theater Company, Berkeley Repertory Theatre, LAByrinth Theater Company, the Massilia Afropéa Festival (France), New Dramatists, PlayPenn, Seven Devils Playwrights Conference, South Coast Repertory, and many others. She is an alumna of The Juilliard School.

Emily Feldman's work has been developed by Roundabout Theatre Company, The Playwrights Realm, Alliance Theatre, Second Stage Theater, American Conservatory Theater, Portland Center Stage, La Jolla Playhouse, and Actors Theatre of Louisville, among others. Feldman is an alumna of The Working Farm at SPACE on Ryder Farm, Interstate 73 at Page 73, the Jerome Fellowship at the Playwrights' Center, the Orchard Project Greenhouse, The New Harmony Project, and Two River Theater's Emerging Playwrights Group. She currently attends the Lila Acheson Wallace American Playwrights Program at the Juilliard School, is a Core Writer at the Playwrights' Center, and is the Tow Playwright-in-Residence at Manhattan Theatre Club. Feldman is under commission from Manhattan Theatre Club, Playwrights Horizons, and Arena Stage. She teaches at Playwrights Horizons Theater School/New York University Tisch School of the Arts. She received her MFA from the University of California, San Diego, and her BA from Middlebury College.

Matthew Paul Olmos is a three-time Sundance Institute Fellowship/Residency recipient, a New Dramatists Resident Playwright, and an alumnus of Center Theatre Group's L.A. Writers' Workshop, Oregon Shakespeare Festival's Black Swan Lab, and the Humanitas Play L.A. Workshop. He has received the Princess Grace and National Latino Playwriting Awards, and was selected by Sam Shepard for La Mama E.T.C.'s Ellen Stewart Emerging

Playwright Award. He was mentored for two years by the late Ruth Maleczech as a Mabou Mines/SUITE Resident Artist, and is a former Emerging Artist Fellow at New York Theatre Workshop, Resident Artist at Baryshnikov Arts Center, and Dramatists Guild Fellow. He is an alumnus of Primary Stages' Dorothy Strelsin New American Writers Group, INTAR's Hispanic Playwrights in Residence Lab, and Echo Theater Company's Playwright's Lab, and is an Ensemble Studio Theatre lifetime member. He was selected by Taylor Mac for Cherry Lane's Mentor Project and is a proud Kilroys nominator. His work has been presented both nationally and internationally, taught in universities, and is published by Samuel French and NoPassport Press. He's currently working on a devised piece, *American Nationalism Project*, developed through New York Theatre Workshop's Adelphi Residency. As part of Center Theatre Group's L.A. Writers' Workshop, he is also collaborating with composer April Guthrie on a play with music entitled *We Walk Along the Christmas Bridge*, exploring the racial polarization of the Left and Right. He is currently developing *The Presidential Plays*, a three-play cycle exploring Americans' tumultuous relationship to our presidents. For more information, visit matthewpaulolmos.com.

ACKNOWLEDGMENTS

We've Come to Believe premiered at the Humana Festival of New American Plays in February 2019. It was directed by Will Davis, and performed by the Acting Apprentices of the 2018–2019 Professional Training Company:

> Amber Avant, David Ball, Silvia Daly Bond, Laura Lee Caudill, Avery Deutsch, Rebby Yuer Foster, Josh Fulton, Ashley N. Hildreth, Rasell Holt, Emma Maltby, Kevin O'Connell, Jonathan Moises Olivares, Ash Patlan, Kayla Peters, Angelica Santiago, Brett Schultz, Julian Socha, Seun Soyemi, Russell Sperberg, and Reagan Stovenour

with casting for specific pieces as follows:

Pure Love Now by Kara Lee Corthron

HERO	Silvia Daly Bond
SISTER EVA	Avery Deutsch
BROTHER GEORGE	David Ball
BROTHER TRENT	Kevin O'Connell
BROTHER PAT	Russell Sperberg
DEVOTEE 1	Emma Maltby
DEVOTEE 2	Reagan Stovenour
MORE DEVOTEES	Kayla Peters, Brett Schultz

Our Impact on the World by Kara Lee Corthron

PETER	Seun Soyemi
MARY	Kayla Peters
POSIE	Reagan Stovenour
BRIAR	Angelica Santiago
RAY	Jonathan Moises Olivares
JODY	Laura Lee Caudill
ARDEN	Ash Patlan and Brett Schultz
JORDAN	Emma Maltby
PEANUT BUTTER JELLY TIME	Brett Schultz and The Ensemble

the asleep… by Matthew Paul Olmos

TOURIST ONE	Rebby Yuer Foster
TOURIST TWO	Angelica Santiago
TOURIST THREE	Ash Patlan
TOURIST FOUR	Ashley N. Hildreth and The Ensemble

how do the lonely live... by Matthew Paul Olmos
melody composed by Carla Patullo

LONELY ....Julian Socha
LENORA... Reagan Stovenour

the awake... by Matthew Paul Olmos

LOCAL ONE .... Rasell Holt
LOCAL TWO... Kayla Peters
LOCAL THREE...Seun Soyemi
LOCAL FOUR ....Kevin O'Connell
TOURIST FOUR ....Ashley N. Hildreth
and The Ensemble

Witches by Emily Feldman

MAN 1... Rasell Holt
MAN 2...Josh Fulton
MAN 3...Seun Soyemi
MAN 4...Julian Socha
MAN 5...Kevin O'Connell
MAN 6..Russell Sperberg
and The Ensemble

The Four Pillars at the Foundation of Winning
at the Games of Life
/or/
I Want To Get Complete With You by Emily Feldman

LEADER ....Josh Fulton
PARTICIPANT 1 ....Russell Sperberg
PARTICIPANT 2 ....Seun Soyemi
PARTICIPANT 3 .... Rasell Holt
PARTICIPANT 4 ....Silvia Daly Bond
BEATRICE... Avery Deutsch
PARTICIPANT 5 .... Reagan Stovenour
PARTICIPANT 5'S SIBLING ....Ash Patlan
PARTICIPANT 6 ....Ashley N. Hildreth
PARTICIPANT 6'S FRIEND ....Amber Avant
PARTICIPANT 7 ....Rebby Yuer Foster
PARTICIPANT 7'S LOVER................. Jonathan Moises Olivares
PARTICIPANT 8 .... Kayla Peters
PARTICIPANT 9 ....Emma Maltby

and the following production staff:

Scenic Designer.. Kimie Nishikawa
Costume Designer..Dina Abd El-Aziz
Lighting Designer.. Heather Gilbert
Sound Designer..Luqman Brown
Stage Manager.. Katherine Thesing
Dramaturg ....Jenni Page-White
Properties Master .... Heather Lindert
Directing Assistants.................. Emily Moler, Rebecca Redman
Assistant Dramaturg.. Susan Yassky
Stage Management Apprentice........................... Em Hornbeck

We've Come to Believe was commissioned and developed by Actors Theatre of Louisville.

The cast of *We've Come to Believe*

43rd Humana Festival of New American Plays
Actors Theatre of Louisville, 2019
Photo by Jonathan Roberts

WE'VE COME TO BELIEVE

PURE LOVE NOW
by Kara Lee Corthron

Characters:

HERO – *charismatic woman*

SISTER EVA – *a devoted follower, female*

BROTHER GEORGE – *a conflicted follower, male*

BROTHER TRENT – *a devoted follower, male*

BROTHER PAT – *a devoted follower, male*

DEVOTEE 1 – *female*

DEVOTEE 2 – *male*

Setting: A peaceful room on the Pure Love Now collective grounds. Everyone is seated except for HERO.

HERO. Breathe in slowly and with purpose. Take in all the love you feel in this room. Hold it. Hold it. Hold it.

Now exhale and release all the worries, doubts, and hate you've suffered from those who don't understand you.

And again.

> (*Pause.* HERO *moves through the room as everyone takes in another breath, holds it, and lets it out.*)

That's it. Good.

Start to feel the floor underneath you. The cool air wafting in from the window. Become present in the space you're in. And when you feel ready, gently, gently open your eyes.

> (*They gently, gently do.*)

Beautiful. Now. While you were away, what did God show you?

> (SISTER EVA *raises her hand.*)

Yes, my sister.

> (SISTER EVA *stands.*)

SISTER EVA. He showed me a long, red road leading to a great palace and said, "This shall be yours."

HERO. Yes. Yes He did, didn't He? Did He tell you when it will be yours?

SISTER EVA. He said "Soon, my daughter. Soon."

> (HERO *smiles big and snaps her fingers. The others follow her in snapping their fingers in applause and bow to* SISTER EVA. *She's*

delighted. BROTHER GEORGE *follows the others, but something is off about him.*)

HERO. What else?

(BROTHER TRENT *raises his hand.* HERO *points to him. He stands.*)

BROTHER TRENT. God showed me a building on fire, people burnt and screaming for mercy.

HERO. Yes.

BROTHER TRENT. He warned me not to be afraid.

DEVOTEE 1. Amen.

BROTHER TRENT. He said, "Only through death can there be new life."

HERO. He knows all things.

(*She leads them in more snaps. Several more hands go up around the room.*)

Yes, Brother Pat?

(*He stands.*)

BROTHER PAT. He showed me a ward full of newborn babies. Glowing, beautiful, alike. They were content. They were happy.

OTHERS. Awwww.

HERO. I like that image very much.

(*Snaps. More hands go up, but* HERO *makes a tiny gesture, signaling that this portion of the day is over and the hands go back down.*)

When we stop and allow ourselves to get quiet and concentrate and see with our heart's eyes, God lets us know that we're on the righteous path. He won't steer us wrong.

DEVOTEE 2. No, He won't.

HERO. Our lives were not meant to be easy.

DEVOTEE 1. No indeed!

HERO. They were meant to be full of service and love and that's what we give.

SISTER EVA. Even though our families don't understand us

HERO. That's right.

BROTHER TRENT. Even if it costs us our marriages

HERO. Right again.

BROTHER PAT. Even when we give up our homes and jobs and assets no matter how scary that can be

HERO. Why do we do it?

ALL. We have a purpose.

HERO. What do they have out there?

DEVOTEE 2. YouTube!

SISTER EVA. Pornography!

BROTHER TRENT. Lying media!

DEVOTEE 1. *Last Week Tonight with John Oliver!*

BROTHER PAT. IRONY!

HERO. Yes yes yes. Nothing. That is what they have. Nothing, nothing, nothing. But what do we have?

ALL. We have a purpose!

HERO. God is good.

> (*Snaps all around.*)

Today is special.

BROTHER TRENT. 4/20!

SISTER EVA. A holy day!

HERO. And to honor this holiday, today marks the beginning of Recruitment Week 2019.

> (*Enthusiastic snaps and whoops from everyone except* BROTHER GEORGE. BROTHER GEORGE *stands up. Everyone looks at him.*)

Yes, Brother George? Do you have a question?

BROTHER GEORGE. Yes.

> (*Pause.*)

HERO. Tell us your question.

> (BROTHER GEORGE *pulls out a disturbingly large kitchen knife. The others panic, scatter.*)

BROTHER GEORGE. My question is what is the fucking security code for the gate?

HERO. Whoa now, Brother George. Clearly you're upset so let's take a few breaths and reassess.

BROTHER GEORGE. I'm getting the fuck outta here! Gimme the code!

HERO. All right. I'll give you the code. Now can you give me the knife please?

BROTHER GEORGE. (*As in no:*) Uh-uh. Code, woman.

HERO. The code is 1152008—the date we began.

> (*Pause.* BROTHER GEORGE *is surprised she gave it to him so quickly; he was prepared for a longer fight.*)

BROTHER GEORGE. Oh. OK. Thank you.

> (*He awkwardly starts to back out of the room.*)

HERO. Is that what you all think? That you're being held here against your will?

DEVOTEE 1. Heavens no!

DEVOTEE 2. We're honored to be here!

BROTHER GEORGE. You people are insane! Wake the fuck up! Why do we have to give up our cars the moment we get here? Why can't we leave the grounds without chaperones? Why, Hero, did it take a big-ass knife for you to tell me how to get out of here? We're prisoners!

(*Gasps all around. Some may not be genuine.*)

HERO. No, you have it all wrong.

You turn over your cars as a vow of poverty to God. Mother Teresa did the same thing.

SISTER EVA. That's true. I heard that she did.

HERO. The chaperones are for your protection.

BROTHER GEORGE. Bullshit.

HERO. Would you like to see the death threats I receive on a daily basis? They're not just aimed at me. Our enemies would like to destroy ALL of us. I send you into the world with guards to keep you and our work alive.

DEVOTEE 2. Amen!

BROTHER TRENT. God bless you, Hero!

HERO. We don't give out the gate code as a security measure. I have a responsibility to protect the 84 members of Pure Love Now that live in this compound. But know this, Brother George—

BROTHER GEORGE. Not my name.

(*A moment.*)

HERO. Know this...Seth Boyers. You are here because you choose to be here and because you believe, like we believe, that God has called you to this important work. The moment you stop believing that, you are not only free to go, I *insist* that you go. Do you understand?

(*Beat. After a moment,* BROTHER GEORGE *nods.*)

We will miss your contribution and your leadership. But we thank you for all you've given us.

OTHERS. Thank you.

(HERO *leads them in snaps and a deep bow of gratitude for* BROTHER GEORGE. *He is touched.*)

BROTHER GEORGE. Well...I appreciate that.

(*Awkward pause.* HERO *and the others are now on one side of the stage and* BROTHER GEORGE *is on the other. They wait for him to leave. He stands there.*)

I—I still feel the same way I did. When I first joined. I'm still that same person.

(HERO *nods. He slowly moves toward the others.*)

To me? The most important thing is feeling free. Knowing that I can leave whenever I want. That I'm not imprisoned here. So. Maybe I'll stay for a bit. I can at least help out with Recruitment Week.

(HERO *reaches out her hand to him and he gives her the knife. The others surround* BROTHER GEORGE *in a giant bear hug.*)

Oh, you guys.

HERO. Wonderful. This marks the beginning of what I know will be a beautiful day. Because what do we have?

ALL. Purpose!

HERO. Now. Things to keep in mind when targeting potential recruits. What do we look for?

(*All hands go up.*)

Just shout it out!

BROTHER TRENT. Depressives!

HERO. Yes!

SISTER EVA. Loners!

HERO. Very good!

DEVOTEE 1. Teens that should be in school, but aren't.

HERO. Bingo! And what will we teach them that Father Ajax has taught us?

BROTHER PAT. That they're special!

HERO. They are!

SISTER EVA. That God loves them!

HERO. Yes yes yes!

BROTHER GEORGE. To self-motivate!

HERO. That's right, Brother George. We want them to know the joy we know. And why are we so joyful?

ALL. We have a purpose!

HERO. What *is* our purpose, brothers and sisters?

ALL. To prepare for the coming genocide of the white race.

HERO. You're all ready! Let's do this!

(*They cheer and file out the exit. They get to the gate and* HERO *hits some keys to open it. They all exit,* BROTHER GEORGE *bringing up the rear. Something's bothering him.*)

BROTHER GEORGE. Hey, Hero? 1152008 is only seven digits. Looked like you put in nine. Or ten? Hero?

(*Blackout.*)

OUR IMPACT ON THE WORLD
by Kara Lee Corthron

Characters:

PETER & MARY – *a typical married couple*

POSIE & BRIAR – *young adult siblings*

RAY & JODY – *young adult couple, not gender specific (either of them can be female, male, or non-binary; same-sex or hetero)*

ARDEN – *precocious 10-year-old sister of* RAY

Use the slash (/) overlap rule where indicated.

Three playing spaces: 1, 2, and 3. An electronic device is the focal point of each, ideally not uniform, i.e. not all laptops or all iPhones, etc.

Lights up on space 1.

PETER. I have to handle this delicately.

MARY. Sure.

PETER. A lot of people loved him.

MARY. They did.

PETER. Ugh! I can't let everyone down. They expect me to be fair and honest, but also biting and sometimes wry. It's so much pressure.

MARY. Unnecessary pressure. The best kind.

(PETER *sighs.*)

PETER. OK. OK. I think I know what to do.

(PETER *types. He hits the delete key a few times, looks pensive, but then types some more. He seems satisfied.* PETER *presses a key, posting his comment. Pause. He is content for a moment. In a flash, he becomes antsy, afraid.*)

Hon? Can you read it? Please?

(MARY *looks over his shoulder and reads what she sees on the screen.*)

MARY. "He was a hero to some, villain to others, but to me, he was a man doing the best he could. #RIP #RealAmericans."

PETER. You think it's OK?

MARY. It's fine.

PETER. But does it sound like I'm letting him off the hook? Oh fuck! What have I done?

(*Lights down on space 1 and up on* POSIE *in space 2.*)

POSIE. (*Looking at a screen:*) Oh are you—are you *kidding* me??

(*As she types:*)

Your entire post reads like *The Onion* circa 2004. If you have to scrape the bottom of the internet barrel to find proof that somebody isn't racist? That person is racist.

(*Pause.*)

And so are you.

(*Hits a key to post. Giddy, then nervous. Lights up on another woman reading her screen.*)

BRIAR. (*As she types:*) Racist??? You're calling me a racist? You are a leftist, New York liberal elitist!

(BRIAR *hits send. The following section is rapid-fire though still a back and forth in response to a post.*)

POSIE. You shared a dug up piece about Sessions being sweet to his kitchen staff—once—as proof that he's not racist. How can you not see the absurdity of that argument?

BRIAR. How can you talk to me like you're some moral authority—

POSIE. How can you believe anything you read on / *Infowars*?

BRIAR. How can you believe the communist propaganda of / Rachel Maddow?

POSIE. How can you defend detaining children? I'd think that would be the one thing we could all / agree on.

BRIAR. I never defended it and that's not the whole truth.

POSIE. There's kindness and there's cruelty. Cruelty can't be defended. You know who does need defending? Fucking toddlers abducted by ICE.

(*Pause. Then:*)

BRIAR. We haven't seen each other in person for four years. You don't know me. You don't know what my life is like every day. You are deluded if you think you're going to "teach" me anything. So in the future, you don't like what I post? Scroll past it. I won't have you humiliating me in front of the whole world.

(BRIAR *posts.* POSIE *needs a breath.*

Lights down on space 2, up on space 3. RAY *stares at a screen.*)

RAY. What makes people so mean?

JODY. Safety of anonymity. It's easy to be cruel when you don't have to look at someone's face.

ARDEN. They're mean even if they can see your pics.

JODY. I'm not talking about a pic. I'm talking about standing face-to-face with someone. Close enough to see them breathing, thinking, their pupils dilating, nostrils flaring. Close enough for them to punch you in the face. People are far more civil when they know they can get punched in the face.

RAY. I sometimes wonder if it isn't worse. Words hurt in a way that punches don't.

JODY. What's upset you?

> (RAY *holds the screen in front of* JODY. JODY *winces.*)

Why did you read the comments?

RAY. It's a BABY! A baby and a kitten! It's cute! What kinda monster would write such a thing about an innocent baby and a kitten?!

JODY. A very disturbed and unhappy person.

> (RAY *grabs the device with new purpose.*)

Please don't respond.

RAY. (*Typing:*) You sound like a very disturbed and unhappy / person

JODY. Oh my god don't write that!

RAY. (*Typing:*) Reach out if you need to talk.

> (JODY *tries to grab the device, but it's too late;* RAY *has posted the comment. Brief silence.*)

ARDEN. That was nice of you.

RAY. Thanks, Artie!

JODY. Why did you do that?

RAY. Because. This person is hurting and probably nobody has ever taken the time to listen to (*Reads name off the screen:*) Beelzejizz666. Maybe I'm the first person to reach out to them. Any one of us can make a difference in the world if we try. We can leave a life-changing effect on total strangers if we put in the effort!

> (*As* ARDEN *speaks,* RAY *listens but keeps eyes glued to the screen.*)

ARDEN. Ashley cried today. Ms. Edwards asked her why she was crying and she said that only three people liked her new Instagram pic and some boy said she had horse teeth.

RAY. That is just awful!

ARDEN. Ms. Edwards got mad and said scientists say social media's causing people to have delusions and psychotic episodes. She said it makes regular people think they're like celebrities—

RAY. Oooh! Seven likes already!

ARDEN. And that everything they say matters and gets seen by the world and they have like some great big impact. They think they have thousands of friends, but they're not really friends. It scrambles your brains.

JODY. There might be truth in that.

ARDEN. I don't want a phone. I don't want to be a zombie.

RAY. They responded!

(RAY *excitedly reads the response then goes quiet.*)

JODY. Are you all right?

RAY. No.

(*Lights down on space 3, up on space 1.*)

PETER. C.J.'s pissed. Says I'm ignoring the war crimes.

MARY. Ignore C.J.

PETER. I can't let his be the last comment of the thread.

I clearly address both sides, don't I? Is there nothing out there that we can all agree on without our partisan bullsh—

(PETER *suddenly looks at the screen.*)

Oh shit. Oh *FUCK!* Mom just wrote: "This man was a prisoner of war for five years. How dare you call him a villain?" That's not what I said! I thought I was clear!

MARY. Ignore it.

PETER. I can't ignore my mother.

MARY. (*Sighing:*) Then call her.

PETER. (*Horror:*) Call her? No. Jesus. *Call her?* I don't wanna *talk* to her!

MARY. Then reply.

PETER. God I hate this so much! I have a persona and it's a burden and I don't wanna hurt anyone.

MARY. Maybe you should hold a press conference.

PETER. Mock me all you want, but I have 2,163 friends who have come to expect certain qualities from me. I cannot let them down.

(*He looks at the screen, incredulous. Flexes fingers.*)

OK you wanna go? Let's go!

(*Lights down on space 1, up on space 2.*)

POSIE. The whole world? I've humiliated you in front of the whole world. Are you insane?

BRIAR. Stay. Off. My. Wall.

POSIE. I will, but I have to address that comment. One, I don't see how disagreeing with you is a form of humiliation and two, your Facebook friend list is NOT the whole world.

BRIAR. You did not disagree with me, you called me a racist and insulted my intelligence. That goes beyond disagreement.

(*Pause.*)

POSIE. I apologize for insulting you. I will stay off your wall. I worry about you, though. I worry about you getting "news" from *Infowars*. You probably won't do it, but here are a couple of better sources you may want to at least glance at some time: *The Progressive, The Nation,* and to a lesser extent *AlterNet.* My best to you.

> (BRIAR *reads what* POSIE *has written.*)

BRIAR. (*To herself:*) This condescending bitch.

> (BRIAR *fumes. She finds an image and posts it as a response. It is a teddy bear wearing a MAGA hat.*)

POSIE. What the—?

> (*Typing:*)

OK?

> (BRIAR *posts it again. This time it has a word bubble coming from its mouth: "The Supreme Court will be ours." POSIE is so mad she doesn't know what to do with herself.*)

I'm about to lose it on this bitch!

> (*Lights down on space 2, up on space 3.*
> RAY *types furiously.*)

JODY. Ray? You're making me very nervous.

RAY. This person is disturbed and unhappy and clearly very uneducated about how the world works and I am doing my best to educate him.

JODY. It's not worth it.

ARDEN. Ms. Edwards says it messes with our natural instincts. When you fight with someone on social media, your brain makes all this adrenaline and cortisol and that used to be necessary back when people had to hunt for their food with their bare hands. But we're not really in danger from an internet fight so all that junk has no natural release.

> (RAY *reads something else on the screen. It's disgusting. Bitter laughter.*)

JODY. Don't write any more. Don't feed this.

RAY. I just have one more—

JODY. Please.

RAY. One more thing to say!

> (*Lights up on all three spaces.*)

PETER. For your

POSIE. Information

RAY. Your words

PETER. Are...

RAY/POSIE/PETER. Uninformed.

POSIE. Ignorant

RAY. Violent

PETER. I

POSIE. Suggest

RAY. You

PETER. Go

POSIE. Fuck

RAY/POSIE/PETER. Yourself.

(*They all post. They all share a moment of deep satisfaction and then tremendous anxiety.*)

MARY. Did you say that to your mother?

JODY. Close the tab.

BRIAR. Un. Friend.

PETER. Of course not! But…what if she thinks I did?

MARY/JODY. This is why it it's always better to say NOTHING!

RAY. I tried to help! He drove me to it.

POSIE. No reaction. Nothing? *Fine!*

ARDEN. Where does all the adrenaline and cortisol go?

PETER. Now I have to call her. Godammnit!

RAY. It's fine. Look. I'm looking at something else now.

POSIE. You want me to keep scrolling, then that is what I'll do.

MARY. Wait. Stop.

(*All at once MARY, PETER, RAY, and POSIE see the same post. It is a video that they all click on. The audience will either hear an audio recording of the following text or perhaps it can be staged. Director's choice.*)

VOICE. I'm Jordan. I am in the 4th grade and nobody likes me. I have no friends. Nobody sits with me at lunch and they pick on me because I'm gay. On my birthday, I shared a pic of me and my mom at Joe's Crab Shack and a bunch of people said that I should kill myself. I think they're right. So that's what I'm going to do.

(*Silence. RAY begins to cry. JODY and ARDEN try to comfort RAY. POSIE slams her fist or kicks something—a violent show of anger. PETER stares for a long, long time then shakes his head.*

A moment. Gradually, they begin to scroll again, away from the horror. They all stop on the same video. We can hear it. It's fucking ridiculous, like the John McCain obit/Dolphin dance video or the perfect Rick Roll. Or it's basic humor like the "waffle-ly wedded wife" video. Either way, we understand why they're laughing. Everyone— the whole cast—sees the video and is captivated. They all start to laugh. Gently at first, but it keeps growing until the entire stage is full of raucous, uncontrollable laughter.

Blackout.)

the asleep...
by Matthew Paul Olmos

The Port of Barcelona at night. Sounds of wind through the palm trees and the running motors of ferries waiting.

This is broken by the ecstatic giggling of several young women in their early twenties.

We hear the clocking of their heels as they move from the plaza and up one of the ramps along the dock.

TOURIST ONE. Omigod, omigod, omigod, omigod, omigod, do you guys hear that???

(They all pause. Sounds of beats in the distance.)

TOURIST TWO. Is there fucking dancing on this boat???

TOURIST THREE. I bet you this ferry is fucking craze.

TOURIST TWO. I bet you Ibiza is un'fucking'hinged.

TOURIST THREE. *(Moans.)* Ugh, how long is the ride again?

TOURIST ONE. How do you keep forgetting *eight hours?*

TOURIST THREE. This ramp feels eight hours. I wanna get to the room.

TOURIST ONE. We don't have a room.

TOURIST THREE. Why didn't we split one???

TOURIST TWO. Ew.

TOURIST ONE. It was a hundred Euros more. And seriously, what is wrong with you, why can't you retain anything.

TOURIST THREE. I'm on fucking holiday in Spain, I left my retention back home.

TOURIST TWO. "That's what she said."

TOURIST FOUR. *What???* That doesn't even—do you even know how that joke works??? No, forget it, nevermind.

Okay look, can we try something.

(They all agree they can.)

Can we maybe try, that sometimes, you three, don't talk.

(A few moments of them walking in silence; finally they stop.)

TOURIST THREE. You've Got To Be Messing. Now there's stairs??? I thought ferries floated on the ocean, not up in the sky.

(Sounds of frustrated heels going up metallic stairs for a few moments. Finally... sounds of beats with full bass.

Appears FOUR TOURISTS, *twenty-something women of color; they are done up as on holiday and carry somewhat poor-looking backpacker backpacks. They all look in awe at the audience.)*

TOURIST ONE. Holy shit.

TOURIST THREE. This is fucking it.

TOURIST TWO. So it.

TOURIST ONE. This...

TOURIST TWO. *Is A Sit-u-fucking-ation.*

TOURIST FOUR. Wow.

TOURISTS ONE and THREE. Yea...

(They step forward. The space turns into Wild On E! *The beats turn into intense electro dance music, lights swirl with moonlight and flash, sounds of champagne popping, glasses clinking, twenty-somethings hollering.*

The women stare; they comically begin to move their bodies slightly, but...

TOURIST TWO *takes off her backpack, but isn't sure where to put it.*
TOURIST FOUR *follows suit, they both can't decide what to do with their bags.*
TOURIST THREE *suggests they stash them someplace.*
TOURIST ONE *tries to show that fun can be had with her backpack still on.*
TOURIST FOUR *tries to agree.*

TOURIST TWO *motions tying the backpacks all together; nobody understands, so she begins tying hers with* THREE*'s.*
They all decide to give it a whirl, they tie their bags off and set them on the side of the stage.
TOURIST FOUR *motions that they need to keep watch.*
All glare at her; she motions: "Fine."
All walk forward, while FOUR *keeps an eye on their bags.*

They feel alive surrounded by foam and spilled drinks; the atmosphere becomes a barrage of skin showing, costumes, masks, and even stilts. The scene is a mesmerizing flourish of color and the colorful.

One by one, each woman is led off into the frenzy, dancing their ass off as they go.

FOUR *tries to keep her eye on their bags, but is caught between responsibility and her age. Finally,* FOUR *lets out a scream for the ages and dives into the scene.*

Sounds of all four women howling at the time of their lives; we wish we were their age again, we wish we were on our way to Ibiza by way of boat.

Just as the revelry reaches a crescendo and the party bursts into legend…all sound, lights, and color are suddenly ended.

Sounds of an engine dying. Darkness. Silence.

Only the sounds of a lapping ocean.

A few moments.

In darkness…)

TOURIST ONE. Uh…

TOURIST TWO. What the fuck happened?

TOURIST ONE. Omigod, omigod, omigod, okay, let's just—

TOURIST THREE. I can't see anything, what happened to the—

TOURIST ONE. Quiet, quiet, d'you hear that?

TOURIST THREE. Hear what?

TOURIST TWO. Yo, I don't hear shit—

(*The lights of the boat sputter up; sounds of a generator kicking in. The three women stare and look around themselves as they realize they are standing in a sea of limp bodies; each one laying haphazardly on the floor.* TOURIST FOUR *is not there.*)

What the fu—

(TOURIST ONE *motions them to stop all movement; they do.*)

TOURIST THREE. …what happened to them…

(TOURIST ONE *motions them both to calm down.*

TWO *motions,* "Fuck you calm, look at this place."

THREE *motions,* "Holy Fuck, d'you think they're dead???"

ONE *motions,* "They were just dancing a moment ago."

THREE *motions,* "Look At Them!"

ONE *motions,* "Alright, just gimme a minute."

Then, "One of us needs to…reach their hand out."

TWO *and* THREE *agree, but make clear it won't be them.*

ONE *huffs, then squats down and reaches her hand out to the closest body, while* TWO *holds her and* THREE *keeps watch.* ONE *carefully pokes their shoulder. Nothing. She shakes their leg; nothing. She regroups, then leans in closer and puts her hand more intimately: movement.* ONE *stands back up quickly.)*

TOURIST ONE. Alright, so they're alive.

TOURIST THREE. Yea, got that.

TOURIST TWO. *So* got that.

(ONE *silences them, then notices* FOUR *is missing, begins to point it out to them.*

They can't believe they didn't notice.

ONE *motions they need to do a search, they agree.*

All begin tiptoeing through the bodies, just as they are almost to a clearing…

The ferry slams into a dock; sounds of wood splintering; they all fall, then quickly scramble up off the unconscious bodies; this is messy.

ONE *motions them to stay put as she goes to the window to see what happened. She does then stops, staring out.)*

TOURIST ONE. Omigod.

(THREE *joins her, then* TWO.)

TOURIST THREE. Is this…?

TOURIST ONE. Ibiza.

TOURIST THREE. You said eight hours, you said—!

(They shut her up.

THREE *motions, "But it hasn't been anywhere near eight hours!"*

They all argue in confusion, finally…

ONE *clears the conversation, then mimes, "Did either of you <u>take anything???</u>"*

TWO *and* THREE *gulp with guilt.*

THREE *raises her hand.* TWO *raises her hand.*

ONE *mimes, "What did you take?"*

THREE *mimes, "Some kind of little pill."*

TWO *acknowledges she took the same.*

TWO *and* THREE *start panicking what they took.*

ONE *remembers that* FOUR *is missing.)*

TOURIST ONE. Wait, where's…?

(ONE *covers her mouth like "Oh Fuck I talked out loud."*

ONE *composes them, then focuses them on:*

"What we need to do is find FOUR."

TWO *and* THREE *finally agree, and all three begin a search.*

All pause as they hear a beautiful melody sounding like nature
TWO *and* THREE *are drawn towards the entrance.)*

TOURIST ONE. What're you…psst, hey, what's a matter with you two—

(*A door opens. Brightness overtakes the space.*

TWO *and* THREE *exit.)*

No, stop, what're you—we can't just—we don't even know what's out there!
I'm serious. It could be—*I don't think we were supposed to be on this boat!!*

(ONE *goes after them, but then is stopped as she stands motionless
and transfixed by the bright. Melodic sounds like nature fill the
space. White-out with* ONE *alone in the bright.)*

how do the lonely live…
by Matthew Paul Olmos
melody composed by Carla Patullo

LENORA *stands looking out at the world.*

LONELY *enters the space looking lonely,*

But walks up to LENORA, *who barely acknowledges.*

LONELY. I apologize for—I don't mean to—I don't even know what I'm
doing here—I mean I never thought I'd be the sort of person who—I just—I
just needed someone to talk to.

(LENORA *gives slight attention.)*

I guess you could say…that I'm, I guess, lonely. Or whatever.

(LENORA *turns to take* LONELY *in, then leans in as though with
empathy;* LONELY *readies for it…)*

LENORA. …there's no guessing about it. Look at you.

(LONELY *looks at themself.)*

LONELY. I used to try better at how I—look to the world, or whatever.

LENORA. I wouldn't worry about it, I don't believe the world is looking
much at you anyways.

LONELY. You're right. This was stupid. I'm stupid. I shouldn't have—

(LONELY *curses themself as they begin to leave. Beat.)*

LENORA. Well, you've come all this way.

(LONELY *pauses.)*

LONELY. I actually live right around the—

(LENORA *quiets* LONELY.)

LENORA. I don't need to know everything. But I do need to know what
happened.

(LONELY *isn't sure how to…)*

Tell me.

LONELY. ...I think a part of me maybe died...?

LENORA. ...how can ya tell...?

LONELY. ...I woke up one day, and half of me was gone. Like some unthinkable nightmare I couldn't wake up from. Just like that, not a whole person anymore.

LENORA. So, what are you then?

> (*Pause.*)

Tell me what's missing.

LONELY. The part that got up in the morning and faced forward. The part that believed good things... The part that made the world worth being a part of.

LENORA. Something you should know, the world isn't worth being a part of. It's isolating and pretends it's not. And it will fuck with your heart so many times over that you'll give your love to anybody, any chance you get.

LONELY. Is this like...reverse comfort or whatever?

LENORA. No. I am simply apologizing on behalf of all what's wrong in this life.

LONELY. ...thank you...?

LENORA. (*Sings.*) "Can you imagine having every key, the gold inside your hand, With nobody left to see, how do the lonely live, how does their aching ease, how could a living life live a life like someone, someone left like me..."

> (LONELY *is completely melted to* LENORA. *Beat.*)

And now for your turn.

LONELY. My...?

LENORA. Show me how you *could* be if the world was how it's supposed to be.

> (LONELY *begins to move their body as if the world saw them perfect; this grows from reluctant to unrestrained.*
>
> LENORA *admires their own work.*
>
> *Finally,* LONELY *is at* LENORA's *feet.*
>
> LENORA *lays touch on* LONELY: *heart orgasm.*
>
> *Lights dim on what could be...*)

the awake...
by Matthew Paul Olmos

The interior of a ferry; it bobs slightly from the move of water. Sounds of coastal birds and an ocean lapping.

Strewn about the floor are numerous unconscious bodies; they lay haphazard and random. The remnants of a wild'ass, but possibly fucked-up party decorate the space.

A few moments before LOCAL ONE *stirs; he sits up, and his eyes go wide as he looks about. He rushes to the window and stares in disbelief.*

LOCAL ONE. It happened, it actually happened. Look.

(TWO *goes to the window, behaves as they're supposed to.*)

LOCAL TWO. It actually did. Look.

(*Various others begin walking to the window to look out; a murmur amongst them.*)

LOCAL THREE. ...could somebody point to something specifically that—

LOCAL FOUR. All of it. Everything that's out there. Can't you see?

LOCAL THREE. I do. See. It's just a lot to—If I may, I'd like to gather the others so that everyone can see...what we're seeing.

(LOCAL ONE *approves. All go to search the boat, except* ONE, TWO, *and* FOUR.)

LOCAL FOUR. If I may, I'd like to lead us in a—

LOCAL ONE. No, you may not.

(FOUR *frustrates silently as* LOCAL ONE *lifts a window up; a bright shines on him; sounds of nature floods; he looks somewhat Godlike.*

Then, the sounds of birds; all of their eyes follow several birds in their view; it seems perhaps too normal for them; awkward.)

LOCAL TWO. It appears so...

(*All look at* TWO.)

...natural.

LOCAL FOUR. The world previous "appeared natural," *this* is how the Earth was actually intended.

LOCAL TWO. Right, no—

LOCAL ONE. Shut up.

(*Enter* LOCAL THREE *leading* TOURIST FOUR, *who can barely walk.*

All stare, not knowing how to react. Finally, LOCAL ONE *goes to* TOURIST FOUR *and examines her, like studying some new species.*)

LOCAL ONE. I, would like for you, to...nod your head, if you can understand...the language which to you I am—

(TOURIST FOUR *kinda does something with their head.*)

Please say something...if you can understand the words, I—

TOURIST FOUR. (*Mumbles something.*)

LOCAL ONE. (*Sighs.*) It seems she's American.

> (*All murmur, then go quickly silent as* TOURIST FOUR *steps forward, a bit wobbly.* LOCAL TWO *raises his hand.*)

LOCAL TWO. May I…observe?

> (ONE *motions him to proceed.*)

She seems…drunk.

> (ONE *examines further and prods* TOURIST FOUR *to see if this is true; confirms that it is.* ONE *speaks in an overtly American accent.*)

LOCAL ONE. *What is it you are doing aboard this vessel?*

> (TOURIST FOUR *clears her throat, all on pins and needles.*)

TOURIST FOUR. …Ibiza…

LOCAL TWO. Did she—

LOCAL FOUR. I believe she said—

TOURIST FOUR. …Ibiza…

> (LOCAL TWO *raises their hand.*)

LOCAL TWO. May I—

> (LOCAL ONE *motions them to get on with it.*)

So, I'm guessing she was taking a ferry to Ibiza.

LOCAL THREE. I mean—

LOCAL FOUR. What.

LOCAL THREE. She kinda *did* take a ferry to Ibiza.

LOCAL ONE. What she took was something sacred that does not belong to her.

LOCAL THREE. So, why don't we just…send her back?

LOCAL TWO. Back to where—

LOCAL THREE. Barcelona.

LOCAL FOUR. There is no Barcelona anymore—

> (ONE *silences all.*)

LOCAL ONE. There is no anywhere anymore. So how is she here? How is some tourist even here standing???

LOCAL FOUR. She's a mistake. A glitch in the—as I see it we have no choice but to—

> (LOCAL FOUR *illustrates throwing her body overboard.*
>
> *All take this in.* ONE *considers, then agrees that is what must be done.*)

LOCAL THREE. …is that really how we wanna begin with all this…?

LOCAL TWO. *This* doesn't belong to her.

LOCAL THREE. So…a drowning then.

LOCAL FOUR. Should she be rewarded for her stupidity?

LOCAL THREE. I don't think she meant to—I think she just got on the wrong boat.

LOCAL FOUR. Look out there, does it look like she simply got on the wrong boat???

> (LOCAL THREE *looks outside, others join.*)

LOCAL THREE. It looks like…

LOCAL TWO. What, what does it look like?

LOCAL THREE. It looks like she wishes she could just go home.

> (LOCAL FOUR *pulls* TOURIST FOUR *with aggression.*
> THREE *moves to stop him, but they are warned off by* ONE.
> As LOCAL FOUR *speaks, attention is given to the audience.*)

LOCAL FOUR. No, they do not deserve a home.

Look at how they live. Just sucking up air with nothing inside them but themselves.

So filled with this wretched neediness that they do any and all things…so many awful, just horrible things, to make themselves feel better.

About what they do.

Who they are.

In a world they treat so poorly.

They spend their entire lives chasing after money and attention.

While their own kind go hungry and alone.

They claim to believe in fairness and the goodness of some god.

While their selfishness grows global and overgrown.

And when finally they find themselves close to death's door,

always they claim, "Well, I did the best I could."

Just absolutely refusing to believe, how much worse all life has become, and will continue to be.

> (LOCAL FOUR *shoves* TOURIST FOUR *to the ground.*
> LOCAL ONE *begins to lead them in a chant.*
> *The chant becomes ritual; it begins with some discipline, but turns towards disrespectful; sacrificial; with violence.*
> *The audience should be unnerved.*
> *Soon, they are underscored by beats and bass.*)

A mad dance happens. It looks like when Ibiza goes wrong.

Several moments of this. Enough for TOURIST FOUR *to sober up and realize nothing good is coming to her.*

Just then, TOURISTS ONE, TWO, *and* THREE *appear outside. The music is cut, all stop dancing and look out the window.* LOCAL ONE *doesn't know what they are looking at yet.*)

LOCAL ONE. What, what is—

LOCAL FOUR. There standing…

(LOCAL ONE *turns to see what everyone has been staring at. We hear gasps and murmurs of "Who are they?" Finally,* TOURIST FOUR *speaks clear and authoritatively.*)

TOURIST FOUR. I know them.

(*All look to her.*)

They are…our new leaders.

(TOURIST FOUR *begins a new chant; others slowly join her.* TOURISTS ONE, TWO, *and* THREE *don't know what is going on at first, then accept. All but* LOCAL THREE *accept this new world. Lights out. End of Play.*)

WITCHES
by Emily Feldman

MAN 1 *and* MAN 2. *1632.*

MAN 1. It's great to see you, Man!

MAN 2. It's great to see you too, Man!

MAN 1. Are you guys still living in the village?

MAN 2. Oh. No. No. No. No. No. We got priced out of the village.

MAN 1. Us too.

MAN 2. Things were different when I moved here in 1624.

MAN 1. 1632 is like a whole different world.

MAN 2. 1632 *is* a whole different world.

MAN 1. Where'd you end up?

MAN 2. We ended up on a little 200-acre farm a little south of the village.

MAN 1. South of the village is very hip.

MAN 2. Yeah, we're not really hip enough to live south of the village, but we like the extra space.

MAN 1. I've been thinking about you. And Fredonia.

MAN 2. We've been thinking about you too!

MAN 1. I've been meaning to write you a letter to see how you are.

MAN 2. We're great! Our eleventh child just turned three.

MAN 1. Time…wow. Three already!

MAN 2. It's such a blessing we all survived the winter…and also a nightmare.

MAN 1. …I wanted to write to you and see how you were doing…with this whole *witch* situation.

MAN 2. I mean. It's crazy! It's a witch hunt!

MAN 1. I guess that's true. It is sort of like they're hunting…witches.

Which is why…I've really been thinking about you. And Fredonia.

MAN 2. Fredonia isn't a witch.

MAN 1. That's great to hear. I sort of heard that she might be. But, that's really great to hear.

MAN 2. Yeah. Fredonia isn't a witch at all.

MAN 1. So, actually. I read this thing. And it turns out.

When a statement is repeated, it starts to feel more familiar and like it might actually be true?

MAN 2. Fredonia is not a witch!

MAN 1. So, actually. It's pretty ineffective to say "Fredonia is not a witch,"

MAN 2. But. FREDONIA IS NOT A WITCH.

MAN 1. Because what you're doing there is sort of reinforcing the frame that she…*is* a witch.

MAN 2. BUT. FREDONIA IS NOT A WITCH!

MAN 1. I'd stop saying it that way.

MAN 2. FREDONIA IS NOT A WITCH!

MAN 1. I'd try to phrase it a different way.

MAN 2. BUT SHE'S NOT A WITCH!

MAN 1. I hear you. But. So. Actually.

It doesn't really matter if Fredonia is a witch or is not a witch /

MAN 2. / FREDONIA IS NOT A WITCH!

MAN 1. Because everyone has sort of come to believe that she is.

    (*A group of witches whisper.*)

WITCHES. Let his days be few.

Let another take his office.

MAN 2. Do you hear that?

WITCHES. Let food bring him no sustenance.

MAN 1. Hear what?

WITCHES. Let sleep bring him only nightmares.

MAN 2. ...Witches.

MAN 3 *and* MAN 4. *1954.*

MAN 3. It's great to see you, Man!

MAN 4. It's great to see you too, Man!

MAN 3. Are you guys still living in the village?

MAN 4. Oh. No. No. No. No. No. We got priced out of the village.

MAN 3. Us too.

MAN 4. Things were different when I moved here in 1942.

MAN 3. 1954 is like a whole different world.

MAN 4. 1954 *is* a whole different world.

MAN 3. Where'd you end up?

MAN 4. We ended up in a little townhouse a little south of the village.

MAN 3. South of the village is very hip.

MAN 4. Yeah, we're not really hip enough to live south of the village, but we like the extra space.

MAN 3. I've been thinking about you. And Freddie.

MAN 4. We've been thinking about you too!

MAN 3. I've been meaning to call you to see how you are.

MAN 4. We're great! We got a television!

MAN 3. Amazing!

MAN 4. We'll have to have you over to watch it. It is pretty amazing. I didn't mean to assume you don't have one yourself, maybe you do, I mean. Whatever. It's pretty amazing.

MAN 3. ...I wanted to call and see how you were doing...with this whole *witch hunt* situation.

MAN 4. You're absolutely right. It *is* a witch hunt!

MAN 3. Which is why...I've really been thinking about you. And Freddie.

MAN 4. Well. We aren't communists. So.

MAN 3. That's great to hear. I sort of heard that you might be. But, that's really great to hear.

MAN 4. We're gay. But, we are not communists!

MAN 3. Amazing.

MAN 4. You can be gay and not be a communist.

MAN 3. Amazing.

MAN 4. And we are definitely not communists.

MAN 3. So, actually. I read this thing. And. It turns out. When a statement is repeated, it starts to feel more familiar and like it might actually be true.

MAN 4. Well. Okay. But. We are not communists.

MAN 3. So, actually. It's pretty ineffective to say "We are not communists."

MAN 4. But. WE'RE NOT COMMUNISTS!

MAN 3. Because what you're doing there is sort of reinforcing the frame that you…*are* communists.

MAN 4. BUT. WE'RE NOT COMMUNISTS!

MAN 3. I'd stop saying it that way.

MAN 4. WE'RE NOT COMMUNISTS!

MAN 3. I'd try to phrase it a different way.

MAN 4. It's a witch hunt!

MAN 3. If you want to call it that, I guess.

MAN 4. ISN'T THAT THE WHOLE THING WITH THE WITCH HUNTS, ANYWAY?

TURNS OUT THERE WERE NO SUCH THING AS WITCHES AND THE PURITANS JUST HUNG RANDOM PEOPLE BECAUSE THEY WERE AFRAID ABOUT ECONOMIC AND POLITICAL AND SOCIAL STUFF AND NOW WE REALIZE THAT WAS REALLY SCREWED UP AND WE SHOULDN'T DO THAT AGAIN! SO, DOESN'T THAT MEAN WE SHOULDN'T DO THAT AGAIN AND THAT WE'RE PROBABLY NOT COMMUNISTS?

MAN 3. I hear you. But. So. Actually.

It doesn't really matter if you're communists or not /

MAN 4. / WE'RE NOT COMMUNISTS!

MAN 3. Because everyone has sort of come to believe that you are.

(*A group of witches whisper.*)

WITCHES. Let shame be his mantle.

Let him meet justice.

MAN 4. Do you hear that?

WITCHES. My witchcraft is strong.

MAN 3. Hear what?

WITCHES. My witchcraft is powerful.

MAN 4. …Witches?

MAN 3. Must be on the TV.

MAN 5 *and* MAN 6. *2018.*

MAN 5. It's great to see you, Man!

MAN 6. It's great to see you too, Man!

MAN 5. Are you guys still living in the village?

MAN 6. Oh. No. No. No. No. No. We got priced out of the village.

MAN 5. Us too.

MAN 6. Things were different when I moved here in 2008.

MAN 5. 2008 was like a whole different world.

MAN 6. 2008 *was* a whole different world.

MAN 5. Where'd you end up?

MAN 6. We ended up in New Jersey.

MAN 5. Oh. How is it?

MAN 6. It's actually pretty nice.

MAN 5. I've been thinking about you.

MAN 6. I've been thinking about you too!

MAN 5. I've been meaning to email you to see how you are.

MAN 6. I'm hanging in.

MAN 5. I've been meaning to email because…I wanted to see how you were doing…with this whole…situation.

MAN 6. It's a witch hunt!

MAN 5. It's great to hear that it's actually not true. I sort of heard that it might be. But, it's great that it's not.

MAN 6. Yeah. I mean. It's a witch hunt.

MAN 5. Yeah. I mean. I know you. And I was totally sure you wouldn't do anything like what I heard you did.

MAN 6. Wait. What did you hear I did?

MAN 5. So, actually. I read this thing. And. It turns out. When a statement is repeated, it starts to feel more familiar and like it might actually be true.

MAN 6. But, what exact version of it did you hear?

MAN 5. So, actually. I don't want to even say it. Because what I'd be doing there is sort of reinforcing the frame that…it *might* be true. And I really don't want it to be true, man.

MAN 6. It's a witch hunt!

MAN 5. Yeah, I don't know if it's really a witch hunt. If it's true, then, it's just a really messed up thing that you really did.

MAN 6. Are you telling me you haven't ever done anything that in the current frame of reference might be seen as being a little messed up?

MAN 5. I'm not sure. I've thought a lot about maybe apologizing for some things I maybe did a long time ago, but if I start apologizing to women I have very little contact with now, maybe I'd just be dredging up stuff that nobody remembers anymore anyway. And maybe that would be unpleasant for everybody. Right?

MAN 1, 2, 3, & 4. Right.

MAN 6. But, that's the whole thing with the witch hunts, right? There never were any real witches. They went looking for communists and silenced everybody's free speech, and made everybody afraid, and held everybody's feet to the fire and said "name names or you're going down in the witch hunt."

MAN 5. Seems like your name has already been named.

MAN 6. But! It's a witch hunt!

MAN 5. I mean…It is and it *isn't* a witch hunt because, even if you did do something fairly messed up to a female subordinate colleague, nobody is going to hang you, or burn you at the stake or anything.

MAN 6. But it's a witch hunt!

MAN 5. You were kind of like my work-wife. And now we have to get work-divorced.

MAN 6. But. It's a witch hunt!

MAN 5. I think we still have to work-separate.

MAN 6. If you were me, if your name was named…would you apologize or would you deny it?

MAN 5. I guess it depends if I did it?

(*A coven of contemporary witches is visible.*)

WITCHES. Let his days be few.

MAN 5. Do you hear that?

WITCHES. Let another take his office.

MAN 6. Hear what?

WITCHES. Let food bring him no sustenance.

Let sleep bring him only nightmares.

MAN 5. Witches.

WITCHES. Let shame be his mantle.

Let him meet justice.

ALL THE MEN. Witches!

WITCHES. My witchcraft is strong.

My witchcraft is powerful.

The spell will work.

So mote it be.

MAN 6 (or maybe ALL THE MEN). See! It *is* a witch hunt!

WITCH 1. Oh, it's *definitely* a witch hunt.

ALL THE MEN. Real witches!

WITCH 2. I'm a witch!

WITCH 3. I'm a WOMAN IN TOTAL CONTROL OF HERSELF. Also known as a WITCH.

WITCH 4. Me too.

WITCH 5. Me too.

ALL THE WITCHES. ME TOO!

WE'RE ALL WITCHES!

AND IF YOU FUCK WITH US, WE WILL HUNT YOU!

SO MOTE IT BE!

THE FOUR PILLARS AT THE FOUNDATION
OF WINNING AT THE GAMES OF LIFE
/OR/
I WANT TO GET COMPLETE WITH YOU
by Emily Feldman

The LEADER *often speaks to the whole room.*

Maybe the LEADER *has a body mic.*

LEADER. I want to tell you a secret. Okay?

Unfortunately, you're not going to like it.

(*A short pause.*)

Okay.

The secret is:

There is no hope.

…

Sorry!

…

It will never get better.

…

Sorry!

…

Life is empty and meaningless.

…

Sorry again!

And that fact that life is empty and meaningless…is empty and meaningless.

…

Okay, I'm done feeling sorry for you.

You have to face it.

You're screwed.

Welcome to being a human being.

You harbor persistent complaints about your life and your relationships.

> (*Maybe the following are pop-ups from the ensemble instead of the* LEADER?)

I'm on the wrong side of 40!

I have a floundering creative career!

I live in a tiny and cluttered apartment!

I don't get along with my sister!

My car is a Ford Fiesta!

…

These complaints—combined with fear—create the life you are living.

You are living a life of shams and illusions.

Everything you do is meant to make you look good or avoid looking bad.

You have no integrity.

You are inauthentic.

Even worse!

You are inauthentic about being inauthentic.

BUT!

There's hope.

Just kidding! Got ya!

There's no hope.

But there is…transformation.

A-ha!

There is transformation that will leave you able to deal powerfully with each and every aspect of your life. But, you're going to have to clean up your act.

And if you do, you can have any result you want for yourself or your life that you invent as a possibility and enroll others in your having gotten.

Do you get that?

> (PARTICIPANT 1 *arrives, or was always there.*)

PARTICIPANT 1. I don't get that.

LEADER. What don't you get?

PARTICIPANT 1. I don't get those words in that order.

LEADER. That's your stubborn need to be right.

PARTICIPANT 1. "I can have any result I want for myself or my life that I invent as a possibility and enroll others in my *having gotten?*"

That's a weird sentence.

LEADER. Every time you insist on being right, you are running a racket.

PARTICIPANT 1. I can't help it. I'm a copy editor.

LEADER. Do you want to win at the games of life?

PARTICIPANT 1. I'm curious, why, in this case, games is a plural noun.

LEADER. Are you ready to cause a breakthrough?

PARTICIPANT 1. I'm here at 11 o'clock at night and I paid $800 so...yes.

LEADER. The first pillar at the foundation of winning at the games of life is—integrity.

(PARTICIPANT 2 *arrives, or was already there.*

PARTICIPANT 2 *is eating a snack.*)

LEADER. You're eating a snack.

PARTICIPANT 2. I'm not eating a snack.

LEADER. Integrity, at its most basic level, is doing what you said you would do when you said you would do it.

Do you get that?

PARTICIPANT 2. I get that.

LEADER. You said, you'd have your name badge visible.

You said, you would stand when you speak.

You said, you would not eat anything in this room or drink anything other than water.

You said, if you are out of your integrity, you forfeit your right to expect transformation.

And here you are. Eating a snack.

(PARTICIPANT 2 *has quickly finished the snack and hid the evidence in a pocket.*)

PARTICIPANT 2. I'm not eating a snack.

LEADER. (*To* PARTICIPANT 2 *and also everyone.*) You behave in this room like you do in the rest of your lives!

You cheat! You lie!

PARTICIPANT 2. I'm so sorry. It's very late at night and I was very hungry.

LEADER. Excuses are rackets.

PARTICIPANT 2. Yeah. I'm sorry.

LEADER. I'm thinking about refusing to coach you.

PARTICIPANT 2. I'm really sorry. Maybe this isn't for me.

LEADER. Maybe not.

(*Taking it out to everyone.*)

You may need to hang on to your rackets.

But hey, it's *your* life.

PARTICIPANT 2. I'll have more than a salad at dinner tomorrow.

LEADER. If you're running these rackets on yourself,

I can only imagine the rackets you're running on other people.

The second pillar at the foundation of winning at the games of life is—relationships.

I want you to speak to someone in your life who you've been running a racket on.

Get complete with them—

Ask yourself: who am I going to complete with regarding these rackets?

(PARTICIPANT 3 *arrives, or was always there.*

PARTICIPANT 3 *holds a bunch of tennis rackets.*

PARTICIPANT 3 *looks forlorn.*)

PARTICIPANT 3. Who am I going to complete with regarding these rackets?

PARTICIPANT 1. Is there any way we could rearrange that sentence, just so I can tolerate being here?

(PARTICIPANT 4 *arrives, or was always there.*)

PARTICIPANT 4. Beatrice, I have been out of my integrity, but now, I am creating for myself and my life the possibility of being transformed and enrolling others in my transformation.

(BEATRICE *arrives, or was always there.*)

BEATRICE. You're what?

PARTICIPANT 4. I have been out of my integrity, but now, I am creating for myself and my life the possibility of being transformed and enrolling others in my transformation.

BEATRICE. You're what? Sorry. One more time.

PARTICIPANT 4. I have been out of my integrity, but now, I am creating for myself and my life the possibility of being transformed and enrolling others in my transformation.

BEATRICE. Okay. Sorry. I'm trying.

PARTICIPANT 4. I have been out of my integrity, but now, I /

BEATRICE. Could you maybe try to put it a different way?

PARTICIPANT 4. No. I think that's the best I've got.

(PARTICIPANT 5 *enters, or was already there.*)

PARTICIPANT 5. Hi.

So.

I'm really sorry we haven't talked lately.

(PARTICIPANT 5's SIBLING *arrives, or was always there.*)

PARTICIPANT 5's SIBLING. Aww. Me too.

It's okay.

You've been really busy and I had a really crazy winter—

Moving,

And then almost changing jobs,

and then having appendicitis,

and then I went to Japan for two weeks,

and then I don't know, somehow, it's already April.

PARTICIPANT 5. Listen. Um.

I think I've been inauthentic with you.

PARTICIPANT 5's SIBLING. Oh my gosh! No, you haven't!

PARTICIPANT 5. Oh, really?

PARTICIPANT 5's SIBLING. Oh my gosh, yeah!

PARTICIPANT 5. Great!

PARTICIPANT 5's SIBLING. Great! See you soon! Love you!

PARTICIPANT 5. Love you too!

> (*Maybe...*
>
> PARTICIPANT 3 *hands out rackets and a tennis ball to* BEATRICE *and* PARTICIPANT 5's SIBLING *and they softly volley somewhere in the space.*
>
> PARTICIPANT 6 *arrives, or was already there.*)

PARTICIPANT 6. I want to get complete with you.

PARTICIPANT 6's FRIEND. I'm not attracted to you. I'm sorry.

PARTICIPANT 6. No, I just. I want to share with you the new possibility I've invented.

PARTICIPANT 6's FRIEND. Okay. Yeah. I've seen this coming for a long time.

I think you're great. I like our friendship so much.

I just don't feel the same way about you.

PARTICIPANT 6. No—I just.

PARTICIPANT 6's FRIEND. Maybe the best thing is if we just don't talk for a little while.

> (PARTICIPANT 7 *arrives, or was always there.*)

PARTICIPANT 7. I want to get complete with you.

> (PARTICIPANT 7's LOVER *arrives, or was always there.*)

PARTICIPANT 7's LOVER. Great. Me too.

PARTICIPANT 7. I think I've been harboring resentments and making you wrong regarding the ways you failed to show up for me when you were drunk all the time, like the time when my father died I was packing for his funeral and I needed you to come to my house and hold me in bed and you were wasted and you said that your optometrist is hot, but not as hot as me naked holding a bottle of Fireball. I want to acknowledge having been resentful in our relationship, and share the impact that's had on my life, and get complete with you.

PARTICIPANT 7's LOVER. Yeah. Definitely. I love that. I could get complete right now.

PARTICIPANT 7. I don't think I'm doing this right.

>(*Maybe* PARTICIPANT 3 *hands other rackets to* PARTICIPANT 6's FRIEND *and* PARTICIPANT 7's LOVER *and they also engage in some soft volleying.*
>
>PARTICIPANT 7 *turns to the* LEADER.)

PARTICIPANT 7. I don't think I'm doing this right. I feel hurt all over again.

LEADER. That never happened.

PARTICIPANT 7. It did.

LEADER. That person's failing to comfort you didn't hurt you.

PARTICIPANT 7. It did. It really did.

LEADER. How you perceived it hurt you.

PARTICIPANT 7. I perceived it hurting me, because it hurt me.

LEADER. You need to stop running this racket.

PARTICIPANT 7. I'm not running this racket.

LEADER. You need to go get complete with them.

PARTICIPANT 7. I can't apologize to someone who hurt me.
I tried.

LEADER. You are living in the past and there is no past.

>(PARTICIPANT 8 *arrives, or is already there.*)

PARTICIPANT 8. I like that idea, can you clarify?

LEADER. You can't commit yourself to a powerful life unless you complete your past.

Something happened, and you developed a way of being around this thing that happened in the past, as a compensation for a failure of being in the present, and that tells you how to be in the future.

And can you see how limiting that is?

The past isn't here now. There is no past!

PARTICIPANT 8. Might this also relate to my credit score?

LEADER. No.

PARTICIPANT 7. I think I get it.

But, I also think I'm physically and emotionally exhausted by all of this and I am desperate to feel like this is worth it.

LEADER. When you get complete with people, you can form powerful alliances

and generate the possibility of being cause in the matter of your life.

PARTICIPANT 1. Yeah, that sentence is also going to be a problem for me.

LEADER. The third pillar at the foundation of winning at the games of life is—existence.

Existence not only means that the game exists, but how it exists.

(PARTICIPANT 9 *arrives, or was always there.*)

PARTICIPANT 9. Is this a cult that exists?

LEADER. What's a cult?

PARTICIPANT 9. (*Looking around.*) I mean—

The unmarked door. The rules.

The multiple levels. The public shaming. The sensory deprivation…

It just seems sort of like a cult.

LEADER. Is this a religion?

PARTICIPANT 9. No.

LEADER. Are you going to follow me?

PARTICIPANT 9. No.

LEADER. Good, because that would be creepy.

What would be possible if you stopped worrying about everyone else—

And started worrying about you?

The last pillar at the foundation of winning at the games of life is—Enrollment.

Enrollment is—sharing with the people in your life /

PARTICIPANT 9. THAT'S THE CULT PART!

WE HAVE TO RECRUIT ALL OUR FRIENDS!

ENROLLMENT IS THE CULT PART!

(*Nobody moves.*

A couple of people we haven't seen or noticed before arrive onstage and very swiftly carry PARTICIPANT 9 *off.*)

LEADER. Enrollment is causing a new possibility to be present for another, such that they are touched, moved, and inspired by that possibility.

PARTICIPANT 7. What was that?

LEADER. Because, remember—

PARTICIPANT 3. Where'd they go?

LEADER. You can have any result you want for yourself and your life that you invent as a possibility and enroll others in your having gotten.

PARTICIPANT 4. Somebody just *having gotten* abducted!

PARTICIPANT 1. Yeah, what happened to them?

EVERYONE BUT THE LEADER. YEAH!

LEADER. Notice all the meaning, interpretations, and stories that you add to what is happening to distinguish the rackets you're running.

>*(Maybe somebody lobs a tennis ball at the* LEADER.)

PARTICIPANT 5. You know what?

The chairs here are very uncomfortable and spaced too close together!

LEADER. Enrollment is causing new possibilities for another, such that they are touched, moved, and inspired/

PARTICIPANT 6. I think we're all feeling touched, moved, and inspired.

>*(The group surrounds the* LEADER.)

LEADER. My intention is to generate bringing forth the possibility of possibility itself!

>*(They circle the* LEADER, *or do some kind of threatening unison movement. The tennis rackets are involved.*
>
>*The* LEADER *looks compromised.)*

LEADER. My intention is to leave you feeling touched, moved, and inspired by your—

EVERYONE. HAVING GOTTEN THAT POSSIBILITY.

LEADER. Okay. Yes. Do you get it?

EVERYONE. WE GET IT!

>*(The group exits, leaving the* LEADER *alone.* PARTICIPANT 3 *stays behind. They look at each other for a moment.)*

PARTICIPANT 3. Wait, could you tell me what a racket is again?

>*(The end.)*

End of Play